Hanging Together

EQUALITY IN AN URBAN NATION

by William L. Taylor

Simon and Schuster

NEW YORK

FIRST PRINTING

SBN 671-20711-3 Trade
SBN 671-20712-1 Clarion
Library of Congress Catalog Card Number: 76-132772
Designed by Irving Perkins
Manufactured in the United States of America

to Harriett

Contents

Preface

Some years ago, Gunnar Myrdal noted that the race problem in this country is intertwined with all other social, economic, political, and cultural problems, adding that its study affords a perspective on the American nation as a whole. Myrdal's observation states the difficulty as well as the challenge: anyone who wishes to make a contribution to the establishment of equality of opportunity for all citizens in this country must first try to familiarize himself with most of the important institutions in American life. Accordingly, in seeking to cover the range of issues—in education, employment, economic security, and housing—that are important to black citizens and other Americans who have been victims of deprivation and discrimination, I have had to deal with the complex systems that govern each of these areas.

And so, to any charge that this book is presumptuous, my plea must be guilty. In taking such a broad approach, I have run the risk of oversimplification and of incomplete analysis, although I hope not of a basic misunderstanding of any set of institutions or problems. But this is a risk that I believed worth taking and, indeed, necessary to the development and testing of the central thesis of the book. Simply stated, my belief is that almost simultaneously we have reached crisis points in two of the greatest challenges facing us as a people: eliminating the stain of racism from American life and creating cities that will enrich our lives and in which all can reside in harmony. My conviction is that neither challenge is insurmountable. Despite our history of slavery and segregation, racism is not an immutable characteristic of the American people, and in fact great strides have been made in recent years in eliminating it. Nor do we lack the resources to build livable cities.

But, while I am optimistic about the nation's capacity to solve each of these great problems, I am equally convinced that they can be overcome only if they are faced together. All of our efforts against racial injustice will fail unless we are willing to restructure our urban system and its institutions to provide freedom and mobility and to allocate to all citizens a share of the responsibility for overcoming deprivation and discrimination. Conversely, all of the efforts to preserve urban values and to make cities a unifying force in American life will be defeated if we are not able to confront and overcome our racial fears.

These convictions—that it is possible to establish racial and social justice and to create livable cities, but only if both challenges are faced together—led to the ambitious undertaking of this book.

In large part, the optimism I retain and what expertise I have to offer stem from an exposure to most of the principal participants and combatants in today's urban arena. I grew up as a second-generation Jewish American in an Italian-Jewish predominantly working class area of Brooklyn, New York. My early professional and social life was spent mainly among middle class blacks and whites, in the city and in suburbia. In more recent years, my work has taken me to the rural South, to the ghetto communities of big cities, and also to the meeting rooms of top-level government officials, school administrators, heads of corporations.

Of all this experience, my exposure to life in the ghetto was the most jarring. It led me, as a person who had been righteous in the knowledge that I was "fighting the good fight," to realize how shallow my perceptions were and to question some of my middle class values and previously unconscious biases. It also made me much angrier about the complacency, obtuseness, and unconscious cruelty of people in positions of authority.

But unlike some who have had similar experience, it impelled me only to modify—not to abandon—many of my middle class values. I still believe that the model of an open, competitive, diverse, and pluralistic society is a sound one, even though it has not been achieved. Although I think I am about as aware of discrimination, cruelty, and hypocrisy as my white skin allows, I still believe that the majority of white America (whether dubbed "silent," "ethnic," "affluent," or whatever) is composed of fair and decent people and that under courageous leadership conditions can be established which will allow their decent instincts to prevail. And I still believe that if the right leadership emerges and if blacks and whites will work together, we can not only create a land of true equality of opportunity, but can make ourselves a people more humane, compassionate, open, humorous, and individualistic than we have ever been before.

But along with many others, my faith in these beliefs is no longer as strong as it once was. And of one thing I am truly convinced: there is not much time left to us to prove these beliefs right.

As in most endeavors of this kind, the author has many debts to acknowledge. Christopher Edley and the Ford Foundation gave me a grant so that I could take the necessary time to write the book. Dean Lou Pollak and the Yale Law School furnished me a congenial atmosphere in which to work along with an inscrutable academic title with which to impress my friends.

John McKnight of Northwestern University, M. Carl Holman, vice president of the Urban Coalition, and Howard Glickstein, staff director of the U.S. Commission on Civil Rights, were good enough to read drafts of several chapters and to give me the benefit of their advice, some of which I was wise enough to take. Mrs. Diane Neustadter and Richard Kluger have been patient, understanding, and constructive editors.

Steve Merchant, a graduate student in economics at the University of Maryland, and Angus Macbeth and John Strait, then Yale law students, helped me research portions of the book. And many dedicated staff people at the U.S. Commission on Civil Rights, in their work in communities throughout the nation, have provided material that I have drawn on freely in writing the book.

Mrs. Christine Meehan and Mrs. Dagmar Aurich typed drafts of the manuscript in New Haven, and Mrs. Klaire Adkins, my long-time associate and friend at the Commission on Civil Rights, typed other drafts in Washington.

There are also debts that are less easy to put into words. I owe a great deal to my parents, Harry and Sarah Taylor. I also owe much to Thurgood Marshall, Bob Carter, Roger Wilkins, Charles L. Black, Joe Rauh, and many others who contributed to my education along the way. My children, Lauren, Deborah, and David, while becoming self-proclaimed experts in the business of writing and publishing books, helped by providing evidence that the world was not as unrelievedly grim as it sometimes seemed within the four walls of my study.

As for my wife, Harriett, a few of her roles can be described; she has been typist, editor, critic, cheerleader, and therapist on this project. But only a few people who know us both very well will have any idea of how much I am really in her debt.

W.L.T.

Washington, D.C.
March 20, 1970

We must all hang together, or assuredly we shall all hang separately.

—BENJAMIN FRANKLIN, at the
signing of the Declaration
of Independence, July 4, 1776

What is needed in our country is not an exchange of pathologies, but a change of the basis of society. This is a job which both Negroes and whites must perform together.

—RALPH ELLISON in *An American Dilemma: A Review*, 1944

PART ONE

"Not Making It"

1

GOALS AND REALITY

Prologue: A Conversation About Goals

> (PLACE: A human relations forum in a white middle-class community. TIME: Any time during the 1960s.)

CONCERNED WHITE CITIZEN: What I'd like to know is what does the Negro *really* want?

CIVIL RIGHTS AUTHORITY (probably white): The very fact that you, an intelligent and concerned person, should ask such a question shows what a mess our country is in. It's a bit incredible that there are so many white people like yourself whose lives have involved so little contact with black people that they can well wonder whether they are speaking of a separate nation or a society with a value system all its own. . . . Still, I suppose the fact that the question is being asked so frequently these days is a mark of some kind of progress. Only a few years ago the great majority of white people so completely ignored Negroes or denied their humanity that the notion that they might have needs and desires never dawned on whites.

CWC: You're patronizing me and you have not answered my question.

CRA: I'm getting to it. First of all, it is a mistake to talk about "the Negro." You are speaking about many people, from differing economic circumstances, with a wide variety of life-styles and values. But if you insist on a general answer, "the Negro" wants what you want. He wants a piece of the action, his share of the benefits this nation has to offer. He wants economic security, job status, a good education for his children. He wants a sense of dignity which can only come from a knowledge that he is contributing something to this society and that others understand and respect him for it. He wants a degree of personal power which can only come from participation in the political process and a feeling that he plays some role in the decisions that affect his life. He wants to be considered a part of his racial group for some purposes and just an American citizen for others.

He wants self-fulfillment and peace of mind. For some, the measure of achievement of these goals, in belief or in fact, is the accrual of resources, economic and tangible. Others require more. For them, fulfillment and peace of mind can only be attained if they live in a society where they can feel that their comfort and security rest upon personal achievement rather than upon the beneficence of those who are more affluent and powerful or upon exploiting those who are poor and weak.

CWC: That's all very interesting, but it doesn't tell me what I'd really like to know, which is when all this racial unrest will come to an end so that we can stop worrying about it.

CRA: Now you are asking a different and more difficult question. Still, if my previous answer is generally correct, it may provide some clues. It suggests that what we should be principally concerned about is the disparity between the status of Negroes *as a group* and that of the white majority. We ought to be concerned too about disparities between the group positions of other minorities that have been discriminated against—Mexican Americans, Puerto Ricans, Indians—and that of the white Anglo majority.

While nobody can say for sure, perhaps we can make a fair guess that our nation will have attained racial peace and racial justice when Negroes as a group and members of other minority groups are distributed over various scales which measure achievement and success in much the same way that whites are. In other words, we may assume that success will have been achieved when roughly the same proportion of Negroes as whites earn $15,000 or more a year, have more than a high school education, hold jobs as professionals and technicians, participate in political affairs, live apart from members of their own group, feel they have some control over their own destinies.

CWC: That sounds pretty radical to me. I've always thought that our system was intended to guarantee equality of opportunity, not equality of results. I gather you want to change all that and to assure colored people that they will share equally with whites whether or not they are willing to work hard and compete.

CRA: Not at all. My fundamental belief is that equality in group status will eventually be achieved by offering equality of opportunity, provided it is *genuine* equality which takes into account past discrimination and not the kind of law Anatole France spoke of which in its majesty "forbids the rich as well as the poor to sleep under bridges, beg in the streets, and to steal bread."

My belief recognizes that all people are not born with the same innate capacities and that equalizing opportunity will not result in equality in the circumstances of all. But it does rest upon an assumption—and this is the critical hypothesis—that differences in capacity are not racially based. In other words, I assume that the differences in the status of Negroes and whites as groups that exist today can be ascribed solely to racial discrimination and the denial of opportunity. Once these are redressed, I believe Negroes will find themselves distributed on the various scales measuring success in roughly the same manner as whites.

It may be, of course, that the hypothesis is wrong and that the view held by Professor Jensen and a few others that Negroes as a race are "biologically inferior" to whites and do not have the same "innate capacity" is correct, despite the lack of evidence to support it. If so, it will be time enough to discover this after everything has been done to remove all the barriers to opportunity that now exist. Of course, it may also be that Negroes as a group are superior to whites, so that when discrimination is eradicated they will rank higher on most indices than their white counterparts.

The key point is that until we take the steps required to equalize opportunity, we will never know which hypothesis is correct.

CWC: It seems to me that what you are dreaming about will be depressingly uniform. Aren't we supposed to be a pluralistic society?

CRA: Sure. But all I have assumed is that equality of opportunity will bring a *rough* equality of results. There is nothing in this notion that is inconsistent with a pluralistic society.

I am not suggesting, for example, that each racial and ethnic group will be proportionately represented across the spectrum of occupations—as nuclear physicists, poets, master plumbers, concert violinists, teachers, nurses. There are differences in occupational choice and status that exist now between Italians, Irish, Jews, Chinese, Germans, and other American groups as well as differences in income, educational attainment, values, and life-styles.

These differences may be attributable in part to cultural factors and in part to past discrimination and the lack of equal opportunity. But none of these groups has experienced discrimination in this country as severe and as long-standing as that suffered by Negroes, and to a great extent by Spanish-speaking Americans and American Indians. And the differences in results are nowhere as gross as the gap that exists between blacks and whites. Once we have redressed this massive wrong, there is every reason to believe that black people and the other minorities will retain separate group identities, that values and life-styles will still be partially distinguishable on an ethnic as well as economic and educational basis, and that there will continue to be differences in attainment in particular areas. But the differences no longer will set apart one or two groups from the rest of society and they will not arise to any significant degree from discrimination.

CWC: One thing I've noticed is that you seem to be all hung up on race. Isn't it true that most poor people in this country are white, not black? Even if we did what you want us to and eliminated racial disparities, there would still be people at the bottom of the heap. Aren't you concerned about them? Are you willing to tolerate the continuation of poverty as long as it is not based on racial discrimination?

CRA: I'm glad to see that your social consciousness is expanding. And I agree with much of what you say.

It is true that two of every three people in this nation who live in poverty are white. At the same time, I am sure you are aware that a much higher proportion of black people than white people are poor.

What you are saying in effect is that racial justice is not quite synonymous with economic and social justice although they are closely related. I am glad to accept your amendment to my statement of goals. We must be concerned with extending opportunity not simply to those who have been victims of racial deprivation but to those who have been victims of other forms of deprivation as well. And we must be prepared to support at a decent standard of living those who cannot be expected to make their own way, whether because they are old, physically or mentally handicapped, are women who do not have husbands and who cannot work because they have young children to care for, or for some other reason.

At the same time, I would defend my preoccupation with race. A great deal of what needs to be done to provide true equality of opportunity for those who have been victims of racial discrimination consists not of special legislation with a racial label on it but general measures of potential benefit to all. It includes efforts to provide good education, decent housing, job training, and jobs themselves to people who have not had access to these things in the past. As such, it will benefit Appalachian whites, white tenant farmers in the rural South, Puerto Ricans, Mexican Americans, and Indians, as well as Negroes.

In seeking remedies, I think there are good strategic reasons for continuing to focus on race. It is an interesting fact that while black people have been the most discriminated against and despised minority in the history of this nation, it is their plight that has provided the cutting edge for reform. It is doubtful that we would have any kind of a war against poverty had it not been for the civil rights movement and the legal victories it won during the 1950s and 1960s. The other side of the coin is that efforts at general economic and social reform are jeopardized by continuing racial prejudice.

Since racial discrimination is the nation's most agonizing moral problem it is neither surprising nor inappropriate that it stands at the center of almost all discussion about social and economic justice. If we are able to triumph over racial injustice a great many people other than Negroes who have been disadvantaged undoubtedly will benefit. If we fail, it probably won't matter much what else we have tried to do.

CWC: So now you want to abolish poverty as well as to establish your notion of racial equity. Can all this possibly be accomplished without hurting many people who have worked hard to get what they have?

CRA: There is no question that some sacrifice will be required. If we seriously want to reach these objectives, a great deal of private spending that now goes into satisfying consumer wants will probably have to be converted into public spending to fight poverty and discrimination. And in spending these public funds, we undoubtedly will be required to decide that it is less important for the nation to be armed to the teeth or for people to be able to fly faster than the speed of sound than that no one in the country go hungry and that there be a job for everyone who needs one.

But this is a far cry from saying that people will have to give up anything that could rationally be considered to be their vital interests. The great advantage this country has in seeking to solve its racial and social problems is that it is capable of large and sustained economic growth. This means that in order to give one man the opportunity for a good job or a decent home it is not necessary to take these things away from another.

The trouble is that while this observation about the advantage of continuing economic growth pertains to the nation as a whole it is no longer true for most of our major cities. We have managed to construct for ourselves a system in which, while wealth is increasing rapidly all around cities, the cities themselves are declining and deteriorating. This means that in the cities, unlike the nation, a decision to create new services or opportunities for one group may well mean that services and opportunities for another group will be decreased. Moreover, the groups that are competing for these scarce resources do not usually include many who are affluent but rather black people who are in poverty and white people who have not emerged from it far enough to feel very secure about their positions. Add to this mixture a long history of racial separation, prejudice, and mistrust and it is a wonder there has not been more turmoil than has already occurred.

If we do not wish to forgo the great advantage that the nation's enormous wealth provides for solving our problems peacefully and rationally, it is essential that we change the system which has made cities places where, surrounded by plenty, people struggle with each other for scarce resources.

CWC: You talk about solving our problems peacefully and rationally, but apparently many Negroes and young white people don't share your view. What is to be gained by all this violence in the cities—rioting, attacking policemen, bombing buildings?

CRA: Nothing is to be gained. But if there is anything as futile and self-defeating as using violence to try to accomplish social change, it is deploring violence without being willing to open peaceful channels to change. While violence cannot be tolerated, the only way to contain and rid ourselves of violence associated with just grievances is to redress the grievances. The racial disorders our nation has experienced in recent years are in part the result of rising expectations. Since the expectations are reasonable and just, the way to curb violence is to demonstrate that change can be accomplished through our political institutions. While violations of the law must be prosecuted, we will accomplish nothing by taking draconian measures against groups like the Black Panthers except win them new allies. And it would be a final cruel paradox if after years of failing to reward patience and redress injustice, we were to use such violations by a few as an excuse for continued inaction on the problems which affect so many.

CWC: I'm sorry that our time has run out, Mr. Authority. I still have many questions. For example, I'd like to know what you mean by providing "genuine equality which takes into account past discrimination." That smacks of preferential treatment to me. And I don't see why colored people can't make it the same way immigrants did. And it seems to me that government has already done an awful lot. I don't know why it should be expected to do more.

CRA: Yes, well . . . I have a book coming out on the subject . . .

CWC: In any case, we are grateful to you, especially since you have agreed to forgo an honorarium. And I'm sure you will be glad to know that the money will be put to good use. It's going into our "Better Speakers" fund.

Disparities

No instruments, however finely calibrated, can fully measure the gulf that now separates white and black America. How, for example, does one gauge the gap of silence between two friends, one black and one white, whose ties are strengthened by similarities in backgrounds, interests, and values but who are divided by differing American heritages of slavery and freedom and, even more, by the contrast in the living conditions and attitudes of their racial brothers?

But yardsticks, even though inadequate, do exist and are necessary as marks of progress or the lack of it and as aids to policymakers seeking public action to reduce the gulf. The most useful of these yardsticks are racial comparisons in the attainment of things most valued by the great majority of citizens—jobs and income, housing, education, health and physical security.

Similar comparisons can be made in viewing the social ills that are usually associated with failure to attain these commonly accepted goals—ills such as crime and delinquency, alcoholism and narcotics addiction, physical and mental illness. The least tangible measures of racial inequality are of differences in attitudes and aspirations, feelings and emotions, views of oneself and the world —all subjective states of mind which are not merely results of the objective conditions of an individual or group but determinants of whether and how far these conditions can be changed.

While disparities between Negroes and whites should be examined on a national basis, the single most important place to view them is in the nation's cities. This is not because deprivation in rural areas is insignificant; indeed, a large portion of poverty in the nation still is rural poverty, and the continuing neglect of people in these areas is in large part the cause of the overwhelming problems that exist in cities. But this is a situation that has changed and continues to change rapidly with the great tide of migration from rural areas to cities, so that it must now be said that whatever efforts are made at this late date to end rural neglect, resolution of the great issues of racial equality and economic and social justice ultimately will rest on what is done or not done in the cities.[1]

Objective Measures

JOBS—Occupation, more than anything else, provides a measure of the standing of a person or a family in this society. A man without a job ordinarily is lacking not only in the income needed to provide adequately for himself and his family but in self-respect and in the respect of others around him.

During the past five years, the nation's economy generally has been a prosperous one, marked by rapid growth and a very low rate of unemployment. Yet, all during this period, some 700,000 nonwhites, the great majority of them Negroes, have been unemployed. While only one white person in thirty-three has been unable to find a job, more than one Negro in every sixteen has been without work.[2] A part of the meaning of the difference may be gauged from the fact that while economists have generally regarded the low overall unemployment rate as reason for satisfaction, they would be alarmed if the Negro unemployment rate prevailed for the work force as a whole. As is the case with many other problems, unemployment has been most serious in the slum areas of the nation's major cities, where the proportion of black people in the labor force without work has frequently been 10 per cent or more.[3]

Unemployment, moreover, is only one part of a large job problem prevalent in big city ghettos. For every black person who is out of work, there are many more who have been able to find only sporadic or part-time jobs, who work full-time but cannot earn more than a poverty wage, or who have dropped out of the labor force entirely. An index developed by the Department of Labor to measure these kinds of underemployment as well as unemployment, and applied in the low-income areas of eight large cities, showed that in 1966, one person in three was afflicted with such "subemployment."* All told, in the disad-

* The definition of "subemployed" included not only those counted in standard unemployment statistics (persons unemployed and looking for work) but also those working part-time but seeking full-time work, heads of households under sixty-five years of age employed full-time but earning less than $60 per week, those not heads of households working full-time but earning less than $56 per week, and unemployed males of working age not

vantaged areas of the central cities of the nation, more than one million nonwhites were subemployed—more than 300,000 unemployed and more than 700,000 underemployed.[4]

The high degree of underemployment among Negroes is a partial reflection of a more pervasive problem—the low status of the jobs held by most black people as compared with those held by whites. Negro workers are found concentrated in the lowest skilled and lowest paying occupations—those which frequently have the least security, involve the most menial and physically exhausting duties, and are regarded as having the least status by the employer, the employee, and the community at large. For example, in 1966, six of every ten white workers were employed as professional, technical, and managerial personnel, clerical and sales people, or craftsmen and foremen—the three job categories where average earnings were the highest and which in general are regarded as having the highest status. Only three employed nonwhites in ten were employed in these fields; the rest had jobs as operatives, service workers, laborers, or farm workers.[5] Many were busboys and dishwashers, construction and factory laborers, carwash and parking lot attendants, janitors and porters—performers of the dirtiest and least rewarding tasks society has to offer.

INCOME AND EDUCATION—The companions of unemployment and low job status, of course, are poverty and low income. In 1968, 25.4 million people were classified as poor in this country; 8 million of them were Negroes or other nonwhites.[6] While only one white person in ten was poor, poverty was the lot of one nonwhite person in every three. The causes of poverty, moreover, are strikingly different for whites and nonwhites. A large percentage

---

looking for work. U.S. Department of Labor, *A Sharper Look at Unemployment in U.S. Cities and Slums.* The problem of people who cannot make more than a poverty wage even though they work full-time is particularly acute. Of 3 million Negro men who worked the entire year in 1966, one-fourth earned less than $3,000. Only 8 per cent of all white males fell into this category. Even in usually better paying categories such as white collar work, Negroes were far more apt to earn less than $3,000 than whites. See U.S. Bureau of the Census, Department of Commerce, Series P-60, No. 58, *Year-Round Workers with Low Earnings in 1966.*

(23 per cent) of the white poor are people who are sixty-five years old or more who have not been able to accumulate enough earnings to sustain them in their old age. But this problem, which may be capable of fairly easy resolution through increases in government old-age assistance, is a relatively insignificant one for nonwhites, accounting for only 9 per cent of the nonwhite poor. Far more prevalent among nonwhites is poverty which strikes adults during the prime of their working lives and which affects their children as well as themselves. As a consequence, the racial disparities in poverty among children are far greater than for any other group in the population. Two of every five children in this country who are poor are nonwhite, and in the cities, where poverty is increasingly concentrated, there are actually more poor children who are Negroes or members of other racial minorities than there are poor white children.[7] In addition, the poverty that exists is usually worse for the minority poor than for poor whites. Negro families with incomes below the poverty line as a group are more deeply impoverished than are poor white families.

The income disparities between black people and white people go far beyond comparisons of those living in poverty. In 1968, for example, the median family income for whites was $8,937, while for Negroes it was $5,360. (In cities, the comparable figures in 1967 were $8,993 for white families and $5,670 for Negro families.) Thus, the earnings received by an average black family were less than two-thirds of those of the average white family. Most Negroes who have escaped from poverty have not escaped very far. If an income of $10,000 a year may be taken as a rough measure of what is required for a family to emerge from the shadow of need, it may be noted that in the metropolitan areas of the nation more than four white families in ten, but fewer than two black families in ten, have achieved this status. If an income of $15,000 or more is taken as a general measure of affluence, then only one Negro family in twenty in metropolitan areas may be said to be affluent compared to one white family in every six.

Lastly, it is worth noting that these great gaps in the income of black and white people cannot be completely accounted for by the explanation that whites receive more and better education than Negroes and therefore are likely to obtain better paying jobs.

There are, of course, large racial disparities in educational attainment. Taking only the age group consisting of people twenty to twenty-four years old (so that recent progress in narrowing the educational gap may be reflected), it may be noted that in 1969, more than two Negroes in every five, but fewer than one white in every five, had completed less than four years of high school. Approximately two whites in every five had completed a year or more of college, while only one Negro in every five had gone as far. Moreover, years of school completed is not a full measure of educational disparities between blacks and whites. A survey conducted by the U.S. Office of Education in 1966 showed that on standardized tests of verbal ability and reading achievement, the average twelfth-grade white student in a metropolitan area performed at or near the twelfth-grade level, while the average twelfth-grade urban Negro student performed below the ninth-grade level.[8] These gaps in attainment and achievement are related in part to major differences in the kinds of teachers, educational facilities, and other resources that are available to Negro and white students, differences which will be explored more fully in the next chapter.

Having noted these differences in educational attainment, it remains true that in the cities of the nation in 1967, the income of a Negro male college graduate was on the average no greater than that of a white man who had only completed high school. The median income of black men who had completed high school was about the same as that of whites who had only attended elementary school. And at every level of educational attainment, the income of Negro men was no greater than three-fourths of that of white men who had reached the same educational level.

These striking differences in the earnings of people with similar levels of educational attainment undoubtedly are due in significant part to the inferior quality of education that many Negroes receive in segregated schools and to the differences in achievement previously noted. But this does not provide a full explanation, for, as economist Andrew Brimmer has pointed out, even in jobs in which the quality of education received does not make a major difference—such as those of carpenters and truck drivers—the earnings of Negroes are far less than those of whites.[9] Thus, although our purpose here is not to provide an in-depth analysis of the causes of disparities but only to describe them, the statistics alone strongly suggest the existence of racial discrimination in the employment process.

HOUSING—One of the chief hardships associated with low income is the inability to obtain decent shelter. In the nation as a whole in 1960, 44 per cent of all nonwhite families lived in housing classified as substandard either because it had structural defects so serious as to meet the Federal Government's definition of endangering "the health, safety, or well-being of the occupants" or because it lacked plumbing facilities. Only 13 per cent of all white families lived under such conditions.*

While a great deal of substandard housing is still located in rural areas, with the rapid rate of migration to the cities, inadequate shelter is becoming principally an urban problem. And in the cities, the racial disparities in occupancy of decent housing roughly paralleled those for the nation as a whole. About 1.8 million nonwhite families in urban areas—more than three in every seven—lived in substandard housing in 1960, while fewer than one white family in seven was in the same situation.[10] Nor did this accounting take into consideration a larger number of families living in housing that was inadequate because it was overcrowded, deteriorating, or had defects that violated local housing codes but that was not bad enough to meet the Federal Government's definition of substandard. While it appears that there has been an overall decline in the number of substandard units throughout the nation since 1960, the disparities between the quality of housing occupied by black and white citizens remain.†

* The structural defects that may cause a house to be classified as dilapidated include holes over large areas of the foundation, walls, roof, floors, or chimney; substantial sagging of floors, walls, or roof; external damage; inadequate original construction, such as shacks with makeshift walls. The racial comparisons are analyzed in Frieden, "Housing and National Urban Goals," in *The Metropolitan Enigma,* pp. 148, 158.

† A recent census report states that the proportion of nonwhites occupying substandard housing declined from 44 per cent in 1960 to 24 per cent in 1968. In central cities, the report says, 25 per cent of the units occupied by nonwhites were substandard in 1960 and only 9 per cent in 1968, while for whites 8 per cent were substandard in 1960 and 3 per cent in 1968. U.S. Bureau of the Census, Department of Commerce, Series P-23, No. 29, *The*

Although the gap in income between black and white people is undoubtedly the major factor in accounting for these disparities in housing, it is not the only one. Case studies conducted in particular cities have shown that Negroes who pay the same rents as whites frequently receive less adequate accommodations for their money and that Negroes who occupy housing that is essentially similar to housing occupied by whites often pay substantially higher rents.[11]

The key to understanding this situation lies in the fact that at every level of income, black people in the cities are far more segregated in their residential patterns than white groups with comparable incomes.[12] In other words, in their efforts to secure decent shelter, Negroes are hampered not only by inadequate income but by racial factors which limit the geographic areas in which they can seek such shelter. In a market where supply is artificially restricted by practices of racial discrimination, the Negro's dollar does not go as far as the white's; he must have a higher income than the white person in order to purchase housing that meets minimal standards, and his income at whatever level cannot purchase housing as good as that available to a white person with the same income.

In short, racial discrimination not only limits the freedom of residential choice of Negroes, but results in the imposition of a "color tax" which makes it more difficult for them to secure decent housing anywhere.

HEALTH—One of the reasons that old people do not account for as significant a portion of the poverty problem among Negroes as they do among whites is that black people simply do not live as long as whites.

In 1965, the life expectancy at birth for whites (71 years) was almost seven years longer than it was for nonwhites (64.1 years). A major factor in this gap is the infant mortality rate; 58 per cent more nonwhite than white babies die during the first month after they are born and almost three times as many during the period

Social and Economic Status of Negroes in the United States, 1969, pp. 56-57. To one who has spent some time in central-city ghettos, the 9 per cent figure is very difficult to believe. It may be well to await the 1970 census for confirmation.

from one month to one year. And, while maternal mortality is no longer a major problem in the nation as a whole, in 1965, 84 nonwhite mothers died per 100,000 live births compared to 21 white mothers.[13]

Poverty, of course, is the principal factor that accounts for the disproportionately large health problems suffered by Negroes. It ordinarily means poor nutrition, inadequate shelter, insufficient clothing, and not enough money to spend on medical care—all factors that contribute to ill health. But as in the housing gap, poverty does not provide a full explanation for racial disparities in health; other elements such as racial isolation and discrimination also have played a role.

Thus, for example, when the U.S. Commission on Civil Rights held public hearings in Cleveland in 1966, it heard testimony that the only public hospital and facility for prenatal care was located on the west side, 3½ miles or more from the east side areas where the majority of Negroes lived. The inaccessibility of the hospital, which required a bus trip of as much as an hour and a half each way for some people, deterred some expectant mothers from seeking prenatal care. And the lack of prenatal care, according to a Cleveland health official, was in part responsible for the high infant mortality rate among Negroes.[14]

THE ENVIRONMENT—Another important element in maintenance of good health conditions is the existence of adequate sanitation services. While there are no statistics that permit precise comparisons, there is much evidence suggesting that residents of slum areas, and particularly of Negro slums, are the principal victims of inadequate services.[15] This may be less a matter of conscious discrimination by municipal authorities than of a failure to take into sufficient account the greater needs for service that low-income areas have, due to their greater density. Whatever the motivation, a decline in sanitation services is frequently a key part of the familiar process by which a well-maintained neighborhood becomes a slum. It is a process which usually becomes manifest when real estate speculators move into an area and, taking advantage of the restricted market conditions created in part by racial discrimination, sell homes to Negro families at inflated prices.[16] To make ends meet, these families sometimes convert single-family homes into two-family dwellings (or two-family units into three), thus increasing the needs for sanitation and other municipal services. It only requires a failure to respond to these new needs (not a conscious policy of discriminating against black neighborhoods, which has been alleged in some places) for sanitation to grow worse and to contribute further to the deterioration of the area.

In addition, as access to health facilities is a major problem for black people in city slums, so too is access to other public services —parks and playgrounds, museums and libraries. Here, too, measurable comparisons are difficult to make. In many places, such facilities are no more geographically remote from low-income Negro areas than similar ones are from middle-class white neighborhoods, although it is not uncommon for the facilities serving white areas to be much better in quality. But physical proximity is not the measure of equality; as a practical matter, access to many of these facilities depends upon the possession of an automobile which many poor black families cannot afford, or upon the availability of superior public transit services which few low-income black areas have.[17]

PHYSICAL SECURITY AND POLICE SERVICES—To be secure in one's person is a right of citizens in our society that is fundamental to the exercise of all other rights. It is also a right which is being threatened by the increase of crime throughout the nation and particularly in cities.

In the concern about crime that pervades the nation, it is often overlooked that the principal victims of most crimes, and especially of those committed against the person, have been members of the lowest income groups in society.[18] And poor Negroes, even more than poor whites, suffer most heavily. So, for example, surveys have shown that nonwhites as a group are almost twice as likely as whites to be the victims of burglary and aggravated assault. They are more than three times as likely as whites to suffer a robbery. And the probability of being the victim of forcible rape is more than three times as high for nonwhite women as it is for white women.[19]

The reasons for the high rate of crime in low-income areas and for the fact that Negroes are disproportionately its victims are complex and lie rooted in the deprivation and social disorganization that exists in the ghetto. A part of the key to understanding lies in the fact that relatively few crimes are committed across racial lines; the perpetrators and victims of an offense are most usually of the same race and, indeed, in crimes against the person, such as murder, rape, and assault, they are frequently known to one another.[20]

While causes are admittedly complex, many people who live in ghetto areas believe that they suffer disproportionately from crime in part because the police do not afford them adequate or equitable protection. In investigating problems in black communities in several major cities, the U.S. Commission on Civil Rights found this to be a pervasive and deeply felt concern, weighing more heavily with most people than concerns about police misconduct. Time and again, the Commission heard complaints that the police did not deploy adequate resources in their communities, that prostitution, bookmaking, and other vices were tolerated when they would not be tolerated elsewhere, that policemen viewed their role as protecting the white population from black residents of the slum.[21] The testimony of the Reverend Virgil Wood, a resident of Boston's Roxbury district, concerning the difficulty one Negro family had in getting the police to respond to a call for assistance was not atypical:

One family had called the police because of an incident in the area. They waited ten minutes, fifteen minutes, twenty minutes and there was no response. Then someone was smart enough to think of calling the police, saying "Get out here quick, there is a Negro beating up a white man." The police were there in two minutes.[22]

Although there are abundant reports of individual cases of inadequate police protection, systematic comparisons of the protection afforded black people in the ghetto with that afforded whites in other areas are more difficult to come by. In Cleveland, however, Commission staff, with the aid of a law enforcement expert, analyzed police communication records in 1965 to determine whether police officers responded to calls for assistance in the predominantly Negro Hough district as quickly as in predominantly white districts. Major disparities were found in almost all categories of crime in the time lapse between the receipt of a call for assistance and the dispatch of a police car—the response almost always being slower in Hough than in the white districts.[23]

Decisions about the deployment of law enforcement personnel are difficult, especially when, as is usually the case, the resources available are so thoroughly inadequate to do an effective job. But there is much to suggest that such determinations by law enforcement officials often reflect a value system that gives higher priority to the protection of property than to protection of the person. The practical result is that in police service, as in other government services, black people receive less than an equal share.

OTHER SERVICES AND EXPLOITATION—Just as the dollar in the hands of a black man is worth less than the same dollar in the hands of a white man in obtaining housing, so the black poor must pay more for other goods and services than most white Americans.

There are many aspects to the problem. Since low-income Negro families have difficulty in accumulating enough cash to make many necessary purchases, they must seek credit. And since standard sources of credit are usually unavailable to them, they deal with lenders who charge high and sometimes usurious rates of interest. This lack of cash also means that they must buy goods in small quantities at prices frequently less economical than larger purchases.

In addition, since major retail chains are apt not to locate in ghetto areas and since black families in the ghetto often are not mobile, they are compelled to trade with small local merchants where prices are almost always higher. The reason for high prices is not necessarily exploitation, since the operation of small enterprises may not be as efficient as that of the chains and since prices may reflect the higher cost of doing business in ghetto areas. But to the black resident the result is the same, whatever the reasons may be. Moreover, while higher prices do not automatically mean exploitation, exploitation does occur. Merchandise such as furniture and appliances is often of inferior quality. And ghetto residents disproportionately often are the victims of fraudulent or deceptive sales practices.[24]

The list of areas where gross disparities exist could be extended to other services, e.g., to the difficulty black businessmen—who almost always are compelled to operate in ghetto areas—have in obtaining insurance, or to differentials in auto insurance rates which result in ghetto residents paying more. But the general point is no doubt clear.

In all of the tangible things that are used to measure success in this nation, black people stand at a gross disadvantage to whites. In most cases, the inferior status of Negroes is associated with poverty and low-paying employment. But poverty does not always provide a clear and simple explanation of the disparities that exist and, in several areas, black families in poverty are not only worse off than affluent whites but also worse off than poor whites. So even on the face of the statistical evidence, without probing into history or investigating racial discrimination, it appears that the disadvantaged status of Negroes continues to be a problem not simply of class but of race as well.

Are Things Getting Better?

In seeking to take a rough measure of the gap between black and white Americans in terms of their objective status and the things they possess, we have omitted, thus far, any discussion of trends. Obviously, trends are important to judging the significance of the disparities that presently exist. If, for example, the present situation has persisted for many years or if, indeed, the gap has grown wider, the most pessimistic conclusions may be justified. If, on the other hand, disparities have been lessening rapidly, a less serious view of their significance may be warranted.

A case can be and has been made for the proposition that important progress has been made in recent years in closing the gap. It is buttressed by statistics which at first glance seem quite impressive. For example, it is true that the median income of Negro families has risen about $1,500 in four years' time—a rate of increase greater than the improvement in family income for whites—and that this has resulted in a narrowing of the percentage gap between black and white family income. It is also true that about three black families in ten now have incomes of $8,000 or more, almost twice the proportion with equivalent incomes in 1960. And it is also a fact that since 1960 the number of non-whites living in poverty has declined from about 11.5 million to 8 million, meaning that while more than half of all black people were poor by government standards in 1960 only one in three is so classified now.[25] The citation of these and similar facts has given rise to the complacent view held in some quarters (apparently including the White House) that while problems of racial inequity and poverty exist, their solution is just a matter of time.

Such complacency, however, does not withstand a closer examination of the facts. In the first place, while it is true that there is a growing Negro middle class, there is also a growing gap in the distribution of income among black people. In short, there have emerged two increasingly distinct groups of black citizens, a middle and upper income group which is becoming wealthier and a low-income group which is getting poorer. While many of the former group have been well enough educated and trained to benefit from the antidiscrimination enactments of the 1960s, most in the latter group have received no benefit from laws which do not deal with their basic problems. It is important to keep in mind this growing contrast in the situations of higher and lower income black people. It aids in an understanding of how, amid general indications of progress, the unemployment rate for black people can stay consistently at about twice that for whites and the circumstances of many black people in city ghettos can continue to grow worse.

Secondly, in considering data showing that the number and percentage of Negroes who are poor have declined markedly by government standards, it is well to remember that poverty is a relative matter. As Galbraith has noted, the poor are those whose incomes have fallen behind the rest of society and the poverty line must always be related to time, place, and possibilities.[26] Recognizing the validity of this observation, most commentators have discarded the habit of comparing the situation of poor and black people in this country with that of people in other societies. Statements that the poverty in the United States is not nearly as wretched as that suffered by many people in South America or that people considered poor in this country might be deemed well off in many parts of Asia or Africa are now dismissed as true but irrelevant. But, while realizing that the situation of the black poor in this country is best judged by comparing it with that of other Americans and not of foreigners, many observers still fail to recognize that the gains made by people who have marginally escaped from poverty have been dwarfed by the progress made by the bulk of more affluent Americans.

So, for example, government analysts may point with pride to the fact that from 1965 to 1968 the ratio of Negro median family income to white median family income moved from 54 per cent to 60 per cent, concluding that the gap is rapidly being closed. But the same statistics reveal that the dollar gap between average Negro income and average white income grew from $3,365 to $3,577 during the same period, indicating that the gap is widening, not closing. And over a twenty-year period, the gap between average Negro and white family income has grown about $1,400, from roughly $2,100 to $3,500—hardly an indication of progress.

Similarly, it is interesting to note that during the past twenty years, there has been no major change in the way income is distributed among the population. In 1967, the poorest 20 per cent of American families had about 5 per cent of total family income, just about the same as in 1947, while the richest 20 per cent had more than a 40 per cent share in both years.[27] Some may conclude from this that the nation is holding its own in the equity with which income is being distributed. But in a nation whose affluence has increased tremendously, what it really means is that the dollar gap between the rich and poor has grown enormously. A family whose income was $2,000 in 1947 and is $4,000 now still has the same proportionate share with respect to a family whose income was $10,000 in 1947 and is $20,000 now, but the gulf between them is now much wider.

So the disaffection of the poor may not be traceable simply to the fact that national television has suddenly made them aware of how affluent Americans live but also to an awareness that their relative position is constantly becoming worse.

Thirdly, even comparisons that take into account the positions of black people and white people now as against their relative positions some years ago may not place problems in full perspective. As economist Rashi Fein has pointed out, such comparisons usually omit the crucial element of time; they do not reveal the time lag by showing, for example, at what point whites reached the level that Negroes have only recently achieved and what, if any, progress is being made in cutting the time gap. In an innovative analysis made in 1965, Fein asked these questions in several areas.[28] He found, for example, that the life expectancy of Negro men reached 61.5 years in 1960, a point that white men had reached in 1932. He found, too, that over a period of years, no progress had been made in reducing the time gap—that Negroes made no more progress from 1920 to 1960 than whites made from 1900 to 1940, even though one might naturally assume that medical advances would make more rapid progress possible in the later period. When viewed from Fein's useful perspective which shows Negroes just now reaching levels that whites reached many years ago and not moving any faster than whites did in an earlier era, the signs of progress look far less encouraging.

Fourthly, if problems are viewed from the perspective of the cities rather than nationally, the notion of progress disappears. In almost every major city, the number of nonwhite families living in poverty has increased substantially during the past decade. In New York the number of such families grew from 68,000 in 1959 to 80,000 in 1967. In Chicago, the increase was from 55,000 to 71,000 and in Los Angeles from 24,000 to 30,000. And lastly, overall descriptions of progress sometimes disguise the fact that the gains are not taking place in the areas which may be viewed as the most critical to lasting solutions. For example, while it is true that since 1960 there have been noticeable improvements in the occupational distribution of Negroes in central cities, what this reflects almost entirely is progress for Negro women who have moved in some numbers from domestic work to clerical and sales jobs. While this is surely progress, it may not be as important as the fact that for Negro men, there was little change in job status.

In short, claims that the nation is making rapid progress in eliminating disparities between blacks and whites and in reducing poverty do not survive close analysis. For perhaps 10 per cent of all Negro families, recent years have brought significant gains, but for another 20 per cent, almost 2½ million of them living in central cities, no gains have been made and for many the situation is becoming worse. Nor do official statistics on the reduction of poverty give great cause for cheer. While some people have escaped from poverty, the greatest number of them are still living on the margins, and in terms of relative deprivation they are far worse off than they were a few years ago. And even when progress is examined in overall terms, it is found that in many areas, Negroes as a group are just now reaching levels that whites achieved many years ago and that their rate of advancement is very slow.

Social Ills and the Psychology of the Ghetto

Just as black people as a group have less of the desirable things of life—good jobs, decent housing, adequate services—so they have more of the social ills. Some, such as higher disease, infant, and maternal mortality rates, have already been noted. Others—family instability and illegitimacy, mental illness, homicide rates in ghetto areas as much as five or six times as high as those in other areas of the city, juvenile delinquency, narcotics addiction, venereal disease—are the familiar stuff of current social comment and analysis, symptoms of social disorganization and malfunction that Kenneth Clark describes as the "pathology of the ghetto."[29]

These social ills are less subject than jobs, income, and housing to precise measurements and comparisons. It is possible, for example, that some contrasts between social problems in black ghettos and those in more affluent white areas may be overstated. Such problems as alcoholism, drug addiction, illegitimacy, juvenile delinquency, and broken homes are more easily shielded from public view in affluent communities, and their extent and seriousness may not be fully reflected in any set of social statistics. Other comparisons, however, such as physical and mental illness, may be understated because in ghetto areas they are more apt to go undiagnosed and untreated. But as difficult as it may be to gauge the disparities accurately, there is no doubt that in sum the social evils that afflict black people in the ghetto are far more serious than those suffered by any other group.

It is also a difficult job to establish precisely the causes of particular social ills. While, for example, family instability is frequently associated with poverty and unemployment, in the rural South where poverty is often as deep and pervasive as in urban areas, broken homes occur far less frequently among Negro families. Nor, for example, can a single factor such as poor housing be isolated from the total environment in seeking the roots of pathology. Improvements in housing in the ghetto unaccompanied by efforts to deal with other kinds of deprivation have not alleviated most social problems.[30] Nonetheless, linkages between deprivation and pathology in the ghetto and between various kinds of social illnesses are abundant and often plain. Whatever other factors may be involved, it is clear that the inability of Negro men to find any but the most menial, low-paying work is a prime cause of the break-up of families and of the unwillingness of many men to enter into formal marriages in the first place.[31] Children who are illegitimate or the offspring of broken marriages, in turn, are more apt than others to engage in delinquent behavior or to become narcotics addicts. And self-destructive behavior often leads to aggression against others, as when heroin addicts turn in desperation to crime to obtain the money they need for drugs.

To gain some understanding of these relationships and patterns and of why the ghetto is self-perpetuating, it is necessary to appreciate the impact that deprivation and discrimination may have upon the soul and spirit of those who have been its victims. It is in this realm, when one seeks to compare the attitudes of black people in the ghetto—how they view themselves and the world they live in—with the attitudes of whites, that disparities become least subject to measurement.

For those who seek an appreciation of the scars that ghetto life can inflict upon the personality, there are abundant sources of illumination—in the moving personal testaments of Claude Brown[32] or Malcolm X,[33] in the "fiction" of Ralph Ellison,[34] in the social analysis of Kenneth Clark.[35] But relatively few white Americans have acquainted themselves with these writings. They have, of course, heard and read a good deal about black attitudes on television and in the press. But lacking any real familiarity with black citizens, many whites seem to have concluded in the wake of riots

and disorders that the feelings expressed have been less than genuine—that they are patterned responses, tactical positions adopted
in an effort to gain political advantage.

Even a limited exposure to life in the inner city would convince
most people that this is not so. Several years ago, before the con-
flagrations of Detroit and Newark and before the media became
interested in detailed reporting of problems in city slums, the
U.S. Commission on Civil Rights undertook a detailed investigation of conditions of ghetto life in cities throughout the nation.
With the help of its state advisory committees, the Commission
conducted hearings and meetings at which it sought to achieve
an understanding of problems not simply by listening to representative organizations and intermediaries but by hearing first-
hand from people who lived or worked in ghetto communities.

Among the striking impressions the commissioners and staff
took away from the hearings was that the dominant attitudes and
feelings of black citizens were remarkably similar in ghetto communities throughout the nation.

For example, one pervasive feeling that emerged from the
testimony of ghetto residents in many cities was that their situation was analogous to being in prison. The same theme kept re-
curring in the statements of witnesses. A mother on welfare in
Gary, Indiana, talked of being caught in "a quagmire, a big quick-
sand," a place where nothing changes and "time stops"; a former
resident of a public housing project in San Francisco's Potrero
Hill said that he and others felt as if they were "in a cage"; to
another slum resident in Gary, her neighborhood was "more or
less a trap."[36]

Closely associated with the theme of imprisonment were feelings of isolation from white society and the larger world. So a
California witness noted that his predominantly Negro community
of East Palo Alto was "more and more cut off from the general
community," so that the younger generation had "no concept of
any social relationship with any people other than Negroes."[37]
And, indeed, the testimony of a Cleveland youngster, Calvin
Brooks, that he had grown up without ever knowing a white person his own age until he was fourteen or fifteen, was not untypical.[38] Implicit in these feelings of isolation and entrapment
was a general sense of powerlessness, a feeling that there was

little if anything that one could do to influence the course of one's own life and that it was useless to try. This sense of futility was not simply vague or generalized, but often was reinforced by illustrations drawn from experience—being rebuffed in efforts to find a job, being uprooted from one's home by an urban renewal project without being informed or consulted.[39]

Perhaps most damaging of all, many black residents have come to share the view they believe that white people have of them—that they are inferior people unable to compete or participate on equal terms in American society. Feeling isolated, entrapped, powerless, and scorned by whites, they reject themselves as worthless and thus engage in the ultimate self-fulfilling prophecy.

It is tragic to see how early this process of self-rejection begins. In the *School Segregation Cases*, the Supreme Court cited the experiments of the Clarks and others showing that even before the age of five, Negro children begin to reject brown dolls in favor of white ones. In the Commission's Cleveland hearings, Dr. Robert Coles, a Harvard child psychiatrist, testified about Negro children in the North. Employing a technique he has used in many places, Dr. Coles had asked children to draw pictures of familiar things. He repeated one youngster's explanation of why she drew a picture of herself sitting in the back of a school bus which took her from her neighborhood to a predominantly white elementary school:

> ". . . they say they are going to stop us from coming here soon, and so no more bus rides."
> I pressed on, "But why are you sitting where you are in the picture?"
> "If we are going to leave anyway, we might as well sit in the back and then we can leave when we have to, then we won't disturb anyone."[40]

Dr. Coles also described the picture a Negro boy drew of his home:

> This house is a shambles. It is a confused disorderly house for a child that can do better and has done better. He has much better drawing ability. The house is deliberately ramshackled. There is a black sky and what might pass for a black sun or in any event a cloud of black. The ground is brown and not green, and there

are no flowers. It is a dismal place. There is a cross on the door. The child told me that the property was condemned.[41]

And, discussing a ten-year-old boy who attended an all-black school:

> But what I was interested in is the way the child drew a Negro and then drew a white . . . I have almost a thousand of these drawings. The white person is more limbed, the Negro is often truncated, the sun is over the white person with a consistency that I could statistically prove much to my horror. I don't like to statistically prove any kinds of human emotion.
> Here are a few other drawings of children who are Negro children, who are having difficulties at five and six coming to terms with their race. They consistently draw themselves as white.[42]

It is only in the context of these pervasive feelings of powerlessness and of self-rejection starting at a very early age and continuing into adulthood that such current abstractions as "black power," "black is beautiful," and the emphasis upon black culture can be understood. Lacking any such background, many white Americans have viewed such notions as threatening or absurd. These they may be in some situations. More often, however, they represent efforts to counteract the corrosive effects of hopelessness and futility in black ghettos—efforts that are very much against the odds because they are rarely reinforced by tangible symbols of self-worth.

For some, self-hatred and rejection eventually become anger directed outward. It is not surprising that the objects of hostility are often white people—the policeman who is viewed as keeping the Negro in line for the white community, the merchant who sells shoddy merchandise and engages in dubious credit practices, the absentee landlord who allows his property to deteriorate after Negroes move in. But, born of despair, the anger is frequently a more general cry of protest against one's fate. James Richards, a black youngster with a prison record who helped stop a riot in the Hunters Point neighborhood of San Francisco, put it this way:

> One minute we are looking ahead . . . and we turn around and again all we can see is darkness ahead.

Describing the conditions under which a typical ghetto young-ster lives, he said:

> . . . he has little brothers and sisters in the house and he sees his mother and brothers and sisters going hungry, half starving and trying to get the rent in. It is a bare house, like it is a cold feeling even to be there and you have to go out on the street and become the subject of the same thing out there. There has to be a breaking point.

And he concluded:

> And sometimes at a time like this all they can do is strike out into the night. They don't know what they are reaching for out there.[43]

Pictures of ghetto life are sometimes overdrawn as unrelievedly grim. Along with hopelessness and despair there are, of course, qualities of humor, dignity, strength, and endurance. Usually, however, these are qualities born of suffering. In Gary, Mrs. Jacqueline Taylor, a mother on welfare, said:

> I try to show my children the beautiful things that are in ugliness. There are beautiful things in ugliness if you look at it, if you have the insight to look at it that way. And then I will tell them about different things and try to put adventure in their souls, they are still young, so they can pull themselves out.
> And maybe if they are strong enough or if I can pull them out, they can reach back and give me a hand and pull me out.[44]

It may be argued that the feelings and attitudes which have such a debilitating effect are products of poverty and deprivation and as such should be viewed as impediments of class, not race. But, as we have seen, race is an inseparable element in the process of degradation which takes place in the ghetto. It sets the black man apart in his own mind and in the minds of others in situations where he might otherwise be indistinguishable from the mass. And while the impact may be much less, many of the feelings of the poor are shared by middle-class black people as well. However economically secure they may become, they are subject to sudden and shattering reminders from whites that they are members of a despised racial group and, to a greater degree than any other group of upwardly mobile Americans, their efforts to become assimilated are apt to be scorned both by the majority and by the poor in their own racial group. It is not then too surprising that much of the anger and militancy that fuels black protest today is supplied by middle-class Negroes.

It may be argued, also, that feelings of powerlessness, frustration, and alienation are not the exclusive property of any single group and that they are in fact shared by a great many Americans. There is no doubt that this is true, but the question is one of degree. It is clearly almost impossible for an affluent white citizen to place himself in the position of a poor black citizen and fully understand his problems. One approach, however, might be for the comfortable citizen to focus on some of his worst frustrations, whether important (such as the loss of a coveted job opportunity) or merely annoying (such as a hassle with a department store over merchandise), and then to try to envision how effectively he would operate if life were like that all the time.

Just as a father's lack of a good job means the inability to provide a decent environment and the necessities of life for his family, and the absence of these impairs the ability of a child to obtain the kind of education needed for a good job, so the frustrations of slum life contribute to a kind of "ghetto of the mind" which also reinforces and perpetuates the cycle of poverty and dependency.

Conclusion

In *Democracy in America,* Tocqueville wrote that "society can exist only when a great number of men consider a great number of things under the same aspect, when they hold the same opinions upon many subjects, and when the same occurrences suggest the same thoughts and impressions to their minds."[45]

If one were to review the public opinion polls taken in recent years he would find that on an increasing number of political and public issues, not simply those confined to race relations, the greatest contrasts in attitudes are not between men and women, old and young, Northerner and Southerner, but between white and black. These often striking differences in opinion arise from glaring contrasts in the experience of most white and black people in the United States. The disparities exist across the board—

in the objective status of whites and blacks, in the possession of goods and services regarded as necessary or desirable, in the ability to avoid social ills, in the feelings people have about themselves and the world.

While there has been an improvement in the absolute position of some Negroes in recent years, the position of many others has grown relatively and in some cases even absolutely worse. The gains made by Negroes have been dwarfed by an enormous increase in the affluence of the nation, and as a whole the gap between white and black America seems to have widened, not closed.

In terms then of the standard offered by Tocqueville, the nation is already, or rapidly becoming, two societies. The possibilities for conflict are increased by the fact that with the mass migration of Negroes to cities, the differences are no longer between a predominantly rural black people and a largely urban white population, geographically remote from each other, but between two groups that coexist uneasily in the same urban areas. And the danger is that if the disparities do not lessen, or if they continue to grow, even the agreement that continues to bind Americans together on fundamental issues, such as the rule of law and democratic processes, will dissolve, leaving no options except conflict and violence.

2

THE IMMIGRANT MYTH

THE BLACK CITY DWELLER, at long last, has begun to shed his cloak of anonymity. For years, most white Americans seemed determined to treat Negroes in the cities as invisible men—people whose presence was hardly to be acknowledged, much less the circumstances in which they lived and their feelings understood. But events have conspired to deprive whites of this cheerful ignorance of their darker city neighbors. For one thing, in most cities there are simply too many of them now to be overlooked. Then, too, in almost every major city, Negroes have made known their despair and anger by sending up smoke signals that even in Los Angeles could hardly be mistaken for smog. And, while urban ghettos remain physically and psychologically isolated from white society, the reporting of television and newspapers has conveyed a picture of the conditions of life for people who are poor and black.

Thus, most white people now are aware that Negro families in the central city live in dilapidated and deteriorating housing; that their neighborhoods are infested by rats; that their children do not have an adequate diet and lack warm clothing in the winter.

Awareness of these facts of ghetto life, however, does not necessarily import an understanding of causes or agreement upon remedy. On these questions, most white people appear to have reached conclusions that rob the problems of a sense of urgency and divest the white community of any responsibility for their creation or solution, instead shifting the entire burden to Negroes themselves.

The touchstone of this set of conclusions is the widely held belief that the situation in which black people now find themselves in the cities is closely analogous to that faced by European and Asian immigrants who came to this nation in the late nineteenth and early twentieth centuries. In this view, the Negro as a migrant to the city is simply the latest in a long line of racial and ethnic groups—Germans, Irish, Orientals, Jews, Italians— in search of opportunity. As the most recent arrival, it is natural that he should be low man on the totem pole, struggling for the least desirable jobs, living in slum housing, and falling prey to a variety of social ills. But this is viewed as a temporary situation; other immigrant groups made their way into American society by dint of hard labor, sacrifice, and perseverance. If the Negro pursues the same course, the analysis runs, there is no reason to doubt that he too will eventually receive his reward. Or, alternatively, it is argued that the reason that Negroes have not yet extricated themselves from urban poverty is that they have failed to apply themselves in the same rigorous way that earlier groups did. The fault, then, is largely theirs.

The immigrant analogy is a popular one. It has enabled many among the millions of white Americans whose parents or grandparents came to the United States in humble circumstances to say in substance, "*We* made it on our own, why can't *they?*" Support for the analogy is not infrequently found in popular journals[1] (one such piece that appeared in *The New York Times Magazine* a couple of years ago was illustrated by a cartoon that depicted a Negro family actually getting off the boat behind little old ladies wearing babushkas and men carrying their belongings in knapsacks). And, curiously, some black separatists who would reject out of hand the parallels drawn between the history of Negroes and of immigrant groups are nonetheless ready to invest their hopes in proposals for remedies—e.g., the establishment of small businesses and other self-help enterprises and the accumulation of political power through control over local party machinery— that essentially grow out of the immigrant experience.

The appeal of the immigrant analogy is not difficult to understand. There are many surface parallels, beginning with the fact that the migration of Negroes in recent years from the rural South to the cities of the North and West constitutes a mass movement of people outranked in our history only by the waves of European immigrants at the turn of the century. (Although Negroes began leaving the South in some numbers soon after the Civil War, the movement has reached a peak only in recent years; from 1940 to 1966 the net out-migration of black people from the South was about 3.7 million. From 1901 to 1921, approximately 14.5 million immigrants entered the United States.[2]) Other similarities between the situation of immigrants and Negroes include their predominantly rural peasant origins and the persecution they suffered before leaving them, their physical and psychological confinement in ghettos once they reached America's cities, and the ill-treatment both groups received at the hands of the majority society. The awareness that immigrant groups were verbally mistreated and abused, while perhaps a potentially sobering lesson about the dangers of stereotyping, may also help some whites to alleviate feelings of guilt about expressions of racist sentiment against Negroes. After all, it is argued, the Irish were once reviled as being lazy and drunk, Jews as being clannish and dirty, Italians and Poles as being ignorant, and each group overcame these prejudices. One may question, then, the seriousness of similar abuse directed against Negroes; it may be regarded as little more than the hazing of the new boy on the block that is quickly forgotten once he has proved his worth and entered the club. Recourse to the immigrant analogy is, finally, comforting; in the optimistic American tradition it promises a happy ending to a story full of strife and bitterness.

But appealing as it may be to draw parallels between the experience of immigrant groups and black people, it is submitted that the analogy is wrong and dangerous. The analogy is wrong because (1) it ignores fundamental differences between the character of the oppression suffered by Negroes and that suffered by immigrant groups, and (2) it overlooks major distinctions between the nature of American society of sixty or seventy years ago and the far more complex, technological society of the 1960s and 1970s, and the barriers that each presented to the advancement of minority groups. The analogy is dangerous because it leads to complacency and to a misreading of what must be done and how much effort is required to create genuine opportunity for black people and to establish harmonious relations between the races.

The Nature of Historical Oppression

Many Irish immigrants arrived in this country as refugees from famine and exploitation. Jews from eastern Europe came to escape pogroms that were only the most recent chapter in a history of persecution that had once included bondage. Immigrants from southern Italy came here to escape the terrible privations of a semifeudal society.

Yet none of these evils could compare in their impact upon the individual to those that the system of chattel slavery imposed in America. Slavery in this country systematically destroyed the Negro family. In law, marriages between slaves had no standing. Adopted as a device to remove any impediment to transactions that would break up slave families, the doctrine also meant that marriages could be dissolved at will, that Negro fathers had neither authority nor responsibility in the raising of their children, that children had no legal protection against the forced separation of their parents.[3] Add to this the fact that women slaves could be sexually exploited because the law recognized few crimes against the Negro except those that would impair his value as his master's property and the strangulation of any real possibility of family life became complete.[4]

Nor did the peculiar institution of slavery in the United States allow much possibility for the Negro to better his condition. By law and by tradition, Negroes were not allowed to learn to read and write, on the theory that they did not have the capacity to absorb an education, that it would be useless to them and that it would only make them rebellious. Restraints against the education of Negroes were not limited to the slaveholding South. During the eighteenth and much of the nineteenth century, most of the free states of the North either excluded Negroes altogether from the public schools or allowed them to attend only vastly inferior segregated institutions.[5] Nor could Negroes in any sig-

nificant numbers acquire the kinds of skills that might stand
them in good stead after the abolition of slavery. They did not
have the opportunity as slaves or even as freed men to acquire
and practice the skills of artisans or tradesmen, a fact that made
slavery in this country even more repressive than similar institutions in Latin American countries.[6]

It is difficult, of course, to measure the contemporary impact
upon opportunities for black citizens of these not so ancient evils.
It is possible that, as deeply destructive as many slave practices
were, their effects might have been all but eradicated today were
it not for the continuance of discrimination against Negroes during the century since emancipation. One suspects, for example,
that the continued instability of family life among poor black
people may be traced at least as much to the persistent denial of
job opportunities to Negro men and to welfare policies that have
made the break-up of families the price of receiving government
assistance as to the lasting effects of slavery. While no neat slide-
rule calculation will provide the answer to such questions, there
is a danger in ascribing too much weight to historical practices,
no matter how severe, as the source of current deprivation. Such
an emphasis lends credence to the prevalent belief among whites
that distinctive "cultural characteristics" of the Negro people provide the principal explanation for their deprived status. There is
a major difference, of course, in the fact that many of those who
subscribe most avidly to theories of cultural difference tend con-
veniently to forget the vicious practices that may have given rise
to these presumed differences. But, whether or not stress upon
cultural differences includes an awareness of the impact of
slavery, the result may be the same—a preoccupation with changes
in Negro family life and values, rather than with changes in external conditions, as the key to progress. So, for example, it appears to be widely assumed among white people that Negro
parents place less value upon obtaining a good education for
their children than other racial and ethnic groups, a conclusion which tends to exculpate public school systems of blame
for the failure of black students. If this were so, it might be explained, without any implication of racial inferiority, as a legacy
of the suppression of education during slavery. But the evidence
does not support this assumed difference in values; in fact, ex-

tensive interviews conducted by the U.S. Commission on Civil Rights in the ghettos of some of our major cities have convinced this observer, at least, that black parents are as concerned as any other group about the education of their children.[7]

If, however, there is risk in relying too heavily upon the practices of slavery as an explanation for the present status of Negroes, it would be equally a mistake to discount them entirely. For, in stripping Negroes of any opportunity for family life, education, and the acquisition of skills, slavery robbed them of resources that would be of crucial importance after emancipation. Many immigrant groups arrived in this country without visible means of support. But each had intangible assets of considerable value. Jews had a long-standing attachment to scholarship that helped them to enter the professions and a reservoir of business acumen that aided in the establishment of small enterprises. The Japanese had similar ties to education and strong family bonds that helped to sustain them through periods when they, like Negroes, were made the victims of racial legislation. The great wave of Irish immigrants had been preceded by a smaller, educated group which had prospered and was in a position to aid in establishing the Catholic Church as a powerful instrument for self-help. Italian immigrants, like others, had close family bonds and some of the skills that would prove useful in building the cities. Even late arrivals, like the Puerto Ricans, came with some assets that distinguished their situation from that of Negroes. Puerto Ricans, unlike Negroes, came to the cities from a place where they were not regarded as a lower caste and, especially during the 1950s, some arrived with skills that had ensued from rapid industrialization of the island (assisted by American investments, subsidies, and tax exemptions).[8]

If slavery had been a less tyrannical institution, perhaps a colorable case could be made for the immigrant analogy. But it was not; Negroes emerged from bondage without the reserves that other groups had to sustain them through the long fight for survival in the cities.

To maintain a belief in the immigrant analogy, another crucial difference must be ignored—the contrast in character and impact between *foreign* and *domestic* oppression.

The immigrant from Europe may have been driven to America

by poverty, economic exploitation, or political persecution rather than attracted by the promise of riches; he may have sustained the shock of being uprooted and of finding himself in new and alien surroundings. But he had left behind his foreign oppressor and in that simple fact there lay hope. Even after he had experienced discrimination in the new world, had been shunned and isolated, relegated to dirty jobs and slum housing, hope could not be completely extinguished. He was not, after all, a member of a small minority; most around him were poor or had recently been poor. And there was solid evidence to support a belief that if he worked hard and persevered, he too might win a place in society.

In contrast, the Negro at any stage in history could hardly maintain the belief that he had escaped from foreign oppression. Perhaps in the days immediately following the Civil War, Negroes journeying to northern cities could imagine themselves entering a new land ruled by a different breed of people. But they soon found themselves subject to laws and policies which disfranchised them and refused them access to public schools, the courts, and other public facilities. Although these laws yielded gradually to the new constitutional amendments, their repeal was not accompanied by much practical improvement in the status of black people. They still were denied the opportunity to acquire skills and a useful education and they found themselves displaced from even the menial positions they occupied by later-arriving groups of white immigrants.[9] And with the Compromise of 1877 which resulted in the withdrawal of Federal troops from the South, the North became a partner in the subjugation of the southern Negro, further dispelling any concept of separate nations.[10]

The later Negroes arrived in northern cities, the more difficult the illusion of a "new world" became. By the time the greatest wave of migration came in the 1940s, most immigrant groups had achieved a measure of economic success and the Negro found himself relatively alone in his poverty and confinement. And then, the employer who refused him a job, the landlord who denied him an apartment, the policeman who abused him, and the merchant who cheated him destroyed any remaining illusion that Northerners were very different from other white Americans of his experience—plantation bosses and southern sheriffs. Given the whole history of northern segregation codes and racial policies directed toward Negroes and of restrictions upon education and economic advancement, black people could scarcely hold a different view. The white immigrant might have looked upon the ghetto as the first rough harbor from a foreign storm; for most Negroes it was simply another mark of their lowly place in American society.

In addition to the pivotal differences already cited, one additional factor should be noted—the inevitable distinction between the character and durability of *racial* as against *ethnic* types of discrimination. For European immigrants and especially for their children, one of the principal routes to success in American society was assimilation. They could drop their foreign ways, perfect American speech, if necessary change their names, and become indistinguishable from the mass of long-settled American citizens. True, it is fashionable these days to conclude that in practice this theory of the "melting pot" has failed, by noting the considerable extent to which ethnic groups have maintained separate interests.[11] In their zeal to make this point some writers have distorted the focus, turning their spotlight almost exclusively on the central city and the still substantial number of older, first-generation Americans who reside there, and away from the increasing ranks of later generations who are located in suburbia. But whatever the perspective from which the problem is viewed, the major point is that for immigrants the melting pot was and is the prevailing dogma, and the measure always has been how close we have come or how far we have fallen short of its promise.

For Negroes (and for the much smaller ranks of other racial minorities) the melting pot theory has never applied. The black person has not had the option of securing equality of treatment by becoming physically indistinguishable from the mass of American citizens. Nor has this even been viewed as a long-range solution, because sexual taboos, no longer enshrined in law but still prevalent, inhibit interracial marriage.

Thus, for Negroes, in contrast to white immigrants, there are no bypaths to full citizenship. Their progress is always measured and limited by the extent to which prejudice and discrimination are overcome. More than a century and a half ago, Tocqueville recognized the importance of this distinction. Looking beyond what he regarded as the inevitable abolition of slavery, he wrote:

> There is a natural prejudice that prompts men to despise whoever has been their inferior long after he has become their equal; and the real inequality that is produced by fortune or by law is always succeeded by an imaginary inequality that is implanted in the manners of the people. But among the ancients this secondary consequence of slavery had a natural limit; for the freedman bore so entire a resemblance to those born free that it soon became impossible to distinguish him from them.
> . . . When I remember the extreme difficulty with which aristocratic bodies, of whatever nature they may be, are commingled with the mass of the people, and the exceeding care which they take to preserve for ages the ideal boundaries of their caste inviolate, I despair of seeing an aristocracy disappear which is founded upon visible and indelible signs.[12]

Tocqueville's despair may have been premature, but the salient fact is that the experience of more than one hundred years since the abolition of slavery has yet to prove him wrong. This alone should give pause to those who have embraced the immigrant analogy and all its comfortable implications.

Continuing Discrimination and the Barriers of a Technological Society

The burden of all that has been said so far is that even if black Americans and white immigrants were entering the nation's cities at the same moment in history, their situations would not be comparable. The arrival, of course, was not simultaneous; the greatest numbers of Negroes came (and continue to come) to the cities many decades after the peak of European immigration had passed. In this gap in time lies another important distinction between the problems confronting Negroes and those faced by immigrants, a distinction perhaps more vital than those previously cited.

For urban, industrialized society has changed drastically in the period since European immigration was at its height; technology has transformed both the character of work and living arrangements, and society has become more organized, complex, and stratified. The traditional avenues of escape from the poverty and meanness of ghetto life—securing a good job, obtaining a good education for one's self and one's family, finding better housing and a healthier environment—may have remained the same, but the changes that have taken place in society have made access to these avenues much more difficult than in the past. It is doubtful in the extreme that *any* group in depressed circumstances could win a place in today's society if it had to rely mainly on traditional techniques of self-help. For black people, the obstacles are made even more difficult by the persistence of racial discrimination.

Employment

For the great majority of newly arriving immigrants, even those without skills, jobs were available. They were dirty, backbreaking jobs in clothing and furniture factories, in the mines and on the docks, in construction gangs building the cities' houses, utilities, and highways. The pay was low and there was no security against illness or layoff. Still, for most immigrants, the jobs were a first shaky step on the economic ladder. And, although opportunities for advancement were limited, they were not entirely absent. Some immigrants advanced to more skilled work in the factories. Some became contractors and distributors of piece goods and eventually small manufacturers. Others started small retail enterprises catering to the special needs of members of their ethnic group. And as some immigrant groups, by virtue of their numbers and organization, gradually won control of local political machines, still more jobs became available in police, fire, and other city government departments and, more lucratively, as contractors who sold the city goods and services.

The black man from the rural South who arrives in the city today without skills or any real semblance of an education may appear to some as the contemporary counterpart of that European immigrant. But the situation confronting him is radically different. During the past quarter century, technology has changed the patterns of job development in the nation in ways that drastically diminish the chances of economic success for new migrants.

One overriding factor is the shrinking need in the labor force for people who command few, if any, skills. It is true that manufacturing, which accounts for many low-skill jobs, still provides a significant share—roughly 25 per cent—of the nation's total employment. But if factory jobs have not declined as rapidly as they have in agriculture and mining, neither are they increasing as fast as the work force is expanding. (From 1964 to 1975, it is expected that there will be about 1.5 million new jobs in manufacturing, a growth rate of about 9 per cent.[13] In contrast, the biggest areas of expansion are in service industries, including government, which are expected to account for 12 million of the more than 15 million new jobs anticipated.[14]) Perhaps even more to the point, the importance of blue collar jobs, in manufacturing and elsewhere, to the nation's economy is declining rapidly. In 1947 such jobs constituted 41 per cent of total civilian employment; in 1964 they were 36 per cent; and by 1975 it is anticipated that they will drop to 33 per cent.[15]

The second major factor is that in competing with white workers in this shrinking area of the employment market (as well as in areas that are expanding), Negroes in the cities face a number of barriers that are peculiar products of contemporary society. In manufacturing and other fields one of the most formidable problems is the increasing inaccessibility of jobs to the great mass of Negroes who live in the inner city. During the periods of great European immigration, employment opportunities were clustered in the central city near the waterfront and rail terminals, and housing grew up around the jobs. But in recent times, manufacturers, acting for a variety of sound economic reasons,[16] have in large numbers moved their facilities from the inner city to suburban locations. With the great population increase of the suburbs, retailers, wholesalers, and service industries have followed suit. During the past twenty years, the shift in jobs has been particularly striking. In 1948 only one-tenth of the jobs in wholesaling in the forty largest metropolitan areas were located in the suburbs, but by 1963 one-third of those jobs were in the suburbs. In manufacturing, the suburbs provided only 37 per cent of the jobs in 1948; by 1963 they accounted for more than one-half. In retailing, almost half the jobs were located in the suburban ring in 1963 compared with slightly more than one-fourth in 1948.

And, in selected kinds of service employment, the suburban proportion moved from 17 per cent in 1948 to 35 per cent in 1963.[17]

For mobile white workers, this mass relocation of jobs has created few problems (and in fact has often provided advantages). But for black people confined to the ghettos by their inability to obtain housing elsewhere, the problems are enormous. The schedules and routes of mass transit facilities are not designed to serve the needs of people who must travel from inner city to suburb in the morning and in the opposite direction at night. People seeking to go that route must often be prepared for time-consuming journeys at rates that are considered expensive even by commuters who hold well-paying white collar jobs.[18] The automobile might provide a satisfactory if similarly expensive alternative to public transportation, but most nonwhite families in the inner city do not own cars.[19]

The increasing physical remoteness of jobs operates to reinforce other factors that also handicap Negroes seeking to enter the job market. The principal of these is the key role that informal networks of communication occupy in the hiring process. Labor experts agree that, while public and private employment offices and newspaper advertising are factors in job recruitment, workers most often locate their jobs by learning of openings from friends, casual associations, or by passing the place of work and seeing help-wanted signs.[20] Isolated from social contact with whites, Negroes never learn of the great bulk of job opportunities at plants that employ virtually all-white forces. (Conversely, when a Cleveland employer, prodded by the government, decided to improve his civil rights record, he found that the most effective first step was to assign the few Negroes already on the payroll the responsibility of finding other recruits.) When, in addition, black people are physically remote from centers of employment, they are deprived of the alternative of learning of job openings by being on or near the scene.

The adverse impact upon Negroes of these seemingly neutral aspects of the employment process (the physical location of jobs and informal methods of hiring) is not limited to handicaps imposed upon the ability to compete for unskilled laboring jobs. They also place beyond the reach of black people a wide variety of jobs—e.g., as craftsmen, clerks, sales personnel—having skill requirements that can be met by relatively short periods of on-the-job training. A further obstacle impeding access by minority groups to many relatively skilled jobs is the tendency of employers to establish formal qualifications for employment that go far beyond the actual requirements of the job. Except during periods of general labor shortage, many of the jobs in question are attractive enough to draw numerous applicants. Employers tend to screen these applicants by the imposition of "objective" qualifications relating to education, moral character, and ability to perform. But these requirements, seemingly neutral on their face, often work to the detriment of minority applicants. Thus, for example, the requirement of a high school diploma may seem harmless enough even when applied to jobs involving largely manual work. But in practice such a requirement works against large numbers of Negroes whose failure to complete high school may be unrelated to their ability to perform satisfactorily on the job. So, too, a ban against the employment of people with criminal arrest records may seem a reasonable way to provide some assurance that new employees will be trustworthy. But the automatic imposition of such a ban is unfair because it ignores the fact that relatively few young people in the ghetto escape some encounter with the law and thus it screens out many potentially reliable applicants.

To the barriers imposed by application of these formal qualifications must be added the negative impact upon minorities of the widespread use by employers of aptitude and ability tests as part of the selection procedures for hiring and promotion. These tests, like the other qualifications cited, frequently set hiring standards far beyond those necessary for the job. Since the tests often are not validated by checking against actual performance, there is a strong possibility that in many cases the scores are not good predictors of how well an applicant will actually do on the job. And, most important, in placing emphasis on verbal skills that may have little relation to the requirements of the job, the tests focus on weaknesses most predominant in members of minority groups and unnecessarily screen them out.[21]

So, in sum, a variety of factors that may be regarded as trappings of an increasingly complex industrial system operate—along with overt practices of racial discrimination not easily rooted out despite the enactment of state and national fair employment practices laws—against black people and other recent migrants to the city when they seek unskilled and semiskilled jobs in factories, offices, and retail establishments. In similar fashion, the changes that have occurred over the course of recent years in other fields—the construction trades, government employment, and small business enterprises—that once provided a foothold for foreign immigrants have rendered them either unavailable or much less useful as stepping stones today.

The character of the construction trades as an entering wedge for the lowest status groups in society has been transformed by the success of the very immigrant groups that once struggled to gain entry through the trades. Over the years they have fashioned a guild which, more than any other group of working men in the United States, has assumed control over access to employment and the terms and conditions under which work is performed. By using this authority to keep the guild small, to reduce hours, and to avert the kinds of technological change that would reduce the need for their services, the craft unions have established an increasingly lucrative profession. The success of the unions has had consequences important to Negroes and other recent migrants to the city. The construction trades resemble in many ways a profitable family business, one which it is natural to pass on to sons and other relatives; without these gains, later generations might long since have sought upward mobility by turning to other occupations, leaving the field clear for other racial and ethnic groups arriving in the cities. In addition, the devices used to restrict access to the field—requiring overlong periods of apprenticeship and other cumbersome tests of qualifications—have been well suited to excluding people whose economic needs are urgent. And the control exercised over the nature and conditions of work has retarded the development of factory-made prefabricated housing, an advance that might have opened new lines of production work for minorities.

Thus, the obstacles placed in the way of Negro entry into the building trades have been formidable indeed. One gauge of the difficulty is that despite protest and some government pressure, very little progress has been made; Negroes still constitute only 4 per cent of all apprentices in the building trades and are fewer than 2 per cent of the apprentices in the best paid crafts—plumbers and electricians.[22] In practical terms, it makes little difference whether the resistance is viewed in terms of the occasional expressions of raw prejudice by local union officers or the somewhat less invidious rationale of "taking care of one's own."[23] The result is the same: exclusion of Negroes and other minorities from one of the few fields in which economic security can still be earned by people who lack advanced education.

Unlike manufacturing, public employment, particularly in state and local units of government, is a rapidly expanding field of opportunity. And, in contrast with private employment generally, Negroes have found jobs in substantial numbers in government, often in proportions equal to or exceeding their proportion of the total population.[24] There, however, the distinctions between private and public employment generally end. As in private industry, black people in government tend to be clustered in the lowest paid, least skilled jobs.[25] As in private industry, their upward mobility is severely limited. Professionalization of many public services and the adoption of "merit" systems and other civil service protections has changed the character of public employment. Where immigrants could hope to progress to better jobs by accumulating experience or political influence, Negroes are faced with the barriers of extensive educational requirements and tests —some related to the actual needs of the job, others not.[26]

Other factors of significance in private industry also operate in public employment. Much of the expansion in government employment is taking place because of the needs for public service in the burgeoning suburbs, but Negroes segregated in the central city lack knowledge of and access to these opportunities.[27] The importance of informal networks of communication to the recruitment process is nowhere as graphically illustrated as in government employment. In many cities, Negroes, nonprofessional as well as professional, are employed in large numbers in departments such as health and welfare but not in others such as finance, budget, and planning.[28] Yet in many of these departments, the skill requirements for office and clerical positions are virtually interchangeable. Finally, practices of racial discrimination, both overt and subtle, persist in some areas of government and have their heaviest impact in excluding black people from jobs such as firemen that do not require extensive periods of training and education.[29]

Of the contemporary relevance of the last-noted route of advancement for immigrants—the establishment of small business enterprises—little need be said. No longer is it feasible to get such enterprises going with relatively small amounts of capital. Even if enough funds are accumulated to start a grocery store or other retail establishment, the prospects for economic success in the face of competition from chain stores are extremely limited, a fact of life evidenced by the very high rate of small business failures.[30] It is conceivable that this discouraging situation could be altered by major infusions of government assistance, both financial and technical, but in the absence of such aid, few people today can hope to emulate the success of European immigrants in starting small business enterprises.

The barriers faced by disadvantaged groups seeking to make their way in contemporary society are, then, formidable indeed. Blue collar jobs, once available in large numbers to European immigrants, are rapidly disappearing. (It is true, as employers occasionally point out in rebuttal, that a few of these jobs are going begging. But they are almost always the most menial, poorest paying jobs, involving work which some black people properly regard as dead-end, traditionally reserved for Negroes and as demeaning as idleness itself.[31]) In competing for many of the unskilled and semiskilled employment opportunities that remain available, Negroes are disadvantaged by a variety of factors ranging from physical inaccessibility of the job to racial discrimination. Jobs that are obtained by minorities frequently offer little or no opportunity for advancement.

Overriding everything is the fact that most of the employment opportunities that are expanding most rapidly (e.g., for engineers, scientists, teachers, managers) require highly specialized training, advanced education, or both. It is to the problems of black people in seeking educational opportunities that we turn next.[32]

Education

Early in the history of the republic, Thomas Jefferson defined the major purpose of establishing a system of public education:

The object is to bring into action that mass of talents which lies buried in poverty in every county for want of means of development, and thus give activity to a mass of mind, which in proportion to our population, shall be the double or treble of what it is in most countries.[33]

In the middle of the nineteenth century, Horace Mann added to the definition the role of education as "a great equalizer of the conditions of men, the balance wheel of the social machinery."[34] With successive waves of foreign immigration, another role assumed critical importance; the public school system was in a position to do what other institutions, e.g., the family and church, could not—transmit common values and, by averting or healing social divisions, help fashion a unified nation.

Measured against these objectives today, there can be little question that public education is failing and failing badly. Large numbers of the poor are emerging from the public schools totally unequipped for participation in society as citizens or wage-earners. And the nation is rent as never before by "social divisions" between black and white that pose a threat to the public schools themselves as well as to other institutions in society.

One part of the problem is that in seeking to carry out its objectives, the public school system must shoulder a heavier burden than at any previous time in history. As should be apparent from the preceding discussion in this chapter, this is the case largely because (1) technological change has cut off alternative routes to economic self-sufficiency, and (2) in facing the task of educating today's poor, the schools cannot expect any great degree of assistance and reinforcement from other institutions such as the family and the church.

In the past, the schools could confess failure in their efforts to educate significant numbers of immigrant children with the comforting knowledge that for many "the talents which lay buried in poverty" would be liberated in other ways—principally through competition in the economic system. Today, this is no longer so; with few exceptions, public school rejects are branded for life as failures. In the past, also, the schools were often aided in their efforts by family, church, and community. But here, too, technological change in combination with the scars that slave practices left upon the Negro community have made a difference. Most

European immigrants had jobs, however menial. Today, however, unemployment is widespread among Negro men and has contributed heavily to the splitting of families and to drug addiction, alcoholism, and crime in the community, all having a major negative impact upon the development of young children. The list of handicaps faced by these children is long. They lack a sufficient diet, adequate clothing, and proper health care. Living in overcrowded tenements, they do not have a place of their own to study or even to sleep. Frequently they do not have toys, books, magazines, or other stimuli that are recognized as important to development in a child's early years. With parents who are often inarticulate or absent from the home, children come to school far less prepared to learn than others who have already had a good deal of practice in developing verbal skills.

Admittedly, then, the task of public education is far more difficult now, in degree if not in kind, than it ever has been in the past. But what is most distressing is that the prevalent reaction among educators to these difficulties is to view them not as challenges to be overcome but rather as excuses for failure. It is a rare meeting of educators these days when the audience is not treated to a lengthy sermon by a school superintendent the burden of which is that the school, since it has the child for only a limited number of hours in the day, cannot be expected to overcome deficiencies of the home and the community. It is true, of course (and always has been), that educational achievement is closely correlated with various measures of family background, such as the education and income of a child's parents.[35] But the test of American public education has always been its ability to fulfill the role set for it by Jefferson and others, by breaking the link between poverty and educational failure. And the tributes accorded to the public school system have stemmed largely from the fact that it has served this role so well for successive generations of children born into disadvantaged circumstances.*

The defeatism now so prevalent in the educational establish-

---

* It may well be true also that given the burdens on the public school system there may be better means for preparing young people for certain trades than through the vocational education programs of the schools. But no one has yet found a satisfactory substitute for the public school system to prepare youngsters for professional careers.

ment might be justified if there were no glaring deficiencies in the public school system as it affects the black and poor or if genuine efforts had been made to correct deficiencies and had failed. But this is far from the case. Experts may, and indeed do, differ in their assessments of the elements that are important in establishing an effective system of education. (There are, of course, important intangible elements of the educational process that defy efforts at categorization; nevertheless, attempts to analyze as best as possible factors which may make a difference are indispensable to educational reform.) Some place great stress upon the socioeconomic and racial composition of the schools and the interaction among students. Some give great weight to the qualifications and attitudes of teachers. Others are concerned principally with the quality of curriculum and still others emphasize the allocation of educational resources as they are reflected in physical facilities or in pupil-teacher ratios.

Important as these disagreements may be in deciding upon priorities for remedial action, the overriding fact is that wherever the spotlight is focussed—teaching, curriculum, the allocation of resources, student composition, or other factors—the public schools serving minority children are sadly wanting. Note that we have said "the public schools *serving minority children.*" For in taking the measure of these inadequacies, one other contemporary fact is of great significance—the splintering of the public school system into two distinct systems, one serving largely the children of the poor and the other catering almost exclusively to the affluent. Thus, it is possible and indeed necessary to judge the inner city public schools not simply in absolute terms, but by comparing them with their suburban counterparts.

STUDENT COMPOSITION—The relevance of the composition of a student body to the performance of children is suggested by the maxim that "students learn as much from each other as they do from their teachers." Indeed, the conclusion of the Coleman Report, a major research project conducted by the U.S. Office of Education, was that the composition of student bodies was not simply relevant but was a major factor in the educational process. The report found a pupil's achievement to be strongly related to the socioeconomic backgrounds of other children in the school.[36] A child from disadvantaged circumstances, it was discovered, is more likely to achieve well and to have high aspirations if he attends school with a majority of children who come from advantaged backgrounds than if the majority of his classmates come from circumstances similar to his own. As a student progresses through school, the importance of the influence of his peers increases and other influences wane.[37]

The importance of the composition of a student body to achievement lies in what one psychiatrist has termed "the hidden curriculum":

> It involves such things as how to think about themselves, how to think about other people, and how to get along with them. It involves such things as . . . values . . . codes, and . . . styles of behavior. . . .[38]

Among the key elements in the process is the influence that family background has upon the aspirations of students and, in turn, the influence that various combinations of students may have upon values established for the entire school. For the children of most middle class parents, the desirability and feasibility of attending college is a foregone conclusion. The predominance of such children in a school may set a standard for the school as a whole. At education hearings held by the U.S. Commission on Civil Rights, a teacher in a predominantly Negro high school in Rochester described the difference in student aspirations between his school (Madison) and Brighton, a more affluent suburban high school. He noted that after an exchange program in which Madison students visited Brighton:

> . . . one of the Madison youngsters said, "At Madison we asked a question, are you going to college? At Brighton the question is always what college are you going to?"[39]

The prevailing view at a given school of what is attainable may have an impact upon the motivation of students to perform well. This was illustrated graphically in Syracuse where the achievement levels of a group of Negro children from disadvantaged backgrounds improved significantly after they were transferred from a school in the ghetto to one in which the student body was composed mainly of advantaged students. The president of the Syracuse school board explained:

. . . at Madison Junior High School [the disadvantaged school], if you cooperated with the teacher and did your homework, you were a "kook."

At Levy Junior High School [the more advantaged school], if you don't cooperate with the teacher and don't do your homework, you are a "kook." Peer pressure has tremendous effect on the motivation and motivation has a tremendous effect on achievement.[40]

Beyond the impact that the composition of a school's student body may have upon aspirations and achievement scores are other consequences, equally important if less subject to measurement. For public schools do not simply instruct students but, in D. W. Brogan's phrase, allow them to "instruct each other in how to live in America."[41] A part of the informal curriculum in middle class schools consists of instruction through student interaction in social codes, practical politics, and organization—lessons that are of great importance to "making it" in contemporary society. In schools made up almost entirely of students from impoverished circumstances, a similar process may take place, but the codes teach adaptation to a society far different from the one which brings status and material rewards to the children of middle class America.

The segregation of children in the public schools by economic and social class was not always so prevalent as it is today. One of the values inhering in the original concept of the "common school" was that of mixing children of varying backgrounds in the same educational facility. In nineteenth-century New England, common schools were established and controlled by prosperous people who could afford the fees necessary to maintain them. They then welcomed all children "who wished to share the education of their betters."*

In many places, particularly in the West, this aspect of the common school persisted well into the twentieth century. In the words of John Goodlad:

Most men and women over 40 recall a childhood schooling in which the sons and daughters of mill owners, shop proprietors,

* See Mayer, *The Schools*, pp. 36-43. It was not until late in the century that compulsory attendance replaced the notion of voluntary schools designed for "the able and ambitious." While in this day the concept may seem elitist and paternalistic, the uniquely American idea was that such able and ambitious children were to be found in all ranks of society.

professional men, and day laborers attended side by side. School boundaries, reaching out into fields and hills to embrace the pupil population, transcended such socioeconomic clusterings as existed.[42]

With the growth of the cities, the attendance of children of different backgrounds at the same school declined. As population densities in the cities increased, school attendance zones were drawn more narrowly and the school became more socially and racially homogeneous. The establishment of suburbs as residential centers for the affluent has virtually completed the process. The "sons and daughters of day laborers" who share classrooms with more affluent students are considerably fewer in number.

RACIAL SEGREGATION—Although not specifically a racial matter, a determination that there is academic value in having children from disadvantaged circumstances attend school with more advantaged students has special significance for Negro pupils. Since the proportion of Negro parents with high incomes and college educations is still very small, any effort to remedy social class isolation would necessarily involve racial integration as well.

Moreover, apart from this necessary relationship between the social and economic class composition of a school and its racial makeup, there is strong evidence that racial segregation has a specific additional impact upon the attitudes and performance of black students. In the *School Segregation Cases,* the Supreme Court of the United States said of the impact upon children of segregation compelled by law in the South that it "may affect their hearts and minds in a way unlikely ever to be undone."[43] After an extensive investigation of racially isolated public schools in the North, the Commission on Civil Rights found that the same conclusion applies to the impact of segregation *not* compelled by law.[44]

The source of the harm, the Commission determined, lies principally in the attitudes that racial isolation engenders in students. Predominantly Negro schools are almost always regarded by the community at large as poor schools. Teachers and parents at black schools often share these community views or are demoralized by them. Students cannot remain unaware of these attitudes for very long. The stigma affects their own view of their schools and impairs both aspirations and achievement.[45]

Recognizing that racial isolation can cause harm some school systems have sought to counteract it through compensatory programs including field trips and exchange visits with suburban schools. But these efforts, designed to stimulate an awareness of the larger community and promote interracial contacts sometimes do not produce the results intended. Thus, a teacher at an all-Negro high school in Cleveland reported that after a student exchange between his school and an all-white suburban high school, a typical reaction by one of his students was: "Well, it was nice of them to come down to the zoo to see us."[46]

Nor do black children who feel this way have an unrealistic view of their situation. For segregation in northern cities and schools is not an accident of fate any more than it is in the South. In most northern states, segregation in the public schools was once mandated by law or official policy and helped to establish segregated housing patterns.* Through the years segregation has been perpetuated by racially restrictive ordinances and covenants, by discriminatory practices of the private housing industry, by housing and planning decisions of state and local governments, and by the policies and practices of city school boards and superintendents. We have in fact reached a point where

* To black people with a knowledge of history, the elevation of the "neighborhood school" to a cherished concept among whites in the North must seem bitterly ironic. Throughout the latter part of the nineteenth century, northern courts rejected lawsuits brought by Negro parents whose children had to walk long distances to school because of laws and policies requiring segregation. In one case, an Ohio court in rejecting the plea of Negro parents whose child had to walk four miles to an elementary school said, "Somebody must walk further than the rest. The only inconvenience complained of is taking a long walk, which walk is not longer than children must take who go to other schools, such as high schools, and less than some must take who go to the University." *Lewis* v. *Board of Education,* 7 Ohio Dec. Reprint 129 (Hamilton Dist. Ct., 1876). The Ohio legislature outlawed separate schools ten years later, but the practice did not die easily. From 1955 to 1958, school authorities bussed 750 Negro children (most of whom lived in a public housing project in a predominantly white school district) 5½ miles to a black school, bypassing several white schools with available space. U.S. Commission on Civil Rights, *Racial Isolation in the Public Schools,* p. 56.

even the modest gains resulting from enforcement of the Supreme Court's decision have made public school systems in the South far less segregated than many systems in the North, where racial isolation has been growing rapidly.[47]

Thus *racial* segregation in the schools cuts far deeper than the ethnic segregation once faced by immigrant groups. Black children who sense in their isolation the ostracism of white society and restraints upon their upward mobility have a firm grasp of reality. There are some who believe that this situation can be altered within the context of segregated schools by massive infusions of racial pride plus the offering of college and job incentives, but that is a proposition yet to be demonstrated.

TEACHER COMPETENCE AND ATTITUDES—Given the greater challenge of educating the children of the poor and the handicaps imposed by race and class segregation, it would be rational to expect that the ablest teachers would be located in central city schools. But this is far from the case.

When the traditional "objective" standards of ability are applied, it is found that in many metropolitan areas teachers in predominantly black schools in the inner city lack the qualifications possessed by their colleagues in other parts of the area. For example, the proportion of teachers who lack certification or who are on probationary or substitute status is often far higher in many Negro schools than anywhere else in the city.[48] While it is true that substantial numbers of probationary teachers in a school may sometimes signify an infusion of young, dedicated people into the system, it is more often a symptom of instability and even chaos. So, in the Roxbury area of Boston, one group of schools was manned by teachers 70 per cent of whom had less than three years of experience and was plagued by a very high turnover rate—factors which both caused and reflected the serious educational problems that afflicted the schools.[49] Moreover, faculties at all-Negro schools score lower on teacher examinations and other tests of verbal achievement than teachers at all-white schools.[50]

A problem perhaps more serious than that of lower levels of competence is the attitudes toward students that many teachers bring to inner city schools. There are, as has been dramatized by a spate of popular books, more than a few teachers in ghetto schools who are overtly hostile toward children and brutal in their treatment of them.[51] Even more prevalent are those who, although well motivated, find themselves unable to cope or communicate with their pupils. Raised in middle class environs, increasingly isolated from the poor, trained at institutions that until recently have provided little practical experience in urban teaching, they arrive at their assignments ill-prepared for effective instruction. Fearful and insecure and frustrated by their own inadequacies, many of these teachers come to the conclusion that their students are incapable of learning—a devastating judgment that frequently becomes a self-fulfilling prophecy.

The low expectations that these teachers have of their pupils lie at the heart of failure in ghetto schools.[52] Time and again in its investigations, the Civil Rights Commission was told of young people whose capacity to meet the challenges of learning was not discovered until they were removed from the environment of the ghetto school.[53] Time and again the Commission heard of apparently well-meaning teachers whose idea of building a child's self-image was to praise him for clearly inadequate work rather than stimulating him to do better. Time and again, we learned of school counselors whose packaged advice to ghetto youngsters was to take up a trade rather than to prepare themselves for advanced education and a profession.[54]

Finally, even teachers who are gifted and sensitive to the needs of disadvantaged children are frequently frustrated by an aging public school bureaucracy seemingly incapable of providing an environment in which learning is possible. Often they and their children must struggle in makeshift classrooms, ill-heated and lacking proper equipment. They must either cope with emotionally troubled youngsters whose disruptive behavior makes learning impossible for others or abandon them to the street. They must make do with ancient texts, often provided in inadequate numbers, with "Dick and Jane" readers whose tales of country life are ill-designed to awaken the curiosity of children of the city, with history books which ignore or defame the heritage and culture of minorities. If such teachers attempt to innovate and improvise by using their own resources, they may be penalized by a system that discourages nonconformity.

FACILITIES AND RESOURCES—Lacking the critical resource of superior teaching, inner city schools are often plagued also by the absence of other resources and facilities which can have an impact on educational outcomes.

The nature of the problem is suggested by growing disparities between the funds available to central city school districts for financing public education and those at the disposal of their more affluent suburban neighbors. In 1965, in thirty-seven metropolitan areas, the average expenditure by the central city school districts was $449 per pupil compared with average suburban expenditures of $573 for each pupil.[55]

These discrepancies arise from the method used throughout the nation to finance public schools—reliance upon relatively small local districts to raise the bulk of the funds for education and the use by these districts of the property tax as their sole source of revenue. Under such a system, the ability of a school board to meet educational needs depends almost entirely upon the taxable wealth available in the community. Such assets vary considerably from place to place, and at the extremes the contrasts are striking. In Illinois, for example, the Monticello school district has taxable property valued at $114,000 per pupil, while the Brockport district has property valued at only $3,000 per pupil. In California, the per pupil valuation of property of the rich Big Creek school district is $306,000 while that of the Olinda district is $1,300.[56]

Recognizing the inequities that result from property tax financing, state legislatures long ago adopted programs of assistance to local districts designed to compensate for disparities in local wealth. But the levels of aid provided are usually so low that, even when combined with Federal aid to poor districts, they fail to have any significant equalizing effect.[57] Thus, the Brockport district in Illinois taxes itself at a rate three times higher than the Monticello district but, even with state assistance, its expenditure per pupil is only two-thirds of that of the Monticello district. In California, per pupil expenditures vary from $265 to $1,353; in New York, from $470 to $1,600.[58]

All of this has had a major impact upon big city schools and the black children who attend them. In the past, the principal victims of property tax financing were generally rural schools (where costs were high because of the small numbers of pupils) and developing suburbs (which had large needs for capital investments). During the last decade, however, the picture has changed drastically. Industrial wealth has fled from cities to suburbs, poor people have flocked to the central city, and increasing social needs such as welfare have placed competitive demands upon central city resources that suburbs do not face. The result is that just as Negroes have arrived in cities in large numbers the capacity of central city school systems to meet urgent educational needs (both in absolute terms and in relation to the ability of suburbs) has declined sharply.

That schools which serve the poor should be so handicapped was hardly the intention of those who guided the formation of the public education system. A part of the rationale for locally financed and operated school systems was the value of choice and diversity.[59] People who placed a premium upon good education, it was reasoned, could locate in communities willing to tax themselves highly for the privilege of obtaining high-quality schools, while those who were less concerned about schools could have the advantage of paying lower taxes. Instead what has happened is that the tax rate bears little relationship to educational expenditure. And people who are locked into the central city because of poverty and racial discrimination have no choice at all.

The harm that flows from inequity in the financing of public schools should be kept in perspective. There is little evidence that the more expensive and modern plant which high tax revenues will buy has any strong relationship to educational outcomes.* And while teaching *is* critical to achievement, the differences in salaries between urban and suburban schools are not usually significant and there is little to suggest that the key to

* The Coleman Report did not find that variations in curriculum account for much variation in pupil achievement, as measured by standard tests. Coleman Report, U.S. Office of Education, Department of HEW, *Equality of Educational Opportunity,* p. 22. It did find, however, that the existence of some facilities such as science laboratories may have a small effect upon performance and that Negro students are less apt than whites to have labs, adequate libraries, and other facilities in their schools. Moreover, a lack of funds often prevents the building of facilities needed to implement innovative programs, such as flexible classroom space for team teaching and nongraded classes. See discussion, Chapter 7, p. 217-221 *infra.*

attracting better teachers to central city school systems lies mainly in providing higher pay.[60]

The conditions provided for learning, on the other hand, may be very important to teachers and to achievement. Many of the most dedicated teachers in the inner city give up in despair when overcrowded classrooms and the lack of supportive personnel eradicate any slim chance of their giving attention to the individual needs of their students. A more equitable division of resources between city and suburbs would enable the lowering of student-teacher ratios and the employment of more health aides, psychologists, and counselors. Moreover, if the standard adopted for judging the use of educational resources is one of *need* rather than just equality of inputs, the defects of the present system of financing become far more glaring. The special needs of inner city schools are pressing—programs to provide free breakfasts and lunches, to start the educational process at an earlier age, to remedy reading defects, to stimulate closer ties between the school and the home. Lacking even the resources available to the suburbs (which have less need for these programs) city schools must either adopt the programs on a selective basis or spread them so thin that they become useless.

CONCLUSION—The dream of American public education—that it would equalize the conditions of men—has never seemed further from realization. Faced with their greatest challenge—to assist a people who had been systematically stripped of the support of other institutions, at a time when public education is more crucial to the poor than ever before in history—the bulk of the education establishment has decided to opt out.

Once educators were regarded as leaders, people who would help set the standards for society. Now the plea of many is that they cannot be expected to do more than reflect society—so the view is that racial and ethnic divisions of the larger community must inevitably be mirrored in the schools.

Once the vision was that of a *common* school where children of affluence and of poverty might study together. Now it seems fair to say that the reality is two school systems, largely distinct except in the middle (since each contains some proportion of children who are neither poor nor affluent). In suburbia, most schools serve as a conveyor belt, processing children along a well-marked route toward affluence, polishing skills and providing training in the rules of the competitive game, conferring badges of status of higher or lower order.

In the central cities, schools serve as conveyor belts also, but the main purpose is to prepare young people for lower status work and to condition them to modes of behavior appropriate to their lesser place in society. (There are exceptions, of course. For a relative handful of the most talented students, the schools may provide assistance in liberating them from the shackles of their environment, but many of those who escape do so without the aid of the public school system, or even in spite of it.) This dominant purpose of the central city school is reflected in its economically and racially segregated student bodies, the low expectations that teachers and counselors have of students, the inferior resources that are allocated to greater needs. Much of the current concern among educators and in the white community is prompted by the failure of the schools to succeed even in their limited objectives—a fact evidenced by increasing disruption of social order within the schools as well as in the community and by the drive for community control.

The overriding fact, however, is that the public schools have become adjuncts of racially and economically separate communities rather than unifying institutions providing opportunity and mobility. As long as they remain so, they no more than the contemporary economic system can provide an escape route for the great majority of people presently trapped in the ghetto.

Shelter and the Environment

As we have seen, the ability to choose one's place of residence today may be critical to obtaining access to employment and to good schools. Conversely, the absence of housing choice—the confinement of people to limited geographical areas—can adversely affect chances for success to a degree never before true in history. In addition, housing has long been viewed as an independent factor in determining one's chances of escaping poverty. Slum housing has been associated with a variety of physical and mental ills; establishing decent homes in a healthy environment has been regarded as an important means of creating conditions in which families might rid themselves of social ills and become self-reliant.

In their efforts to secure decent housing and a better environment, Negroes throughout history have been faced with obstacles more formidable than those encountered by any other group. Until after the Civil War, black people, both slave and free, were widely restrained by law from making contracts and acquiring property. Once these restrictions were lifted, they were replaced in many areas by racial zoning ordinances designed to confine Negroes to separate sections of the city. When the Supreme Court declared these ordinances unconstitutional in 1917,[61] racially restrictive covenants—private agreements among adjoining landowners not to sell to members of specified racial, religious, or ethnic groups—accomplished much the same purpose. Although these covenants often included several minority groups, the prime targets usually were Negroes, and while ruled judicially unenforceable in 1948,[62] they continue to be employed as private arrangements. Throughout the same period, the prevalent and accepted practice of the housing industry also has been to restrict black people to limited geographical areas. Builders have refused to sell or rent homes to Negroes in new developments intended for whites, brokers have pursued similar practices in settled neighborhoods, and lending institutions have refused to make credit available. These discriminatory actions were sanctioned and even reinforced for many years by government at all levels, and now are yielding only very slowly to laws prohibiting them. The net effect, then, has been to place a blanket restriction upon mobility and the exercise of choice by black people; those who were not restrained in their search for decent housing by economic factors have been confined to the ghetto by racism.

Meanwhile, the efforts of immigrant groups to escape the ghetto and to secure better housing were having very different results. They were able to participate successfully in a movement to establish better living conditions for the vast majority of American citizens. And, strikingly, the success of this movement for members of immigrant groups and others has resulted in the erection of a new set of barriers for Negroes at the very moment when they seem ready to emerge from the shadow of racism.

There is evidence that suggests that even as the most impoverished newcomers, immigrants were not as completely segregated in ghettos as Negroes have been.[63] Certainly, as they achieved some measure of economic security, immigrants dispersed much more rapidly than Negroes in similar situations. The key element in this dispersal has been the migration to suburbia which began in earnest during the 1920s and became a mass movement after the end of World War II. Two factors facilitated the process of suburbanization—economic and technological advances (particularly the development of the automobile) which benefited large numbers of citizens and the intervention of the Federal Government to assist people in their efforts to secure better housing. The entry of government into the housing field in a significant way, initiated as an emergency measure to prevent the housing market from collapsing entirely during the Depression, later became the spur which permitted mass development of suburban areas. But the programs in question were ones which provided subsidies in the form of credit and insurance to people who had already achieved a measure of economic self-sufficiency; for those who still were poor a different form of aid was provided (the public housing program) and it was one that did not work nearly as well.[64]

So the assistance of government permitted a great many Americans including immigrants recently emerged from poverty to establish at least a beachhead in the effort to achieve a better environment. It was a position they then sought to consolidate by building viable communities that would provide needed services and amenities without imposing a major tax burden upon their citizens. In order to accomplish this objective, these newly established residents of suburbia adopted measures that made it difficult for others to follow in the same path.

Prime among these measures have been land-use controls, particularly zoning regulations. Such regulations in a variety of forms have been upheld by the courts as reasonable efforts to protect members of a community from uses of land that would diminish the value and enjoyment of their own property.[65] But increasingly zoning in many communities has been used as a means of permitting only the most profitable uses of land, of requiring newcomers to assume the major costs of services provided to established residents and of fencing out members of groups regarded as undesirable.

Initiated as a practice only half a century ago, land-use regulations have spread rapidly to the point where more than two-thirds of all the local governments in metropolitan areas have adopted zoning ordinances.[66] In one-quarter of the municipalities in metropolitan areas large-lot zoning regulations prohibit the construction of single family homes on lots of less than one-half acre. And in some places the restrictions are pervasive, e.g., in Cuyahoga County, the central county containing Cleveland, two-thirds of all vacant land is governed by laws requiring lots of one-half acre or more.[67]

The impact of such controls is to reduce significantly the amount of desirable land available for housing and to raise the costs of housing far beyond the means of people of low and moderate income.[68]

Other factors also operate to place decent shelter far beyond the reach of people of very modest means. The American housing industry, it has been said, is the one segment of the economy virtually untouched by the industrial revolution. It is affected by the multiplicity of local building codes which while originally designed to protect health and safety now constitute a jumble of antiquated provisions that raise the costs of building by preventing the use of modern materials and mass production techniques.[69] Similar problems result from the power of craft unions to impose restrictive building practices (such as on-site rules that limit the use of prefabricated products) and to raise labor costs by extracting high wages.[70] High interest rates (in an industry where credit is of crucial importance) and high property taxes also operate to make the price of housing prohibitive for many people.[71]

In a land-rich nation (it has been noted that if all Americans were to move to Texas and Oklahoma our population densities would then be comparable to those of the United Kingdom and West Germany)[72] access to property has always been important to advancement. At critical points in history, the Federal Government has intervened to assure an element of fairness in the distribution of our abundant resources. In the late nineteenth and early twentieth centuries, millions of Americans, including earlier generations of immigrants, were able to acquire free land under the Homestead Acts. In the 1930s new opportunities to secure land and shelter were extended to a later generation by the massive extension of housing credit under the New Deal.

Now, however, the frontiers are closed. Land is still abundant, but the property that would be valuable to the wage-earner in an urban society, i.e., land in the still undeveloped parts of metropolitan areas, is largely controlled by small groups of well-off citizens who are able to use it to enhance their own positions while excluding those less fortunate.

Cut off from decent shelter by suburban land controls, continuing discriminatory practices, and the inability of the housing industry to produce it at modest prices, the impoverished black man remains confined to the ghetto. There, since the normal channels of the housing market are denied to him, he is compelled to deal with speculators and landlords who charge what the traffic will bear and refuse to provide the services necessary for a habitable environment.

Thus, absent the kind of government intervention needed to deal with the contemporary facts of housing deprivation—facts which differ in significant ways from those faced by the immigrant—the hope for a livable environment as a means of escaping poverty is no less a mirage than similar hopes for good jobs or effective public education.

Conclusion

Two further observations are pertinent on the dangers of easy recourse to the immigrant analogy. First, the message, expressed or implied, of those who are fondest of the analogy is that given the successful experience of the immigrants we can afford to be reasonably confident that today's "immigrants" will make their way without major assistance by government or sacrifice on the part of its more advantaged citizens. To reach this conclusion, however, proponents of the analogy tend to overstate both the rapidity with which immigrants overcame barriers and the degree to which they have become full participants in the benefits of American society. As the Kerner Commission report has pointed out, among the last great wave of immigrants from southern and eastern Europe, only those who came from urban environments managed within a relatively short period of time to escape from poverty. Others, who, like Negroes, came from a rural background are still struggling after three generations to win their place in society.[73] And many among them have not yet made it; in income, job status, and education, they lag behind the great majority of citizens.[74] Only by glossing over these facts is it possible to avoid a hard question—whether, even if the immigrant analogy were entirely sound, it would be possible from a humanitarian or practical point of view to wait three generations or more for the solution to problems of racial injustice.

Second, resort to the immigrant analogy feeds another trend in policy-making—to deal with problems of deprivation and discrimination not preventively at their source but only after they have festered in the cities. Although the rate of migration has slowed, there are still thousands of young black people in the rural South who each year are leaving their homes for the cities. Many have been brought up without proper nutrition or medical care, and have attended wretchedly inferior segregated schools where it has been assumed that they were fit only for lesser vocations and then have been trained in skills for which there is no demand.[75] Since in any case there are few jobs available to them where they live, the only logical graduation gift is a Greyhound bus ticket to the city, where they arrive almost totally unequipped to make their way. If these were *foreign* immigrants we were talking about, there would be little that government could do except to extend a helping hand once the traveler reached the city. But they are *American* migrants who have been victims of *American* oppression and neglect, and the logical way to help those who are still in the rural South is to begin the process long before they arrive as refugees in the cities. Use of the immigrant analogy helps blind us to this simple truth and permits continuing neglect of the rural poor.

There is not one answer to the suggestion that "immigrants made it on their own, why can't Negroes?"; there are many. The contrasts in the character of historical oppression. The destructive impact that slavery had upon the development of institutions capable of use as vehicles for self-help. The continuation of official policies of segregation resting upon a doctrine of racial inferiority, long after slavery had been abolished. The effect that domestic repression necessarily had upon the confidence and aspirations of many of its victims.

The bar that color poses to achieving acceptance through assimilation. The persistence of practices of racial discrimination even where prohibited by law.

Of great importance, the critical ways in which American society has changed during the past fifty years. The decline of unskilled jobs. The screening out of potential workers through formalistic job requirements and qualifications. The diminishing effectiveness of political organization as an instrument of economic advancement. The growth of big business, foreclosing the prospects of the small entrepreneur.

The consequent growth in the importance of education as a means of escaping poverty and the waning effectiveness of schools in serving this objective. The fragmentation of public education into separate systems for the affluent and poor.

The economic factors that lead to physical concentrations of resources and affluence. The isolation of the poor from jobs, good schools, and services.

The emergence of small power blocs that maintain position by exclusionary practices which, intended or not, have a racial impact (a phenomenon inadequately expressed or grasped in the term "institutional racism"). Craft unions limiting entry to the trades. Civil servants weaving a protective web around their jobs. Employers seeking sheltered tax status. Small groups of property owners acting as public corporations to enhance the value of their holdings.

All of this suggests at a minimum that if black people are to have a fighting chance against the forces that keep them in poverty, government must intervene on their behalf to a much greater degree than was necessary for earlier immigrant groups. (Much the same can be said, too, about the need for government assistance to other minority groups arriving late in the cities.) Some people, of course, believe that government has already intervened strongly to aid Negroes. It is to this question and the quality of government's response that we turn in the next section.

PART TWO

The Federal Effort

To many white Americans the least comprehensible aspect of the current racial situation is the failure of more Negroes to respond to the ministrations of the Federal Government. Conceding, as some do, that prejudice and discrimination still have not been banished from the hearts of individuals, or from private institutions and local governments, they nonetheless regard the Federal Government as the special guardian of the interests of Negroes. Viewing the past thirty-five years from the New Deal to the Warren Court to the New Frontier and Great Society as a history of almost unbroken concern and action to advance the cause of Negroes, they have concluded that those black people capable of responding to a helping hand already have done so and virtually all of the vast majority who have not responded must be congenitally hopeless cases.

But no fair reading of history will sustain a verdict so favorable to the government. Only when compared with the long periods of neglect and active support of discriminatory practices that preceded it, does the record of government concern and action during recent years, particularly the past decade, appear creditable. Examined in light of the need created by oppression, the record has been halting and episodic, marked by very limited perceptions of what the problem is and the magnitude of the resources required to deal with it, and barely visible or tangible to the masses of the Negro poor.

3

THE CIVIL RIGHTS EFFORT

The New Deal

Hardest hit by the depression (in 1935, 65 per cent of all employable Negroes were in need of public assistance), black Americans of course benefited from the recovery measures instituted during the New Deal. They participated in the new welfare systems, in jobs created through public works programs, in public housing. But, in the main, the New Deal reforms were intended to deal with the immediate effects of a national economic disaster and to build a floor under poverty, not to provide remedies for minorities operating under special handicaps. Some recognition was given to the obstacles faced by Negroes and members of other minority groups in laws and regulations prohibiting discrimination in jobs created by public works programs.[1] These, however, simply constituted policy declarations of limited effect because no administrative machinery or effective sanctions were provided for enforcement.[2] In practice, under NRA, Negroes either had to accept racial differentials in wages or run the risk of displacement by unemployed white men.[3]

Even the pioneer Tennessee Valley Authority hired Negroes only for unskilled positions and excluded them from TVA training programs and from residence in the TVA town of Norris. The policies of crop reduction embodied in the Agricultural Adjustment Act actually worsened the economic situation of Negro sharecroppers who were forced off the land when white landowners reduced their acreage.[4] And the Federal Government, while establishing the first sustained programs of housing assistance, also instituted policies sanctioning the residential patterns of economic and racial isolation which now characterize every American city.[5]

The Courts

In the 1950s, the long campaign of the NAACP Legal Defense Fund to establish equality through litigation in the Federal courts began to pay its greatest dividends. In *Brown* v. *Board of Education*[6] a unanimous Supreme Court in 1954 stripped away the legal fiction, sanctioned by the Court a half-century earlier, that separate public schools could provide equal educational opportunity for Negro children. There followed a series of decisions by the Supreme Court and lower Federal courts outlawing practices of segregation in public parks and golf courses, on interstate and local buses and trains, in publicly assisted housing.

It would be wrong to minimize the importance of the school desegregation cases. The decision, as Jack Greenberg, chief lawyer for the NAACP Legal Defense Fund, has said, "proved to be the Declaration of Independence of its day."[7] It both reflected and significantly advanced a growing national consensus that officially promulgated doctrines of racial inferiority, no matter how rationalized, had no place in American life. It gave new energy to the civil rights movement, which, through community action, lobbying, and protest, brought about the elimination of racial practices in areas such as public accommodations that were then untouched by court decisions. And in places where desegregation actually ensued, the decision fulfilled one of the higher functions of law, not merely establishing new standards, but helping to create habits of conformity to them. By providing contact and the opportunity for dialogue, the decision began to breach the barriers of misunderstanding that segregation law had helped to create.

It is clear, however, at least in retrospect, that the court decisions alone could not bring about the fundamental changes needed to create equality of opportunity for the mass of the

Negro poor. Measured against this goal, they were subject to a number of important limitations, some inevitable, others not.

The rulings had little direct application in the North. The immediate impact of *Brown* v. *Board of Education* was upon the laws of seventeen southern states which required or authorized racial segregation in the public schools. The decision dealt with specific governmental enactments unmistakable in motivation and intent. In the North, segregation of the schools and other public facilities, although in many places as severe as in the South, generally was the result of a complex skein of public and private practices. Because such segregation was not immediately affected by the decisions of the 1950s, the increasing numbers of Negroes who lived in the North derived little if any direct benefit.[8]

The rulings could not by themselves redress economic and social injustice. Like all civil rights laws, the court decisions simply promulgated a set of ground rules which could not operate effectively if other conditions of social and economic justice were not present. The opportunity to attend school on the same terms as everyone cannot be meaningful to a child who by the time he has reached school age has been irreparably harmed by the effects of an inadequate diet or the lack of medical care. President Johnson put the matter succinctly in a speech proclaiming that steps affording legal protection for human rights dealt with only one aspect of the problem:

"You do not take a person who, for years, has been hobbled by chains and liberate him, bring him up to the starting line of a race and then say, 'You are free to compete with all the others,' and still justly believe that you have been completely fair."[9]

Without the enactment of measures to alleviate "inherited, gateless" poverty, to provide training and skills, decent housing and adequate medical care, court rulings abolishing segregation practices could hardly be effective. Such measures were not forthcoming in the 1950s.

The rulings were widely ignored and violated. The widespread flouting of Supreme Court rulings on public schools and other civil rights matters by now is a familiar if shameful chapter of current history. State governments and local school districts, taking advantage of President Eisenhower's failure to give either moral or practical support to the decision and of the Court's reasonableness in permitting implementation "with all deliberate speed," either ignored or threw roadblocks in the way of compliance. In the face of massive resistance by most of the states of the deep South, progress became dependent upon the successful completion of hundreds of lawsuits in which every tactic of delay was employed by the defendants. The token results were reflected in the annual mournful litany of school desegregation statistics; in 1961, when a new Administration took office seven years after the *Brown* decision, only one Negro child in every fourteen enrolled in the public schools of the southern and border states attended school with white pupils.

The Kennedy and Johnson Administrations

By the time John F. Kennedy assumed the Presidency in 1961, a major concern of civil rights leaders had become an effort to secure more active involvement of the executive branch in the enforcement of existing civil rights law. One principal objective was the promulgation of executive orders and regulations which would condition the granting of Federal assistance upon the agreement of recipients not to engage in racial discrimination. Civil rights leaders invested great hopes in the approach as a means of dealing with intransigent resistance to civil rights laws. Beginning with the New Deal, grants-in-aid to state and local governments and to private institutions had become an increasingly important mechanism for performing governmental functions, growing in volume from $2.3 billion in 1940 to $10 billion in 1961.[10]

In general, political scientists have viewed grants-in-aid as a useful device for promoting cooperation between different levels of government in a federal system. National needs are identified and dealt with through the more efficient revenue-raising system of the Federal Government. At the same time, by the placing of administrative control in the hands of state and local governments, universities, corporations, and other private institutions under regulations which limit Federal interference, the dangers of centralized and undue Federal control are avoided.

Although all grant-in-aid programs contained some minimum Federal requirements, the policy of noninterference in the administration of grants for years had been applied to permit "neutrality" with respect to the racial practices of the recipients. The results of this policy had hardly been neutral, for under it the Federal Government had helped to perpetuate inequality in education, to build all-white suburban neighborhoods, to provide new employment opportunities which were made available principally to whites, and, generally, to subsidize the discriminatory practices of local governments and institutions.

It was this policy of "neutrality" that civil rights leaders sought to reverse; the priority they accorded to action in this area rested on the belief that administrative rules broadly applied would be more expeditious than protracted case-by-case legal proceedings and that the sanction for noncompliance— termination of assistance—would be effective.* While the principal benefit to be derived from requiring nondiscrimination in Federal grants was vastly improved enforcement of existing civil rights laws in the South, it also had potential significance in the North, particularly in dealing with segregated housing and hospitals subsidized by the Federal Government, and promised to be a partial wedge for dealing with economic injustices, by opening up more job opportunities to Negroes.

John Kennedy campaigned in the big cities on a pledge of bold executive action in civil rights but, once elected by an exceedingly narrow margin, his Administration quickly retreated. The dilemma the Kennedy Administration faced was a real one, for the closeness of the victory was accompanied by a loss of Democratic strength in Congress which bolstered the always disproportionate influence of southern committee chairmen. The potential gains of forthright executive action in civil rights had to be weighed against the adverse effects it might have upon the prospects for social and economic legislation (measures, it was pointed out, that would also be of great benefit to Negroes). The

* The faith that state and local governments faced with a choice of abandoning racial discrimination or forgoing Federal assistance would choose the former was based in part on the importance of Federal grants as a source of state revenue. In some states, particularly in the South, $1 in every $4 or $5 comes from the Federal Government.

result was a retreat from campaign promises to a far more limited operating principle, generally believed but also politically serviceable, that securing the right to vote would be accorded first priority and that litigation brought by the Department of Justice (not administrative action or other techniques) would be the principal means of enforcing this and other rights. *

There were only two departures of significance from this narrow theory of civil rights action, one in the field of housing and the other in employment.

HOUSING—In housing, the President issued an executive order (E.O. 11063) almost two years after taking office to redeem his campaign promise to ban discrimination in federally assisted housing by a "stroke of the pen." The order, however, was exceedingly narrow in its coverage. It applied only to new housing for which commitments were made after November 20, 1962, thus exempting discrimination in all future transactions on housing built before that date, even public housing. And while it prohibited discriminatory practices in units insured by the Federal Housing Administration and Veterans Administration, the order excluded housing which was "conventionally" financed by savings and loan associations and commercial banks regulated and insured by the Federal Government. As a result of these restric-

* No effort is being made here to assess the overall record of the Kennedy Administration in civil rights since it was directed principally to the rural South. The rationale for giving voting first priority—that once the franchise was secured all other rights would follow—had little application to the North, whatever its validity may have been in the South. But it is worth noting that the effort to deal with mass disfranchisement of Negroes in the South through litigation proved a failure, despite the investment of thousands of hours by capable lawyers in the Civil Rights Division. Negroes were registered in large numbers only after President Johnson secured enactment of the Voting Rights Act of 1965 (first recommended by the Commission on Civil Rights in 1959), which suspended the use of literacy tests in several states and established a network of Federal administrative officials to register Negro applicants where local registrars refused to do so. More than 1.2 million Negro applicants were registered between the enactment of the law in the summer of 1965 and late 1967 in eleven southern states, the percentage of voting-age Negroes who were registered changing from 35.5 to 57.2. From 1957 when the Department of Justice was first authorized to bring voting suits until 1965, the gains were minimal.

tions,* in 1967, five years after the issuance of the order, it covered about 2 per cent of the total national housing supply of 65 million units.

The limitations of the housing order were particularly striking in light of the history of Federal complicity in the establishment of segregated patterns of residence. During the 1930s, when the Federal Government first became substantially involved in the private housing market, racially restrictive covenants were a major instrument for maintaining segregated neighborhoods. The covenants, typically private agreements among adjoining landowners that they would not sell to members of particular racial and religious groups, were promoted by builders and real estate brokers, and were enforceable in the courts until 1948. The FHA during this period encouraged the use of restrictive covenants as a means for assuring racial homogeneity. Its underwriting manual of 1938 declared:

"If a neighborhood is to retain stability, it is necessary that properties shall continue to be occupied by the same social and racial groups."

The manual carried this principle a step further by setting forth a model restrictive covenant and recommending its use. This policy, along with a similar one later adopted by the VA, remained in effect without substantial modification until 1949, more than a year after the Supreme Court held that racially re-

---

* In part, the issue of coverage was a legal one. Officials of the Housing and Home Finance Agency and the Civil Rights Commission took the position that the assistance the Federal Government furnished banks which provided conventional financing afforded a basis for prohibiting discrimination. Justice Department lawyers took a contrary view, noting that the Federal agencies which regulated banks traditionally were somewhat immune from Presidential direction. The Administration flirted briefly with the broader view. During one session in which I participated, Attorney General Robert Kennedy, confronted with the argument that the banking agencies were independent, called for a list of the members of the Federal Home Loan Bank Board and the Federal Reserve Board. After perusing it, he noted that the Boards were "independent" only for several months, the date when the terms of a majority of the members appointed by President Eisenhower expired. He also mused that one of the members had a son who worked for the Kennedy Administration, a fact that might affect his independence. While the discussion might have proved illuminating to political scientists, it did not influence the final decision.

strictive covenants were not enforceable in the courts.[11] Thus, during the post–World War II years of greatest expansion of the suburbs, the Federal Government actively encouraged the creation of racially segregated neighborhoods and communities. And the expansion itself was made possible by government assistance. In 1965, there was outstanding some $150 billion in mortgage loans, insured or guaranteed under FHA and VA programs, which represented more than 15 million housing units, most of them financed during a period when the Federal Government fostered racial discrimination.

During the same period—from the Depression to the 1950s—the Federal Government also subsidized the construction of low-rent housing on terms that led to economic and racial segregation. Policies of segregation in assigning tenants to public housing developments were accepted until ruled unconstitutional by the courts, although an effort was made to assure "racial equity," i.e., that Negroes would have access to a proportionate share of the housing built. More important, the Public Housing Administration (and its predecessors) neither required nor encouraged the dispersion of low-income housing within metropolitan areas. The selection of sites was left to local housing authorities whose jurisdiction under law generally extended only to the central city. If a local housing authority wanted to acquire land for public housing in the suburbs, it could do so only with the permission of the suburban governing authority. As a result, of 250,000 units built in the nation's 24 largest metropolitan areas, only 76 were located outside the central city.[12]

In the face of these long-entrenched patterns of segregation, established with the help of the government, there was little prospect that an executive order so limited in scope could have a significant impact. Any chance, however, that even moderate gains would be made was dissipated when Federal housing officials permitted the order to go largely unenforced. Instead of setting forth specific procedures for compliance, the Federal housing agencies have left enforcement largely to the discretion of their regional officials. These officials, in turn, often have been satisfied with perfunctory written assurances from builders that they will not discriminate; builders have not been required to make efforts to reach the Negro market by advertising or even by making it known to potential buyers that they are subject to the executive order. For enforcement, principal reliance has been placed upon the filing of complaints by the victims of discrimination (an unsatisfactory method for the average home-seeker whose aim is to secure suitable housing for himself and his family rather than to win a legal point) and the resolution of complaints has been a slow process, often taking many months.[13] In the few instances in which complaints have been resolved by making a house available to the complainant, this usually terminated the case; rarely have sanctions been imposed or the builder subjected to special surveillance to assure that the violation would not be repeated.[14] A compromise provision of the order which authorizes the Justice Department to bring lawsuits in certain cases where assistance cannot be withheld has not been utilized at all. And the housing agencies have not even established reporting procedures which would enable them to evaluate how well or badly compliance efforts were going.*

It was not until 1968 that additional tools were provided to buttress the lagging executive orders. In that year, Congress enacted civil rights legislation containing broad provisions designed to bring an end to racial discrimination in almost all housing transactions, and the Supreme Court interpreted a century-old civil rights law, which declared that all citizens should have the same right to acquire property, as affording Negroes a right to sue when they have been discriminated against in seeking housing.[15] While the new legal measures are very broad in their application, they do not provide for enforcement by an administrative authority, depending instead upon individual law-

---

* In part, this failure of implementation has been attributed by housing officials to the fact that FHA financing no longer provides great benefits to builders and that they are free to finance their construction through conventional channels if they wish to continue discriminating. This point, which motivated the housing agencies to seek in the first place to bring conventionally financed housing under the order, is supported by the fact that the combined FHA and VA share of the market which once was more than 35 per cent had dropped to 17 per cent in 1964. But even in San Francisco, where FHA still retained 51 per cent of the market, its vulnerable position in the market was offered as an excuse for failing to enforce the order. "Transcript, Hearing Before the U.S. Commission on Civil Rights in San Francisco, Calif.," p. 183.

suits brought by aggrieved parties or by the government. The Attorney General may secure the opening of a large new suburban subdivision to several Negro home-seekers by suing the builder before he disposes of all the units, but failing widespread voluntary compliance, there is no way in the short run to change the racial patterns of suburban communities built under the discriminatory policies of the 1940s, since almost all homes are individually owned. Thus, whether the present Federal laws will prove effective in dealing with the one limited area of the problem they are designed to cover—removing the barrier of discrimination for those Negro families who have the means to afford decent housing—remains to be seen.

EMPLOYMENT—The other problem on which the Kennedy Administration sought to bring the resources of the executive branch to bear was discrimination in employment which had a Federal connection. Here the Administration was not innovating, but building upon a program begun in 1941 when President Roosevelt, concerned that full use be made of the nation's manpower in the defense effort, issued an executive order establishing a Fair Employment Practices Committee. The Committee survived in truncated form through the Truman and Eisenhower Administrations. The principal application of the Roosevelt, Truman, and Eisenhower orders was to jobs in companies which held contracts with the Department of Defense and other Federal agencies. While not nearly as far-reaching as the fair employment legislation long sought by civil rights groups, the orders did cover a substantial number of jobs, estimated at about 20 million in 1961 and perhaps as many as 30 million during the Vietnam war.

Soon after taking office, President Kennedy issued a new executive order (E.O. 10925) which strengthened in several ways the potential utility of contract compliance as a means for securing better job opportunities for Negroes and members of other minority groups. The order placed responsibility for enforcement on a new President's Committee on Equal Employment Opportunity, which, along with the contracting agencies, had power to impose sanctions for noncompliance. The sanctions, spelled out clearly for the first time, included the power to terminate contracts, to debar noncomplying employers from future contracting

and to recommend lawsuits by the Department of Justice to enforce the nondiscrimination provisions of the contract.

Equally as important, the drafters of the order sought to impose upon employers a concept of their responsibilities broader
than the simple duty to avoid overt discrimination. They did this
by requiring that contractors "take affirmative action" to assure
equal employment opportunity. The concept of "affirmative action," deliberately stated in terms which were broad and vague,
constituted a recognition that a simple change in formal policy
by companies that long had practiced discrimination and exclusion would not be sufficient to accomplish meaningful improvement. At a minimum, it meant that employers had to make
special efforts, e.g., through visits to Negro colleges and advertise-
ments in Negro newspapers, to assure that information about
new job opportunities was conveyed to those previously discriminated against. Along with a broader definition of employer
responsibility went improved methods of detecting possible violations. Complaint procedures were established, but complaints
were no longer viewed as the principal vehicle for implementing
the law. Instead emphasis was placed upon compliance reviews
undertaken by the Committee and by contracting agencies on
their own initiative and upon the analysis of detailed information
which each employer was required to supply showing patterns
of employment by race. Racial statistics were not to be used as
proof of the presence or absence of discrimination, but as aids
in identifying areas of concern where further investigation and
negotiation might prove fruitful.

With improved machinery for the enforcement of the law and
with the hiring of fair employment specialists to assist contract
managers in each department in implementing the nondiscrimination requirements, there were great hopes for progress. These
hopes have not been fulfilled. Although more gains have been
made than under previous directives, the order has not proved to
be a vehicle for achieving major improvements in the employment status of Negroes or members of other minority groups.[16]

The reasons are several. Perhaps the most important is that
despite the strong sanctions set out in the order, there never was
agreement in the executive branch that firm enforcement was the
best means of achieving results. A competing approach, urged by

some of the public and private members of the President's Committee, was that of voluntary action. This approach, embodied in the "Plans for Progress" program, entailed efforts to secure broad agreements with the largest employers (many already covered by the executive order) that they would take voluntary steps to improve employment opportunity for minority groups.[17] Voluntarism was given major emphasis and it helped to undermine the credibility of the compliance procedures and sanctions. In several communities where the Commission on Civil Rights conducted investigations, it found that only small gains had been made, particularly in professional and white collar jobs where Negroes had been most underrepresented. Frequently the large "Plans for Progress" companies had the worst records, poorer than those of other government contractors and sometimes poorer than employers who were not subjected to Federal regulation at all.[18] The sanctions were not used; no contract was canceled during the Kennedy or Johnson Administrations for violation of the nondiscrimination clause, and temporary suspension or debarment was utilized only during the latter days of the Johnson Administration and then not to any significant degree. It was argued that the threatened imposition of sanctions was a "literally incredible weapon" made impractical by the disproportionate penalty it would visit upon employers and by the interference it would impose upon the orderly procurement of important government supplies (the latter a contention which received increasing weight as the government became more involved in the Vietnam war). This argument against sanctions was based on a value judgment shared by most agency heads and contract managers, that civil rights objectives are subsidiary to their main mission—the efficient flow of goods and services to their programs—and that where the two goals come into conflict, civil rights considerations must yield. But the argument prevailed, and it prevented a fair test of the thesis that the invocation of sanctions in only a few cases would impel many contractors to make greater efforts to comply with the order and that methods of enforcement, e.g., investigation of the practices and performance of bidders *before* the contract is awarded, might be adopted that would mitigate the damage and disruption feared.

A second failing was that the order did not apply directly to labor unions, with whom the Federal Government had no contractual relationship. The impact of this gap in coverage has been most severe in the building trades where unions maintain control of the hiring process through referral systems and hiring halls. Although employment in the building trades is not numerically a major source of opportunity (in the absence of much larger public works programs than presently exist), it is of considerable practical and symbolic significance to Negroes. Jobs as skilled plumbers, electricians, and sheetmetal workers pay well and do not require college degrees; thus they constitute one of the few short-term avenues of advancement for people who do not have a great deal of formal education. Yet Negroes are notoriously underrepresented in the skilled trades. When the Commission in 1966 held hearings in Cleveland whose population was roughly one-third Negro, it found that Plumbers Union Local 55 had four Negro members of a total of 1,428 journeymen, that there were no Negroes among the 1,786 journeymen ironworkers and only a single Negro among 1,519 journeymen pipefitters. The pattern has been similar elsewhere. Efforts to probe the reasons for these racial patterns with union officials and contractors usually led to discussions of the uncertainties and complexities of the construction industry, the lack of full employment, strict limitations on the number of apprentices, and the existence of long waiting lists of young white people who had applied for apprentice opportunities. Yet union officials freely admitted practices of nepotism under which relatives and friends of union members, almost all of whom were white, were favored in selecting among applicants for union membership and apprenticeship programs.[19] And further probing sometimes evoked statements of raw prejudice, as when the secretary-treasurer of the Plumbers Local in Cleveland, asked to give his personal feelings on segregation, replied: "I think everybody has got a place and everybody should stay in the place where they belong."[20]

The relationship of the Federal Government to construction employment is not insubstantial; the executive order covers not only construction that the government undertakes directly (such as post offices) but projects in which it provides assistance to states and localities (such as the building of highways and hospitals). But, lacking a clear mandate to deal directly with unions, the officials charged with administering the order generally have contented themselves with requests that employers take a number of formal steps requiring the cooperation of the unions.[21] Where employers have reported that unions were uncooperative or that the steps taken did not result in the actual employment of Negroes, the government ordinarily has not pursued the matter further. In a few recent situations, the government has tried a firmer approach, insisting that the efforts of the contractor and unions result in the employment of minority group members in all trades on the job and in all phases of the work. This approach, first used in Cleveland in 1967 (and which later reemerged as the "Philadelphia Plan" in the Nixon Administration) stirred vehement objections from unions that government was imposing a "quota" system, objections which resulted in a peace-making meeting between Secretary of Labor Willard W. Wirtz and union officials and assurances that the government would continue to be flexible in enforcement. One additional enforcement tool, the authority of the Department of Labor to refuse to register apprenticeship programs, has not brought any better results. Although registration allows the payment of less than journeyman wages to apprentices on Federal construction projects, this assistance apparently is not regarded as crucial by contractors and unions.[22] And the enforcing authority, the Bureau of Apprenticeship and Training—an agency which consists in large part of retired officials of construction unions—has tended to accept without further investigation the assurances of employers and unions that they are in compliance.

In the construction field, as in other areas, the government's reluctance to invoke sanctions has hampered progress. A more consistent application of the tools used in the Cleveland dispute —suspension of the contractor followed by hard negotiations aimed at placing excluded minorities in all trades and in all phases of the work—might well have induced more unions to abandon their exclusionary practices. But in construction, unlike most other employment, the employer's ability to eliminate discrimination is limited. An effective attack upon the problem would have required the government to challenge the protection the law now gives building trades unions in their control over the hiring process, a step that Federal officials were loath to take.[23]

Another area in which the interests of labor unions impinge upon efforts to promote equal job opportunity is in the establishment of seniority systems. It is in this area that steps taken to remove racial discrimination are likely to raise competing claims about what constitutes equitable treatment for Negro and white employees. If, for example, a plant has long maintained separate departments in which Negroes and whites have performed similar work at different pay scales, the law clearly requires the elimination of segregation and differential treatment. The departments are likely, however, to have maintained separate seniority rosters, entitling those with the most service to protection in the event of layoffs and to other benefits. The adjustment of these seniority rights may become the subject of bitter controversy. A decision to place Negroes at the bottom of the seniority list of the newly merged department would clearly make their victory a hollow one. Yet whites may claim that it is unjust for their position to be prejudiced by efforts to remedy past discrimination even though they may have derived benefits from it.

Failing to deal directly with unions in a field where union interests and influence clearly are significant, the executive order was an inadequate instrument for resolving problems involving seniority. Its defects were remedied in part when, in 1964, Congress enacted a long-sought Fair Employment Practices Law as part of the Civil Rights Act of 1964. Title VII of the Civil Rights Act provided for the extension of the nondiscrimination requirement to all employers with twenty-five or more employees (not simply those who hold Federal contracts), and it directly imposed upon unions and employment agencies as well the obligation not to discriminate. But the new law had major deficiencies too; the agency established to implement it—the Equal Employment Opportunity Commission—was not given enforcement powers. It cannot, after finding that an employer or a union has practiced discrimination, issue a cease and desist order, but can only conciliate and negotiate, and, as a last resort, refer the case to the Attorney General with a recommendation that he bring a lawsuit. In addition, Congress indicated some concerns about the application of the law to problems such as seniority by inserting a general proviso stating that ". . . it shall not be an unlawful employment practice for an employer to apply different standards of compensation . . . pursuant to a bona fide seniority or merit system . . ." With these deficiencies and admonitions, it seems inevitable that more subtle practices of discrimination will yield slowly if at all. Civil rights organizations and the Attorney General have filed a number of lawsuits and have obtained judgments to protect the rights of Negroes in seniority disputes, but the efforts are still new and progress is piecemeal.[24]

A final set of limitations upon the effectiveness of the executive order and other equal employment enactments has to do with the inherent bounds of what can be achieved by traditional civil rights legislation. The "voluntary action" approach of the Kennedy Administration recently has begun to pay dividends for reasons that government officials could not have foreseen when the program was first undertaken. Shaken up by the riots in the big cities, many large employers have focussed for the first time on the impact of job discrimination and unemployment in Negro communities. For a variety of reasons—the importance of stable communities as a business consideration, moral concerns, a desire to be in compliance with the law—many employers, particularly large businesses, have undertaken new efforts to recruit Negro applicants. Thus, in 1968, Plans for Progress was able to report a 37.2 per cent increase in the employment of Negroes, Spanish-surnamed Americans, and members of other minority groups since 1966. Included in the increase was a gain from 59,000 to 225,000 in the number of white-collar jobs held by members of minorities, bringing them from 2.8 to almost 5 per cent of the total white-collar work force. Even allowing for the fact that aggregate figures often disguise important deficiencies, such as continued exclusion of members of minority groups from particular industries and job categories, and that the performance of the largest companies now may be better than that of smaller businesses, the report clearly reflects progress. But what it reflects primarily is the new will of many businessmen to locate and utilize at least a part of the pool of talented people who possess standard qualifications and who previously have been excluded from good jobs in industry. For many Negroes and Mexican Americans who have college degrees and needed skills, the opportunities multiplied during recent years. But employers as a whole have yet to come to grips with the problem of upgrading minority group employees who for years have been under-utilized and underpaid. And for applicants who do not have the standard qualifications and skills and who may have other disabilities, the doors frequently are still closed.

Civil rights enactments standing alone are an inadequate instrument for overcoming many of the barriers faced by the disadvantaged. One such obstacle lies in the aptitude and ability tests commonly utilized by employers as part of the selection procedures for hiring and promotion. Testing is a seemingly neutral method of determining which prospective employees will function most effectively on the job. Where, however, employers are not faced with shortages of applicants, tests often set hiring standards far beyond those actually necessary, and since many employers do not go to the trouble of validating their tests, there is often a strong possibility that the scores are not a good predictor of actual performance. Most important, the kinds of tests given frequently prejudice the chances of Negroes, Mexican Americans, and members of other minority groups. By placing a high premium on verbal proficiency in English, they focus on skills in which members of minority groups may be weakest and which may be only peripherally related to the requirements of the job. Since tests generally are drawn by middle-class white Americans they may also contain a cultural bias that works against many Negroes and others from disadvantaged circumstances.

Similar observations may be made about other "objective" qualifications such as the requirement for high school diplomas even where the completion of high school may have little relation to the demands of the job. A further major obstacle to employment is the tendency of personnel offices to screen out all applicants who have records of criminal arrest or conviction without examining the recency or remoteness of the event, the seriousness of the crime, or other circumstances which may be extenuating. If the estimate of the President's Commission on Law Enforcement that 50 to 90 per cent of all Negro males in urban ghettos have criminal records is even roughly accurate such employment practices are a serious impediment for a great many ghetto residents. And again, for many reasons, there may be little relationship between the fact of an arrest or conviction and the applicant's reliability on the job.

The agencies charged with implementing equal employment laws have recognized the significance of these tests of qualifications and have sought to induce employers to reexamine their hiring procedures. But the role of Federal officials in these matters necessarily is limited to the provision of information, technical assistance, encouragement, and persuasion. It is difficult for the government to prove that seemingly neutral hiring procedures constitute discriminatory practices, even where they clearly work to the disadvantage of Negroes. In this area too, Congress has contributed caution by providing in the law that it shall not be an unlawful practice for an employer to act upon the results of a professionally developed ability test if the test and its administration are not intended or used to discriminate.[25] So, in general, Federal civil rights agencies are limited in their efforts to encouragement and persuasion techniques which usually are effective only with those already predisposed to change.

Similar efforts to convince employers to adopt a broader view of their responsibilities are needed to deal with distance as a barrier to employment opportunity. As noted in Chapter 2 the migration of industry from the central city to suburban areas increasingly has placed jobs beyond the effective reach of ghetto residents who are precluded from moving to the suburbs by the absence of moderate-income housing available on a nondiscriminatory basis. In California, for example, the Lockheed Missile and Space Company, an employer with a respectable overall record, maintained a plant in the Santa Clara area—where Negroes faced difficulties in acquiring housing—which in 1967 had only 400 black employees (less than 2 per cent) in a total work force of more than 22,000. For employers to deal with the problem of distance, they would have to assume the responsibility of negotiating with local authorities to assure a supply of moderate-income housing available without discrimination and adequate to meet the needs of employees and prospective employees. In doing so, large employers would have considerable bargaining power by virtue of the economic benefits they bring to the community. But thus far, few companies have viewed the housing needs of their employees and prospective employees as within the orbit of their equal opportunity concerns, and Federal agencies have not encouraged them to do so.

Perhaps the most serious limitation on the effectiveness of traditional civil rights enactments in attaining job opportunities for disadvantaged people is that the laws do not deal with lack of training and education for needed skills. In partial recognition of this, the Kennedy Administration in 1962 secured the enactment of the Manpower Development and Training Act, a law initially designed to retrain experienced adults whose skills had been rendered obsolete by technological change, but whose focus gradually has shifted to training for the disadvantaged. The operation of that law will be assessed in a later section, but a few observations are pertinent here. The training conducted under Federal sponsorship is of two kinds—"institutional" training conducted by government agencies or manpower specialists under contract to the government, and on-the-job training conducted by employers. In the view of many, on-the-job training is potentially the most useful part of the program, since successful completion of the training provides assurance of a job. But as recently as 1967, on-the-job training still constituted a relatively small portion of the total program, and despite many public statements by industry leaders that it should be used as a vehicle to provide opportunities for the disadvantaged, only 10 per cent of those enrolled were nonwhite and only 20 per cent could be categorized as disadvantaged. On-the-job training, it appears, has been used by employers principally as a tool for upgrading the skills of their own employees.[26]

Where training is not provided by the employer, efforts to assure that programs are conducted in skills for which there is a demand and that those successfully completing programs are placed in jobs become critical. One logical way to approach this would be for the agencies enforcing equal employment laws to focus on employers with poor records of employing minorities, identify their principal manpower needs and then work with them to secure the establishment of training programs which will help to fill the needs with members of minority groups. This has not been done. Manpower programs and equal employment programs operate within the Federal Government as separate bureaucracies, with minimal contact and no coordination. Thus, the Commission on Civil Rights found in its investigations repeated instances of persons successfully completing institutional programs who were unable to find jobs in the fields for which they had been trained.[27] And fair employment investigators continue to be faced by employers' claims that their poor civil rights records are accounted for by the lack of qualified people.

TITLE VI—Events in 1963 worked a radical change in the cautious approach of the Kennedy Administration to civil rights problems. In May, peaceful protests led by Martin Luther King in Birmingham, Alabama, were met by violent repression on the part of police authorities who used police dogs and fire hoses and made massive arrests. In June, the murder of NAACP leader Medgar Evers by a sniper in Jackson, Mississippi, brought protests and demonstrations throughout the nation.

In February 1963, President Kennedy had submitted to Congress a mild civil rights bill reflecting his continuing belief and that of his chief advisers that voting was the main priority and litigation the chief instrument for securing progress. But in the summer, sensing that public opinion would now support, if not demand, a stronger response to the tragedies of the spring, the Kennedy Administration proposed new legislation.

The most far-reaching provision in the new bill was Title VI, a requirement that every Federal department and agency administering a program of Federal assistance assure that there be no racial discrimination in the receipt of benefits under the program. The requirement was backed by sanctions, including authority to terminate assistance to state and local government agencies and private institutions which continue to engage in discriminatory practices.

Some Kennedy aides viewed Title VI as the dispensable part of his program, to be junked when the Congressional going got rough.[28] But the sentiment for effective legislation was greater than anticipated. The massive, peaceful, and spirited group which assembled for the "March on Washington" in August made an impression on Congressmen who in the past had often gauged public sentiment by the absence of mail favoring civil rights legislation. And church groups throughout the country for the first time asserted themselves as an effective lobby for new civil rights laws. When the bill took shape in Congress in the fall, it included not only the key provisions proposed by President Kennedy, but

Title VII, a fair employment practices measure that the Administration had resisted as impossible of attainment and likely to jeopardize passage of the entire bill. The national soul-searching which took place following the assassination of President Kennedy, and President Johnson's strong appeal to the Congress, helped to assure the final enactment of the program without substantial modification in July 1964.

Title VI of the new law was an important response to the demands of civil rights groups for new tools for enforcement. Responsibility for carrying out civil rights laws was no longer the sole province of a small group of lawyers in the Department of Justice but of twenty-two Federal departments and agencies administering more than 200 programs involving more than $18 billion in benefits. Vindication of rights no longer depended entirely upon lawsuits which sometimes took several years to conclude but upon the invocation of administrative remedies which promised speedier relief in many cases. And with the principle of executive action now sanctioned by Congress, there was the hope that Federal officials carrying out civil rights responsibilities would be less subject to pressures than when they acted on the authority of the President alone.

After six years, the record of action under Title VI is best described as a mixed one of success and failure. Federal agencies, particularly the Department of Health, Education and Welfare, have had greatest success in utilizing it as an instrument for eliminating discriminatory practices that are overt and blatant. Thus, in many places in the South, cities as well as rural areas, Negroes no longer are compelled to occupy separate wings, wards, or rooms in hospitals, to receive segregated treatment in clinics, welfare facilities, or local employment offices.* Contrary to the predictions of a number of Federal officials (including former At-

---

* Success, however, has been far from uniform. Some states and local welfare agencies continue to employ only white caseworkers and discriminate against Negro clients. Negro families in rural areas are still subjected to gross discrimination in services financed by the Department of Agriculture. For example, some extension service offices have a policy which permits employees to service only clients of the same race, which means that Negro farm families will receive much less attention from overburdened Negro staff than white families receive from white staff.

torney General Nicholas de B. Katzenbach) who believed that
political leaders in the South would be willing to forgo Federal
assistance rather than desegregate and that Title VI thus would
harm the very people it was intended to benefit, change often
has come swiftly and with little resistance.

In areas such as public education, where the elimination of discriminatory practices is a more complex process, change has
come more slowly. Viewed from the optimistic perspective, Title
VI can be counted a success because in the first three years of its
operation more black children were placed in desegregated
schools than in the previous decade following the Supreme
Court's decision in the *Brown* case. Yet in the 1966–1967 school
year there still were more Negro children attending all-black
schools in the South than there had been at the time the Supreme
Court decided *Brown.* Progress, in other words, had not even
kept pace with the increase in the black school population
(which has continued to grow despite the migration of Negroes
to the North).*

However the value of Title VI in the South may be assessed, its
impact in the urban North has been minimal. In the field of public education, Congress made clear in enacting the law that it
was concerned with segregation compelled by law, not separation which comes about as the result of segregated patterns of
residence.† Segregation in northern city schools is not always
the fortuitous result of separate housing, as a number of court
decisions have established, but intensive investigation generally
is required to uncover the decisions of local officials which
brought it about.[29] HEW has not undertaken such careful inquiry. In 1965, the Office of Education of HEW made an abor-
tive effort to defer the granting of funds to school authorities in
the City of Chicago on the grounds of a possible violation of

* From 1967 to 1969, some additional progress was made, by the degree
of integration in many places in the deep South is still very small. More recently, the Nixon Administration has undermined Title VI enforcement,
thrown the burden back on the courts, and made it doubtful whether progress can be sustained.

† Periodically, Congress has reemphasized the point through the attachment of riders to education bills forbidding the use of Federal funds to
compel the remedying of racial imbalance in the schools.

Title VI. The action was ill-considered in several respects. Although Federal officials were responding to a well-drafted complaint filed by Chicago civil rights organizations, their action to withhold funds was taken before they had conducted an independent investigation to determine whether segregation was attributable to intentional action by Chicago school authorities. Moreover, HEW's entry into northern school problems was completely *ad hoc;* the Department had established no guidelines or criteria which would enable its investigators to determine what actions by local officials, e.g., in selecting sites for schools, in establishing district boundaries, might constitute violations of Title VI or what remedies might appropriately be invoked if violations were found. Finally, from the standpoint of political decision-making, HEW officials could not have chosen a worse place for the first real exercise of Title VI authority in the North. Without serious preparation, they had taken on Richard Daley, a mayor whose political influence had been clearly demonstrated and who exercised tight control over a large Congressional delegation, and Everett Dirksen, a Senator whose whim could determine the fate of major portions of the Administration's legislative program.

At the behest of President Johnson, who had not been consulted or informed before the original deferral action was taken, negotiations were undertaken to release the funds and HEW beat a hasty retreat. It did not reenter the field until 1968 when it issued cautious guidelines for northern school investigations. The guidelines made it clear that Title VI could not be invoked in the absence of evidence that school segregation was the product of intentional action. And the unspoken strategy was to apply Title VI initially only to small and medium-size cities, where political opposition would not be overwhelming and where integration might be attained without vast new Federal expenditures.

If HEW's efforts to cope with discrimination in the North were misconceived, other agencies have made little effort to deal with the problems at all. It is generally recognized that decisions made in the course of administering programs of assistance in the North may result in discrimination even when they are not overtly racist in character. For example, site selection often is a key part of the administrative process. A decision to locate a low-income housing project in the heart of a Negro ghetto assures that it will be a segregated development. Similarly, decisions about the location of health and recreational facilities may be made in a manner which assures that they will be segregated or that the services provided will be inaccessible to members of minority groups. In employment, local officials while eschewing overt discrimination may apply seemingly neutral standards—such as the requirement that persons be trained in fields in which there is a "reasonable expectation of employment"—in a manner which results in Negroes not being placed in (or being referred away from) programs which may lead to meaningful job opportunities.

The regulations drafted to implement Title VI recognized the possibility of discrimination by subtle means. They prohibited all forms of discrimination including "the use of criteria or methods of administration which would defeat or substantially impair the accomplishment of the program's objectives for individuals of a particular race or color." But enforcement of the regulations requires the allocation of sufficient staff resources to give careful scrutiny to local decision-making, and the collection and evaluation of racial statistics showing how federally assisted facilities are utilized. Federal agencies have not done this. Frequently they have been content with paper assurances of compliance received from state agencies which themselves have neither the staff nor the incentive to deal with discriminatory practices on the local level. The result has been that no significant restraints have been placed upon the tendency of local authorities in utilizing Federal funds to make decisions that reinforce existing patterns of racial separation.

In the general neglect of the urban North, some Federal agencies have not even dealt with more blatant instances of discrimination. In Cleveland, for example, the Commission found in 1966 that seven of eleven public housing projects were at least 90 per cent Negro or 90 per cent white. Testimony indicated that housing assignments were manipulated to maintain this pattern of separation. Whites consistently waited less time for housing than Negroes even though there were more Negroes on the waiting list. And the director of the local housing authority admitted that despite long waiting lists, no Negro had ever been offered an apartment in a development which had been 100 per cent white for twenty years. The regional office of the Public Housing

Administration had accepted the local authority's statement that it was in compliance with Title VI without conducting a review.*

Conclusion

During the past fifteen years major changes have occurred in the legal status of Negroes in the United States. Two of the most important restraints upon the ability of government to afford legal protection to black citizens have been removed. The first, the maintenance for sixty years of the enormous fiction that state laws which separated and excluded a whole race from participation in public communal life provided equal protection, was swept away by the *Brown* decision in 1954, and the cases that followed. The second restraint, the doctrine that the Federal Government was empowered by the Constitution to prohibit only discriminatory practices imposed by government and not those of private institutions, has yielded gradually. Initially the doctrine was predicated on the theory that state governments would act to prevent private discrimination which significantly disadvantaged Negroes. When this expressed hope could no longer be sustained and when government assistance to private institutions had blurred the lines between public and private action, the courts began to chip away at the doctrine by prohibiting discriminatory acts by private institutions in which the government was significantly involved. Congress went further in 1964 by using its commerce powers to bar discriminatory practices by private employers and proprietors of places of public accommodation. And in 1968, Congress and the Supreme Court rendered

* HUD subsequently sought to revise procedures which led to segregated public housing. In 1967, it modified its "freedom of choice" policy under which applicants could refuse to accept available units until they were satisfied, without losing their position on the waiting list. HUD also sought to eliminate segregated offices for the acceptance of applications and required periodic compliance reports from local authorities. Implementation remains the key question. An earlier HUD directive, aimed at preventing low-income housing from being located in "areas of racial concentration," has been more honored in its breach than in observance. See "Comment, Title VI—Civil Rights Act of 1964," 36 *George Washington Law Review* 824, 999.

"state action" limitations almost obsolete by utilizing authority provided under different clauses of the Constitution to outlaw discriminatory housing practices by builders, bankers, and real estate brokers.

Yet, far-reaching as these changes are in legal terms, they have had very limited practical meaning for the great majority of black citizens. The reasons for this are several:

The work of the courts and Congress in establishing legal equality is still far from complete. Although the courts have disposed of the myth that "separate" could be "equal" and have found the means to protect Negroes against private as well as governmental discrimination, they still generally are disposed to act only when the practices challenged are overt, unmistakable in their intent to disadvantage Negroes, and where responsibility can be affixed clearly. In the urban North, segregated public schools generally are the product of racial housing patterns which government helped to establish and of decisions by local authorities on the organization of school systems which often are ambiguous in intent. In these situations, courts have been reluctant to intervene, in large part because to do so would necessarily entail extensive remedial action, involving the courts, for example, in major reorganizations of school systems. While the reasons for this reluctance are understandable, the result is that patterns of segregation in the North—indistinguishable from those in the South in that they are imposed upon Negroes rather than reflecting individual choice—remain immune from legal attack.

The gap between the declaration of legal rights and their effectuation, while narrowed, still remains. It took ten years of almost total frustration of the rights declared in the *Brown* decision for Congress and the executive branch to recognize and act upon the limitations of court litigation as a means of vindicating civil rights. Under ordinary circumstances, lawsuits are a reasonably effective instrument for securing redress for an individual who has suffered harm at the hands of another. But they are not easily adapted to deal with mass deprivations of rights occurring in many areas of the nation, especially when resistance to change is deeply ingrained and when the offending parties have the power and resources to resist that are available to state governments and other large institutions. In these circumstances, the national government must weigh in heavily if it is to tip the scales in favor of the individual seeking to secure his rights.

In recent years, the Congress has provided for a more significant Federal involvement by requiring the executive branch to use its administrative authority to prevent discrimination in Federally assisted programs by authorizing the Attorney General to bring lawsuits on behalf of individuals deprived of their rights. Use of these new tools has brought progress, but in many cases long-entrenched patterns and practices of discrimination still have not yielded. In part, the continuing gap between profession and practice reflects the timidity of government's approach. Most Federal agencies still play a passive role, responding only to complaints and reacting to crises, rather than seeking out problems and moving affirmatively to remedy them. And the reluctance of these agencies to impose the sanctions provided by law has impaired the government's credibility, leading many employers, unions, and state and local governments to conclude that paper compliance will suffice.[30]

Civil rights laws alone cannot bring about major improvements in the opportunities available to poor people. During the long period when there were few civil rights laws or enforcement mechanisms, little attention was paid to the potential limitations of such laws. It would in fact have been counterproductive to have focussed on limitations; to have done so would have added a string to the bow of those who opposed civil rights legislation. But with the enactment of new laws and procedures, the restricted potential of civil rights policies for improving the lot of poor people has become increasingly apparent. A law assuring that all people will be considered for employment on the basis of merit rather than race will not secure a good paying job for a black man who lacks skills, training, and education. A law prohibiting discrimination in housing will not secure a good home in a decent neighborhood for a Negro family when it does not have the financial means to afford such housing. Poor education leads to poor housing and unemployment or poor-paying jobs. Poor housing may make jobs inaccessible and provide an unfavorable environment for raising children. A family without adequate income cannot provide adequate nutrition, a good environment, or educational opportunity for its children. The familiar cycle of poverty prevails. Unless government intervenes effectively at some point to provide economic assistance and needed social services, legal guarantees of equality are hollow. It is to government's efforts in the economic and social spheres that we turn next.

4

ECONOMIC AND SOCIAL PROGRAMS

IF THE AVERAGE BLACK CITIZEN in the ghetto sees no tangible change in his life resulting from Federal efforts, many affluent white citizens also are mystified. They read that the Federal Government is spending $4 billion for education, almost that much for welfare programs, $3½ billion for economic opportunity programs, and $1 billion each for labor and manpower programs and for urban community development including low- and moderate-income housing. They listen to the claims of the Johnson Administration (or whatever Administration is in power) that during the period from 1958 to 1968, the number of federally assisted public housing units has grown by almost 70 per cent, that enrollees in vocational education programs have increased by 80 per cent, that new programs are strengthening the education of 8½ million disadvantaged schoolchildren and making privately sponsored low- and moderate-income housing available to 117,000 families. They hear that during the short space of four years, the Federal Government has helped to create 7½ million new jobs, to reduce unemployment to less than 4 per cent, and to reduce by 6½ million the number of people living in poverty.[1]

In the light of these claims, it is not difficult for many white Americans to draw comforting conclusions. The programs of the New Deal as improved and brought up to date by the Great Society appear to be making a significant dent in the problem of poverty; perhaps we can look forward to the day when, without materially increasing Federal effort or even while reducing it, poverty will cease to be a problem. On the other hand, the physical evidence seems to contradict many of the political claims. Cities continue to deteriorate, welfare rolls grow, and there is more disorder and discontent.

Some citizens may draw the conclusion that many poor people are simply incapable of responding to government assistance. Or alternatively, perhaps the Federal Government is the wrong institution to look to for solutions; if we had vested our confidence in private enterprise or state and local governments and limited the Federal role to providing financial resources, perhaps we would be much farther along the road toward solutions.

The foregoing conclusions are obviously not completely consistent, but they point to a single policy judgment—that the Federal Government is not the institution upon which to place principal reliance for devising and implementing solutions to problems of poverty. If its resources are needed they should not be on a scale much larger than that being employed at present, and any new programs should be planned in a manner which will avoid the imposition of Federal standards or controls.

Yet an analysis of the operation of Federal programs from the New Deal through the 1960s yields quite a different set of conclusions. The economic and social measures undertaken during the past thirty years have failed to assist many people, not because of a surplus of resources wastefully used, but because of a scarcity of resources allocated; not because poor black people are incapable of responding to Federal assistance, but because they have not had access to meaningful assistance; not because of a heavy-handed imposition of Federal standards and controls, but because the Federal Government's deference to local interests has resulted in the imposition of *local* conditions which often defeat the purposes of the program. In this view, the principal deficiencies of Federal programs are along the lines following:

The Federal Government, in every important area, has failed to commit resources adequate to solving the problems.

Nowhere is the gap between profession and practice so wide as in the provision of standard housing to those who cannot afford to purchase it on the private market. The goal, implicit since the initiation of subsidized housing programs, was made explicit in the Housing Act of 1949: "A decent home and a suitable living environment for every American family." Yet the public housing program has provided fewer than 700,000 units in more than thirty years, barely more than 1 per cent of the national housing inventory. To this may be added 46,000 units built under Section 221(d)(3) of the Housing Act of 1961, a program designed to provide inexpensive rental housing for families with incomes too high to be eligible for public housing but not high enough to obtain standard housing in the private market, and a handful of units provided under the rent supplement program. The total, fewer than 800,000 units, can be measured against need in various ways. It is about the same as the number of substandard housing units estimated to exist in New York City in 1968.[2] Nationally, there are some 6 million substandard housing units, and well over that number of families lack sufficient income to rent or buy standard housing without spending more than 25 per cent of their income and sacrificing other essential needs.[3]

When special needs such as those of large families are examined, the gap grows even wider. A report prepared for the National Commission on Urban Problems, surveying the needs of poor families with five or more members in seven large cities, concluded that there were 103,000 such families with incomes too low to obtain standard housing in the private market, and only 20,000 units of public or subsidized housing available to them. When the gap was projected for the sixty-one largest cities in the United States, the deficit was estimated at 529,000 units, involving more than 2,570,000 children.[4]

The Kerner Commission recommended that the need be met through a program to provide 6 million units of housing for low- and moderate-income families over a period of five years. The Johnson Administration and Congress responded with a program which contemplates meeting the goal over a period of ten years. Even stretched out over a decade, the program would require the construction of almost as much housing in one year as has been built in thirty years under the public housing program.*

* Although the program is now authorized, the problem, as is usually the case, is in securing funding. For the first year, Congress provided only $25

Obviously then, whatever potential public housing may have as an instrument for helping families to extricate themselves from poverty has not been realized by millions of people simply because they have not had access to the program.[5]

The entry of the Federal Government into the field of retraining people to provide them with needed skills is of more recent origin, dating principally from the enactment of the Manpower Development and Training Act in 1962. From 1962 to 1966, approximately 600,000 people were enrolled in training programs and fewer than 350,000 completed training. Of those completing training, it has been estimated that some 170,000 were drawn from poor families, of whom 130,000 were believed to be in jobs relating to their training.[6] A very rough measure of the adequacy of the program can be gained by comparing its achievements with estimates that in 1968 there were about 2 million people unemployed and 6.5 million who worked full-time and earned less than the annual poverty wage.

Even in the wake of the stepped-up level of activity the government has engaged in recently, the gap does not appear to be materially reduced. In 1965, training projects were approved for 215,000 trainees, about .003 per cent of the entire labor force. Many European nations make a significantly greater effort, and a Swedish economist has suggested that the experience of his country shows there is an annual total training need of 1 per cent of the labor force.

If the 1 per cent standard were accepted in the United States, it would mean increasing the employability and earning power of approximately 900,000 persons each year for the next decade. At an unemployment rate of 3 per cent it would mean that one unemployed person in every three would acquire new job skills each year, compared to one in every sixteen under the 1965 pro-

---

million each for the two major new programs authorized, one to assist low-income families in becoming homeowners and the other to subsidize rentals in private developments. The amount appropriated was one-third of the Administration's request and will finance only 33,000 units under each program, hardly a promising step toward the proclaimed goal. The housing built under the home ownership program, moreover, is likely to be beyond the means of the lowest income families, even with the subsidy. See Bailey, "Housing, Yes, Cities, No," *Architectural Forum*, p. 37, Sept. 1968.

gram when the unemployment rate was more than 4 per cent.[7] In short, the retraining of 1 per cent of the labor force annually would require a level of expenditures by the Federal Government more than triple its effort in recent years.

Again, without considering the issue of whether training programs are operating effectively for many of the poorest, least educated people who do have access to them, it may be concluded that the programs have failed in that hundreds of thousands of citizens who need training and jobs simply are not reached by them.

If manpower programs are designed to provide assistance to people who are employable, public welfare programs serve an entirely different constituency. Of the 4 million people who received assistance in 1965 under the Aid to Families of Dependent Children program (AFDC), the largest of the welfare programs, the great bulk were eligible for assistance because they were in families where the father was either dead, incapacitated, or absent from the home. Of the approximately 1 million adults participating in the program, 900,000 were mothers, 100,000 disabled fathers, and only 50,000 unemployed fathers. *

Thus, the major purpose of AFDC is to provide decent living conditions for those who are unable to work, and specifically for children, to provide them with an environment which will enable them to develop their own abilities in ways which increase their chances of escaping from poverty.[8] The extent to which the program falls short of its intended purpose can be gauged in part by the average payments made to families. In 1964, the national median payment for public assistance, including payments for medical care, was $141.80 per month for a family of four, or $1,701.60 per year.[9] This was little more than half the amount ($3,335) that the government had established as the "poverty" level for a family of four living in an urban area. Since

---

* Whether it would be sensible to adopt a national policy of treating mothers of small children as employable is a moot question in the absence of programs designed to provide training and job opportunities and day-care centers to provide for the children. In 1967, Congress, disturbed by the rapid growth of the AFDC program, decided to cut down on the welfare rolls by disqualifying mothers who could find employment. But in the absence of major efforts to provide training, jobs, and day-care centers, the Congressional policy had little impact.

each state is authorized to set its own standards, payments vary widely from state to state. In part, the low national average is accounted for by rural states, such as Mississippi, which in 1964 expected a family of four to survive on $390 per year (the payment has since been raised to $446). But even industrial states such as Indiana, Ohio, and Michigan furnished payments of less than $2,000 a year, and only a handful of states approached the official poverty level.

Whether viewed in humanitarian or utilitarian terms, a welfare system which permits people to be sustained only in degrading poverty is self-defeating. Lacking any opportunity for meaningful training or work, families receiving government aid that allows them to live only in the meanest circumstances are apt to turn in desperation to illegal or asocial practices to supplement their income. Mothers seek paramours to scrape up enough money for food or the rent bill. Children learn at an early age that various forms of "the hustle" are the most accessible means for bringing in income. For many who do not supplement their incomes, inadequate levels of government support mean ill-nourished children who sometimes are kept out of school because they lack proper clothing. Thus, the objectives of the welfare programs are made a mockery by the failure to commit adequate resources to their implementation.[10]

The failure of government to commit adequate resources to solving social and economic problems stems in part from its treatment of the interests of the poor in receiving assistance as privileges rather than rights.

In responding, for example through old age insurance or programs of veterans' benefits, to certain kinds of social needs, Congress has tended to view the interests of the people who are to be benefited as rights rather than privileges. In consequence, it has defined with some precision the class of people to be benefited and the standards of eligibility, and decided at least in general terms the level of assistance required to respond to the need. The funding of the program has been determined in large part by this view that assistance is a matter of right.

In contrast, the interests of poor people in obtaining decent homes and opportunities for training and jobs have been treated by Congress as privileges subject to charitable dispensations by the government. True, the goals of programs in these areas are sometimes broadly stated in the legislation in terms suggesting that citizens have rights, for example, the goal stated in the Housing Act of 1949 of realizing "as soon as feasible . . . a decent home and a suitable living environment for *every* American family" [emphasis added]. But the executive branch and Congress have not implemented the programs in a manner consistent with the stated goals. They have not funded the programs by making a determination that a particular level of investment is necessary either as a matter of morality or of strategy. Thus, Congress has not said, "We determine that a person who is unable to work needs X amount of dollars so that he and his family can survive" or "It will take X amount of dollars to provide a standard housing unit for everyone who is not able to afford one." Nor has it said as a strategic hypothesis or determination that "We believe that if we spend X amount of dollars to provide a person with a better environment or training for a job, he is likely to become a more productive citizen who will contribute to society rather than require subsistence." Instead, levels of expenditures for these programs are likely to be determined in the budget-making and appropriations processes by external considerations. These include what is "left over" for the program after determining the expenditures for programs such as agricultural price supports, whose costs are regarded as "fixed," and whether, taking other costs as fixed, increased levels of expenditure would require tax increases that may be politically imprudent, or running deficits which might prove inflationary.

Admittedly, to determine expenditures by treating the interests of the poor as rights and estimating what is needed to reach particular strategic or moral objectives would result in large-scale increases in expenditures. The estimates of necessary levels of expenditures might be far beyond the capacity of our national economy to sustain, without a great increase in economic growth or a change in national priorities and a redistribution of resources. But such an approach at least would force a dialogue and decisions about national priorities and the planning of steps toward the achievement of goals, rational elements sorely lacking in our national decision-making processes now.

Some programs ostensibly for the benefit of the poor have

failed to serve them or have actually worsened their position. Frequently this results from the mixing of social with nonsocial goals in the same program or from a choice of means ill-adapted to social purposes.

Perhaps the classic example of good intentions gone awry is the urban renewal program. It was established initially as part of the Housing Act of 1949, a law which recognized the existence of a serious housing shortage and, as noted, articulated the noble goal of providing decent housing for all citizens. While there is no reason to doubt the general goodwill of the framers, the only fair conclusion after twenty years of experience, is that the urban renewal program, far from proving a boon to the poor, has succeeded only in adding hardship to their lives.

The Achilles heel of the urban renewal program has been the failure of Congress to address itself to the means for solving the serious housing shortages, particularly those facing poor people, that the law recognized. It provided only that public housing monies would continue to be authorized for the cities, and families displaced by renewal would be relocated in existing housing. But this general statement of intent did not work out in practice. Public housing was located on urban renewal sites in only a handful of projects, and alternative sites for low-income housing were not developed. From the inception of the program through the end of 1965, urban renewal had resulted in the demolition of more than 330,000 homes, and had replaced them with only 84,-000—less than one-fourth of the number eliminated, and for the most part beyond the reach of the poor families displaced.

Urban renewal has had widely varying success from city to city, but whether the program has lagged or moved forward vigorously, the effect upon people living in blighted areas has been adverse. In Cleveland, the program was the victim of poor planning and shoddy implementation. Although an urban renewal plan for a portion of the Hough ghetto had been in effect since 1962, the changes planned were piecemeal and minor and by 1966 all that had been accomplished was the condemnation of a number of widely scattered houses, some leveled and others left standing vacant.

The results were disastrous for the people living in Hough. With the threat of the bulldozer and wrecking ball hanging over them, many families simply left the community. The houses so vacated and those condemned and left standing became targets for vandalism and gathering places for vice. The houses leveled became trash-filled vacant lots. Small grocery-store owners and other businessmen whose enterprises were modest but stable found themselves threatened by bankruptcy because customers had moved and the neighborhood had deteriorated. To cap it all off, city housing authorities decided without publicity to stop enforcing the housing codes in areas designated for urban renewal. The action was prompted by "sound business reasons." To have required landlords to make costly repairs would have driven up the costs of slum property when the city was ready to acquire it for urban renewal. But the decision was immoral; the city was not prepared to move ahead and the result was simply to make the lives of people living in Hough more miserable.[11]

In contrast with Cleveland, the New Haven urban renewal program is regarded as one of the most successful in the nation. With Federal Government assistance of $130 per city resident just for one of several costly projects, New Haven has revitalized its downtown area, attracting new businesses, providing commodious housing for middle-income families, and significantly improving services available to the poor.[12] Yet from 1956 to 1968, the urban renewal and highway programs combined had resulted in the demolition of 6,500 housing units, mostly low income. To replace them, New Haven had built only 951 low-income dwellings since 1952.

In New Haven and elsewhere, the displacement of people for the purposes of urban renewal is subject to a general Federal requirement that they be relocated in areas not generally less desirable, at rents within their means, and in decent, safe, and sanitary dwellings. Given the absence of programs to provide housing within the reach of people of low and moderate income, faithful adherence to requirements for relocation would bring urban renewal to a halt in most communities. The problem has been circumvented in many places by an exercise in fiction. Local public agencies responsible for relocation make general and theoretical estimates that suitable dwellings are available. And the Federal Government accepts these assurances without question, although it knows that they are not realistic. Little is known about what actually happens to families displaced by renewal, but in many instances, it appears that they relocate on the fringes of the renewal area, finding housing which is substandard or for which they pay higher rents, and sometimes introducing a problem of overcrowding into the new area.[13]

While the reasons for the failures of urban renewal are complex, it seems fair to state that a major part of the problem stems from conflicts between the goals declared and the means adopted to achieve them. Congress determined early that the objectives of urban renewal should be fulfilled through private enterprise and that the program should meet standards of economic soundness. But it did not provide the means for meeting these standards and at the same time fulfilling the social aims of the program. As a result, social concerns about meeting the needs of residents of the inner city have yielded to business concerns about minimizing risks, producing the greatest returns on investment, and maximizing the tax yields from city land.[14]

Other Federal housing policies, seemingly neutral and fair on their face, in application have worsened the plight of Negroes in the cities. FHA operations, for example, long have been governed by principles of "economic soundness" which restrict the agency to making loans and offering mortgage insurance on buildings whose economic life is judged sufficient to warrant the financing. In practice, FHA has implemented this policy by "redlining" certain areas of cities, determining in effect that they were so threatened by deterioration that no building within their borders was acceptable for government investment. Frequently the areas red-lined have been older neighborhoods occupied or available for occupancy by Negroes. The effect of the FHA's withdrawal has been that no reputable institution would offer financing in the area, leaving prospective residents prey to speculators and shady operators.

In the West Lawndale neighborhood of Chicago, for example, whites began moving out and Negroes began moving in in 1960, and the FHA stopped insuring mortgages in the community shortly thereafter. Whites sold their homes to real estate speculators who resold them to Negroes. In a typical transaction, the real estate speculator purchased a home for $14,000 (an amount roughly equal to its appraised value), and resold it a few weeks later to a Negro family for $25,000. The terms of the contract provided for a twenty-one-year mortgage at a 7 per cent rate of interest, the maximum then allowed by Illinois, and the total obligation of the Negro buyer was more than $47,000, $22,000 of it in interest. With monthly payments of more than $200, some Negro purchasers made ends meet by converting two-family dwellings to three-family units, thus contributing to the decline of a neighborhood already burdened by inadequate services.

At a minimum it may be said that the effect of FHA's policy was to assist in building a trap for the unwary. But this really understates the case. Even if they were aware of the likelihood of being exploited, Negroes in search of a home had few alternatives available to them, because patterns of racial separation, created with the assistance of FHA's "racial homogeneity" policy,[15] had closed many markets to potential Negro buyers. Thus, Federal housing policies had made exploitation and deteriorating neighborhoods almost inevitable.*

Food, no less than shelter, has been the subject of Federal legislation that has badly served people who are in need. In 1946, Congress enacted the National School Lunch Act, a law designed "to safeguard the health and well-being of the nation's children," in part, by supplying "lunches without cost, or at a reduced cost to all children who are determined by local authorities to be unable to pay the full price thereof." While the goal declared in the law was unexceptionable, twenty years later fewer than 2 million of the 18 million children participating in the program were able to obtain free or reduced-price school lunches. More than 4 million children were in dire poverty (with parents receiving ADC benefits or with incomes of less than $2,000 a year) and did not participate in the program at all.

In part, the failures of the school lunch program to reach millions of children in need stem from the mixed motives that

---

* In 1966, FHA modified its economic soundness requirements by permitting all buildings to be considered acceptable risks in "riot or riot-threatened areas." But the change came too late to help persons who had been the victims of exploitative contracts. In West Lawndale, some relief was obtained through the formation of the Contract Buyers League, a citizens' organization assisted by a group of seminarians, which, through demonstrations and other pressures, persuaded a number of contract sellers to renegotiate the terms of the sale.

prompted its enactment. For Congress, while articulating its concern for the welfare of children, also declared that the purpose of the law was "to encourage the domestic consumption of nutritious agricultural commodities and other foods," i.e., to distribute surpluses that the government is required to purchase in order to support agricultural prices.

In practice, the administration of the law has reflected these business concerns of Congress more than its welfare objectives. The 1946 Act specified that Federal funds in addition to surplus commodities would be made available if each Federal dollar was matched by $3 from "sources within the state . . ." Whatever the original intent of Congress may have been in using such language, most states have utilized it to avoid placing any drain upon government revenues; in the great majority of states, the cost of the program is borne by the children, with little if any contribution from the state or local governments. Moreover, the unit of administration for the program is generally each individual school. A school with many affluent children may be able to finance a free or reduced-price lunch by selling other lunches at full price. For poorer schools that cannot make ends meet, the alternatives are to discontinue the program or to raise prices. A rise in prices frequently eliminates children who had just managed to pay the full price and thus makes even less money available to provide free or reduced price lunches for needy children. To make matters even more inequitable, about 9 million children cannot participate in the school lunch program because their schools do not have the facilities to provide lunch. The greatest number of schools without facilities are located in the slum areas of large cities.

Although Congress through the years has added provisions to the school lunch and other laws to provide additional resources to meet the needs of poor children, the assistance provided has been minimal and the basic inequities of the program remain. They will continue as long as need is a matter for local determination and the Federal Government neither requires state contributions sufficient to assure that all in need are fed nor undertakes the responsibility itself. And these reforms are unlikely to occur until Congress decides that the business values in the law do not define the limits of its humanitarian concerns.[16]

The inadequacy of Federal programs is attributable in large measure to the delegation of policy-making authority and administration to state and local governments.

The dominance of states and localities in the performance of many governmental functions is an ancient and honored tradition in this country. Fears of a too powerful central government prompted the men who wrote our Constitution to limit the authority of the national government and to provide for a federal system. In some fields of governmental authority, the roots of localism go even deeper. The present autonomy of states and localities in administering the welfare laws, for example, derived from the concept of "local responsibility" for the poor which found expression in the Elizabethan poor laws.

In education as in welfare, local communities were deemed the institutions closest to the family and best suited to carry out functions which could be performed adequately neither by the family nor the church.

Thus, it is not surprising that when needs for national assistance became compelling, the legislative response preserved to a great degree the authority of local communities and the states. Frequently, Federal legislation simply has made funds available to states and communities, leaving to them the responsibility of determining how liberally assistance should be distributed or whether, indeed, it should be distributed at all.

If states and local units of government had been responsive to the needs of disadvantaged citizens and if there had been some rough consensus throughout the nation both on priorities and the willingness of states and communities to raise revenues in order to take advantage of Federal assistance, the system might have operated equitably, even without specified national standards. But this has not been the case and the results of permitting local control have been crippling to the goals of national legislation.

One consequence, already noted in welfare programs, has been vast disparities in the identification of need and the allocation of resources in different states and areas. In these programs, each state is permitted to define the standard of living it will use to determine the eligibility of needy persons to receive benefits. The definitions states have adopted of who is needy and what is the appropriate level of support have differed widely not simply in different regions of the country, but even among states within the same region. Thus, for example, in 1965 a Michigan family of four was considered eligible for ADC benefits if its income was less than $223 a month, while the same family in Ohio could qualify only if its income was less than $165 a month.

The inequities inherent in a system in which each state is permitted to define its own standard of need without restrictions of any sort are magnified when states are not even required to make payments conforming to their own standards. The net result is that families living in states with the least generous welfare programs are required to exist on payments five or six times smaller than those that have striven most successfully to meet a standard approximating the common definitions of a minimum level of decent living.

Beyond the problem of gross disparities in the operation of programs nationwide is the selective refusal of some states and communities to participate at all in some programs. For many years, more than 300 of the poorest counties in the United States refused to participate in either of the major programs—food stamps and surplus commodities—designed to make food available to the poor. The situation began to change in 1968 only when the Department of Agriculture, utilizing power it had previously refrained from employing in the name of principles of federalism, instituted or threatened to institute the programs directly. Similarly, although Federal funds had been available for a number of years to provide assistance to families with parents who were unemployed, in 1966 only 21 of 54 jurisdictions had initiated such a program.

Nor does the Federal Government exercise any kind of leverage upon states and localities to induce them to accept programs for the benefit of the poor. States and their political subdivisions are free to accept Federal aid for programs that they deem advantageous, while continuing to reject others they do not consider useful. Thus, Santa Ana, a large school district in California with substantial numbers of Mexican American students from poor families, was not restrained from following a policy of accepting all Federal aid to education except under programs where the funds were earmarked specifically for the benefit of disadvantaged children.[17] And suburban cities and counties throughout the nation have exercised their option to shun Federal programs which provide assistance for the construction of low-income housing, while continuing to benefit in substantial measure from Federal assistance for the construction of highways and community facilities.[18]

A final aspect of deference to state and local authority is that Federal programs which have been widely heralded as providing special help to the disadvantaged frequently do little more than partially redress inequities against the poor created by state and local systems. This is particularly true in the field of public education where present systems of financing result in great disparities in expenditures per child, both within and among states. As noted in Chapter 2, public school systems are supported principally through the imposition of local property taxes, and the consequences of employing this method of raising revenue is that local districts with good tax bases are able, with the same or even a lesser tax effort, to raise more money for their schools than districts with fewer resources. While many states have adopted legislative formulas that purport to equalize educational expenditures by providing variable amounts of state aid to local districts, the formulas are rarely sufficient to alter the basic pattern. The chief beneficiaries of the system are children living in affluent suburban areas. The chief victims are poor children living in cities with inadequate tax bases and enormous needs for non-educational services, along with many children residing in rural areas.[19]

Title I of the Elementary and Secondary Education Act of 1965 (ESEA) was designed specifically to assist school districts with large concentrations of poverty. Monies appropriated under the law *have* had an equalizing effect, although it has not been sufficient to close the large dollar gap between city and suburban expenditures in such metropolitan areas as Cleveland and St. Louis.[20] While the assistance provided under Title I undoubtedly is useful, its effectiveness is severely limited by the fact that it is superimposed upon inequitable state and local systems for financing public schools. The ESEA was billed by its sponsors, and is generally regarded by the public, as a measure furnishing "special" help to needy students to compensate for their disadvantaged circumstances. With this understanding, and with approximately $1.5 billion allocated each year to implement the law, great expectations have been created. If dramatic improvements in the achievement scores of disadvantaged children do not follow, people are apt to conclude that they (through their government) have done their bit, and that responsibility for failure must rest elsewhere.*

But these expectations and conclusions rest upon a false premise. Title I is not labeled correctly as legislation to provide special assistance to the needy, but more accurately should be called "a bill to eliminate or at least reduce discrimination visited upon less affluent schoolchildren by states and local school districts." (To some extent Title I represents an effort by the Federal Government to compensate not only for state and local discrimination, but for inequities fostered by its own programs. Apart from Title I, the largest program of assistance to elementary and secondary schools is the Impacted Areas program under which the Federal Government aids school districts in meeting the costs of educating the children of Federal military and civilian employees. A good portion of this assistance goes to affluent school districts, such as Montgomery County, in Maryland, one of the richest areas in the nation.)

The discrimination, in fact, is so pervasive, and the resources available to poorer schools so inadequate that those administering the law are faced with a dilemma—either, in the name of fairness, distribute aid so widely among poorer schools that it is likely to have a minimal impact any place or, in the name of effectiveness, concentrate it on a small group of schools and so deprive all the rest of assistance.[21] For the Federal Government to institute a program which would really provide special educational assistance to the needy, Federal resources far beyond those presently allocated would be necessary, but the burden would be lessened if Congress were prepared to stop deferring to what

* I do not mean to suggest in this discussion that educational expenditure is the only, or even the most important, factor in raising the level of student achievement. But it is significant enough to cause concern when there are major disparities between the states or districts.

it regards as state and local prerogatives—in this case, the prerogative to discriminate in favor of the wealthy.*

If Federal aid to education operates against a handicap of wide differences in the financing of education within states (differences which favor the wealthy), the disparities between states and regions are an equally formidable barrier. In 1965, the disparities in per-pupil expenditures ranged from $318 in Mississippi to $869 in New York, from $265 in rural Georgia to $1,211 in suburban Scarsdale, N.Y.[22] Like the differences within states, interstate disparities in school expenditures arise less from differences in tax effort than from differences in wealth and resources. The state of Mississippi, for example, which has long ranked last in the nation in per-pupil expenditures, has been among the leaders in the percentage of personal income of its citizens that it devotes to school investment. While Mississippi, like all other states, might improve its educational system by reordering priorities for state and local spending, the basic problem is that its resources are inadequate to support a decent educational program.

To an extent, the Congress takes into account these differences in wealth, and the formula for allocating aid is weighted toward the poorer states, rewarding states which make a significant effort in proportion to the income of their citizens and penalizing those which do not. But here again, the equalizing effect of Federal assistance has been very small; the need to secure broad political support for Federal education legislation has militated against allocating a seemingly disproportionate share of assistance to the poorest states. A rational approach to meeting educational needs would require that Congress set forth some standard to define the level of expenditure per pupil necessary to maintain an acceptable educational system. To implement such a standard, it would be necessary to resolve a difficult set of problems—how to

* In Detroit, Chicago, Los Angeles, and other cities, the city school boards and parents have filed lawsuits against the state, claiming that the present system of financing the schools violates the Constitution when it results in greater expenditures for children in affluent suburban areas than for children in the inner cities. In the first of the cases to reach the Supreme Court, *McInnis* v. *Ogilvie,* 394 U.S. 322 (1969), the Court dismissed an appeal from a ruling that there was no violation of the Constitution.

define the kind of effort that states and communities should engage in to make their contribution to meeting the standard, what kinds of incentives or penalties it would be appropriate for the Federal Government to impose in order to induce other units of government to meet their responsibilities, and what to do about educating children if states and local governments fail to do so. But the difficulty of settling these questions must be weighed against the wastefulness and ineffectiveness of a policy which results in providing token assistance to thoroughly inadequate school systems while giving aid to other wealthier systems which by any comparative standard do not need it.

It must be acknowledged that the issues of how authority should be allocated among the various levels of government in our federal system are often difficult and complex. But whatever else may be said, it is clear that the current Federal policy of almost complete deference to states and local governments in the administration of social and economic programs has contributed heavily to the ineffectiveness of the programs.

It has been suggested by some commentators that the failure of the Federal Government to set a national standard of need for welfare programs constitutes a kind of mindless national migration policy that runs counter to sensible objectives by inducing people to leave rural areas where welfare payments are low and migrate to cities where the payments are higher but which are already overcrowded and burdened by inadequate services. This proposition may be open to question because of insufficient evidence that people come to cities to obtain higher welfare checks rather than better job opportunities. But it is certainly true that it is foolhardy to try to deal with the problems of a mobile population without any standards which are national in application. A child born to a poor family in a rural Georgia county that refuses to take advantage of Federal food programs may reach school age in such poor health that his ability to learn is impaired. If his family then moves to Atlanta, the school authorities there may spend thousands of dollars in special remedial programs in an effort to deal with a problem that arose outside their control but could have been averted. A youngster who grows up in rural Alabama and attends a school whose curriculum is thirty years out of date will graduate without any job skills that he can market anyplace. If he then moves to New York City on the theory that his chances are better there, public officials in New York may spend thousands of dollars to put him through a job training program or to sustain him on relief.

Let us put aside then the question whether deferring to state and local authority can be justified in the name of representative government in a nation in which thousands of such jurisdictions historically have disfranchised black citizens and where they still are not able to participate fully in the political process. Put aside too the moral and political issue of whether in any event the basic economic security of minority groups should be made to rest upon the consent of local majorities. From the standpoint of cost effectiveness alone, it makes little sense to delegate control over programs to solve economic and social problems to thousands of independent sovereignties, each of which, by refusing to act, may aggravate the problem, shift the cost burden to others, and increase the total costs.

Conditions imposed upon the receipt of benefits under social and economic welfare programs have often served to defeat the purposes of the programs.

When the interests of the poor in receiving assistance from the government are conceived of as privileges rather than rights, it does not seem illogical to attach conditions to the receipt of benefits. Such conditions have been added freely to programs of Federal assistance, particularly in the welfare field, by writing them into the enabling legislation, Federal regulations, state or local procedures, or by imposing them as a matter of administrative discretion without any written authorization. Most frequently the purpose of attaching conditions to the receipt of benefits is to induce the poor to conform to standards of behavior deemed desirable or to assure that assistance is not "wasted" or fraudulently misused. But little attention has been given by government to the actual impact of the conditions imposed upon the poor. In many cases what evidence there is suggests that the rules, far from being of assistance, tend to defeat the purposes of the programs.

The definition of who is eligible for the benefits of a program may in itself constitute a self-defeating condition. For example, except in states that have adopted the special program providing assistance to families with parents who are unemployed, a family will be disqualified from receiving AFDC benefits if there is an employable male in the household. There is evidence that this condition of eligibility has prompted some families in desperate straits to split up (or to give the appearance of having split up), with the father leaving home so that his wife and children may receive assistance. This condition of eligibility thus operates to defeat one of the cardinal objectives of the welfare program—family stability.

Another condition imposed by most states until the Supreme Court declared it unconstitutional in 1969 was that individuals have resided in the state for specified periods of time before being eligible for welfare assistance. These requirements were a relic of the Elizabethan poor laws. In colonial times, the concept of "local responsibility" embodied in the poor laws was applied to require that a person be settled in a community before becoming eligible for aid, and to provide for the removal of indigent people back to their states of origin. Removal provisions fell into disuse along with the statutes requiring paupers to wear a badge with the letter "P" and other ostracizing laws, but residence laws remained on the books in many states.[23] They were justified as dissuading people from coming to a state principally to take advantage of its welfare benefits, although there was little evidence to support this supposition and although the laws operated to deprive people of assistance at a time when they needed it most.

While not, strictly speaking, a condition for receiving assistance, administrative rules governing the treatment of income earned by welfare recipients also have operated to defeat the purposes of the program. Until recently, when Federal law was amended to provide for the retention of some earnings, most states required that welfare benefits be reduced in the amount of any income earned by a family receiving assistance. The effect of these policies has been to discourage people from finding jobs that would help them to supplement inadequate welfare aid and perhaps eventually enable them to become self-sufficient.

In the field of housing, local authorities have the power to set standards for the admission and retention of families in public housing units. Many local authorities have vested broad discretion in their officials to exclude applicants and to evict tenants for various forms of antisocial behavior—for having records of criminal arrest or conviction, for having illegitimate children, for drug addiction. In part, the use of this power to exclude applicants or tenants may reflect not simply a tendency of bureaucrats to engage in moral strictures, but a real dilemma. In the absence of needed social services in many areas, the efforts of housing officials to create a decent environment for some poor people may be prejudiced if others with severe disabilities such as drug addiction are permitted to become members of the community. But without well-defined standards, exclusionary policies have been applied far more broadly than can be justified in the name of protecting the community and, in any event, the policies, however well motivated, prevent assistance to people in the greatest need.

The exacting of conditions as a prerequisite to the receipt of governmental assistance provides a useful focus for examining together some of the defects of Federal programs previously cited. As noted, the tendency to impose conditions flows from the treatment of the interests of poor people obtaining assistance as privileges rather than rights. In some measure, the conditions imposed may then become a means for rationalizing inadequate resources. If Congress has provided resources that do not meet the need, e.g., not enough low-income housing to serve all those who are eligible, it is natural for officials administering the program to find ways to choose among those eligible, to select the most "deserving" of the poor. These standards, in turn, become a means for rationalizing the continuation of inadequate resources; once categories of "less deserving" are devised they are easily placed outside the market to be served.

The doctrine of state and local control over Federal programs heightens the potential for harm in imposing conditions on the receipt of benefits. If all conditions were prescribed nationally by Congress or the agency administering the program, they at least would be subject to public scrutiny and there would be a degree of accountability. But when local officials are free within very broad limits to set their own standards there is a temptation to use Federal assistance programs as instruments for imposing or reinforcing political and social controls which keep people in a dependent state. The most blatant examples of this sort of control have occurred in the rural South where Negroes have been threatened with cut-offs of various kinds of welfare benefits to deter them from exercising their civil and political rights and where some benefits, e.g., food assistance, have been furnished only at times when the presence of Negro labor in the community would serve the economic interests of employers.

In the North, such gross abuses of governmental authority do not occur frequently. Yet the imposition of numerous conditions is in itself a form of control which has had adverse effects beyond those specifically noted above. The conditions attached to Federal benefits generate in the poor feelings of dependence and impotence, feelings that inhibit the development of the very attitudes of self-sufficiency stated as the objectives of the program. These feelings are reinforced by the absence of procedural safeguards in the administrative process. For under many programs, a person not only lacks the assurance that the rules governing the receipt of benefits will be reasonable, but also that they will be fairly applied to him. When he believes that he unjustly has been declared to be ineligible for benefits or to have violated the conditions attached to their receipt, he often has none of the protections of ordinary due process—fair notice, the right to a hearing, the right to be represented by a lawyer—available to right the wrong.* These circumstances lead to an impoverishment of the

* See, e.g., Reich, "Individual Rights and Social Welfare: The Emerging Legal Issues," 74 *Yale Law Journal* 1245. In recent years the absence of legal protections has been a principal focus of attention of the many new organizations of lawyers concerned with poverty law. Their legal challenges have met with a measure of success in the courts. For example, the Supreme Court held in 1968 that Federal law did not permit states to disqualify a family from AFDC benefits on the ground that a "substitute father" (a male not married to the mother) visited the home when aid was conditioned on the continual absence of "a parent" from the home. The Court said that, under amendments to the Social Security Act and administrative rulings, it was "inconceivable . . . that Alabama is free to discourage immorality and illegitimacy by the device of absolute disqualification of needy children" (*King* v. *Smith*, 392 U.S., 309, 326). Previously HEW had outlawed the practice of local welfare agencies making "midnight raids" to determine if there was a "man in the house" and it has since strengthened its rules providing for fair hearings. HEW has also encouraged local agencies to experiment with systems calling for a simple declaration and spot-

spirit as well as the body. And these conditions may be aggravated still further by the attitudes of local administrators toward their clients and by the approaches they take in administering their programs.

Many local officials refuse to accord poor people any voice or opportunity to participate in decisions which affect their lives.

A bright exception to the general pattern of relationships between government officials and poor people may help to illuminate the general rule.

In 1967, a group of tenants of Coronet Village, a private housing development located in an industrial suburb of Chicago, formed a tenant union. The concerns of the tenants, almost all of whom were black, were not unusual. The development, a group of about a hundred attached townhouses and apartments built after World War II, was deteriorating rapidly. It was rat-infested, major appliances and heating systems were unserviced, window sashes were rotted and broken panes unreplaced, screens were not provided by the landlord.

But if the complaints of the tenant group were commonplace, its antagonist was not. During the 1950s, the developers and subsequent owners of Coronet Village had run into a series of financial troubles. Later, the savings and loan association that held the mortgages on the property became insolvent and was taken over by the Federal Savings and Loan Insurance Corporation, a Federal agency that insures and regulates private banking institutions. Thus, when the tenants' organization presented its demands for recognition and the negotiation of a collective bargaining agreement, along with a threat that rents would be withheld if the demands were refused, the landlord it was dealing with was the United States Government.

After an initial rebuff from regional officials of the FSLIC, representatives of the tenant union asked the U.S. Commission on Civil Rights to serve as an intermediary and to take the matter

---

checking as a means for determining eligibility rather than having extensive investigations of each applicant. In New York, where such a system was tried, a spot-check showed no greater rate of ineligibles than in the ordinary investigation system. The experience suggests that the supposition that considerations of efficiency and the prevention of fraud and waste always require placing onerous burdens on recipients may not always be correct.

up with the leadership of the Federal Home Loan Bank Board, the parent agency. The first response of the top officials of the Bank Board was not encouraging; recognizing a tenant union, they said, would be unprecedented, and besides, the tenants themselves were responsible for the condition of the property. The rat problem was caused by tenants throwing garbage around the premises, and much of the physical damage to the premises was also brought about by the action of tenants. In return, the Commission suggested that if the government decided to deal with the union, these problems too might be made a subject of the bargaining, and the tenants' union asked to assume some responsibility for assuring the proper maintenance of the property.

After some discussion, which included the helpful intervention of an aide to the President, it was decided to undertake negotiations with the tenant union. The first meeting between government officials and representatives of the union was tense, but after several sessions an agreement was negotiated. The contract, signed in September 1967, specified a wide range of tenant rights and landlord responsibility, including maintenance of utilities, extermination services, landscaping and decorating, a reduction and equalization of rents among tenants. The responsibility of the tenants for maintaining their households in an orderly condition was also set forth in the contract, and grievance machinery culminating in binding arbitration under the supervision of the American Arbitration Association was established to resolve disputes.[24]

When officials of the Civil Rights Commission visited Coronet Village six months later, the changes were striking. Many of the apartments had been renovated and painted, the streets were free from litter, and the rats were under control. Negotiations were underway with local officials to clear and develop a vacant lot into a recreation area for children. Crime and vandalism had decreased markedly. Most impressive was the spirit of the leaders of the tenant union. For the first time they felt a real stake in their community and they were exerting pressures upon others who did not take proper care of their property or who were delinquent in their rents to shape up or ship out. The majority did not want to see their newfound pride and the gains they had won jeopardized by the thoughtless actions of a few.

The relationship established by the government with the tenants of Coronet Village hardly represents the usual pattern. The success of the effort was largely due to the skill and commitment of one man, the late Jerry Worthy, a soft-spoken Alabama banker, who was director of the FSLIC. Worthy participated personally in the negotiations and despite initial rough treatment by the tenants (which he attributed to his southern accent) eventually won their confidence and respect by dealing with them on a basis of equality.

Unfortunately, Worthy's approach to the tenants of Coronet Village is hardly typical of the way government officials ordinarily operate. In its hearings and investigations, the Commission learned that the general disposition of most administrators (Federal, state, or local) was to keep their clients at arm's length, to divulge to them as little information as possible about the workings of the agency and its plans, and not to consult them or seek their advice except to the extent required by law. The very appearance of most public housing units is testament to the absence of contact between government officials and the people they serve. In Cleveland, for example, several people testified that they continued to live in deteriorated private apartments although they were eligible for public housing which would have provided them with objectively better accommodations at lower rents.[25] They did so because they did not like the institutional character of public housing, the paradoxical combination of impersonality and a lack of privacy. Coming as many of them did from rural southern areas, they would have felt more at home if they were provided with even a tiny patch of garden they could call their own. Some of these problems could have been overcome without significant extra costs if the planners of public housing had thought it relevant to ascertain the views of tenants and prospective tenants about their own needs. But this has not been the practice.

Nor are tenants of public housing usually thought to have any contribution to make to the successful operation of their project. Many public housing projects are beset with all of the problems that existed in Coronet Village—vandalism, crime, deterioration of property, etc. But, despite the formal organization of tenants' councils in many projects, it is a rare public housing manager who has felt that tenants might be helpful in meeting these problems. Instead, the occupants of public housing projects find themselves governed by detailed sets of rules and restrictions, promulgated without consultation and often without explanation. It is not surprising that many feel that they are regarded and treated as "inmates," rather than leaseholders.

Similarly, local planning agencies often have regarded residents of areas designated for urban renewal simply as potential obstacles to progress. Until recently urban renewal officials did not include local residents of the affected neighborhoods on city-wide advisory committees and often scheduled public hearings very late in the planning process so as to preclude the development of effective organization in opposition to the plan. As a result, low-income people have found themselves uprooted from their homes, sometimes more than once, without ever having received an adequate explanation of the reasons for the public action or information about the services available to assist them, much less an opportunity to participate in the planning for their communities. In some cases, the failure to consult local residents is simply a reflection of the untenable character of the urban renewal program. If a local official is unable to demonstrate that the program will improve the lot of people in the area to be cleared, he naturally may regard public discussion and consultation as simply an embarrassment. But the habit of ignoring local residents seems so ingrained that even urban renewal plans that are on a sounder footing have received little public discussion. It should hardly be surprising then that the feelings of ghetto residents about urban renewal almost everywhere are deep and bitter, that they characterize the program as "Negro removal" or "urban destruction."[26]

These observations about the attitudes of housing officials toward their low-income constituents are generally applicable to local officials responsible for welfare and other social services. What it is important to note in this pattern of unresponsiveness to members of low-income communities is that, contrary to the general indictments issued by conservative and even some liberal spokesmen, the offending parties are not remote Federal bureaucrats issuing fiats from Washington but local officials on the scene. The theory of those who urge decentralization in the administration of Federal programs is that officials at the local level are more likely to be aware of special community needs and more likely to be responsive to them. As we have seen, the theory frequently does not work out in practice. In fact, in the one instance cited as an exception to the general practice—the case of Coronet Village—it was a Washington bureaucrat far removed from the scene who was sensitive to local interests and who worked out a settlement which took them into account. In other situations, it has been local officials who operate with considerable authority and with few constraints imposed by Washington who have been least attuned to the concerns of local citizens. Some possible explanations for this will be explored later on, but it seems reasonable to conclude at this point that more decentralization and local control do not alone provide the answer.

Finally, it should be noted that while community participation in government programs is easy to support in theory, it is, as experience with the poverty program has shown, much more difficult to put into practice. When poor people have been voiceless so long it may be hard to ascertain who represents their interests. The banner of community participation may be waved by individuals or splinter groups interested only in political self-aggrandizement, or in being bought off to secure their support of the program. While local groups war among themselves or define their interests only in the narrowest and most immediate terms, programs that would be of great ultimate benefit to the community may be delayed or deferred indefinitely. All of this is not intended to suggest that the denials of dignity and self-respect that have attended the administration of many government programs must be accepted as the price for securing efficiency and speed. Indeed, few programs have operated efficiently or speedily when the community has had no voice. It does suggest, however, that between paternalism and anarchy lies a very narrow path, one that may be negotiated only by a careful balancing of means and ends.

The War on Poverty

The War on Poverty, initiated during the Johnson Administration, departed sharply, at least in its early stages, from the usual pattern of relationships between government officials and members of low-income communities. The premise of those who conceived the program was that what was needed was not simply major increases in cash transfers to low-income people or improvements in social services, but the adoption of structures and techniques which could help bring about drastic changes in attitudes among the poor. Diagnosing the problems of many poor people as stemming from a lack of confidence that they could shape their own lives and destinies, and believing that many traditional programs reinforced these psychological problems through paternalistic attitudes and modes of administration, the framers of the War on Poverty hoped to establish an environment in which the poor could gain confidence in themselves by influencing decisions on issues important to them. Thus, the emphasis upon programs of "community action" and the Federal requirement that there be "maximum feasible participation of the poor."

No detailed assessment of the War on Poverty is possible here, but on the basis of general observation, the judgment may be ventured that the program has not thus far rendered invalid the conclusions previously drawn about the failings of Federal economic and social programs and that it does not seem likely to do so in the near future. The principal problem lies in the futility of an approach that seeks to deal with one of the major deficiencies of past Federal efforts—their paternalism and failure to involve the poor—without attacking others. In this case, the failure of the poverty program to provide significant new resources and to create new opportunities has proved extremely damaging.

In the economic sphere, the program has not sought to deal directly with the income problems of a large segment of the poor, e.g., the aging, who are outside the labor market. It has not involved an effort to overhaul the welfare system so that it would meet the basic needs of those who should not be expected to work. Even in focussing on employment as the major economic problem, the program has been limited in approach. It has tended to concentrate on youth and to regard the principal causes of unemployment and underemployment as structural, i.e., stemming from such factors as inadequate motivation rather than from insufficient growth of the economy and of aggregate demand that would produce more jobs.

Although it is true that lack of skills and motivation *are* a major source of unemployment and low income (and that insufficient economic growth has faded temporarily into the background in the inflationary economy created by the Vietnam war), a single-minded approach nevertheless has major limitations. It does not provide assistance to those who have the necessary motivation and who in fact *do* work, but at jobs that do not produce adequate income. And, if few new employment opportunities are created or those which are created appear to be jobs without much dignity or future, it becomes very difficult to motivate people to complete training programs.*

Moreover, the poverty program has not dealt directly enough with the need for reform of the major institutions which presently provide and administer the bulk of economic and social benefits. It was hoped, of course, that the competition furnished by the program would stimulate other agencies to improve their services, and that in helping the poor to find a voice, they would become an effective force for institutional reform. These hopes have materialized only to a very limited extent.

Certainly, the Neighborhood Legal Services program has impelled the organized bar to recognize an obligation to provide legal representation for the poor. But by and large, lawyers perceive this obligation as a new form of charity, a duty to devote some time and resources to casework in order to assist deserving individuals in meritorious cases. There has been only the most limited recognition that justice for the poor can be achieved only through an examination of the way legal systems operate to their detriment and through affirmative efforts to achieve law reform.

Surely, too, some government agencies have been led to im-

---

* It is not being suggested that any of this is easy to accomplish. One of the more promising aspects of the War on Poverty is the "New Careers Program," an effort to create new jobs in public service for people as teachers' aides, police aides, welfare aides, etc. The general theory is that the professionals would be freed from burdensome ministerial chores to perform their main responsibilities better and that new jobs would be created for people who need them. But if "new careers" are to be attractive to young people, not principally to mothers on welfare, some system for upward mobility must be built into the jobs, and this is easier said than done. One of the major obstacles, however—the opposition of public employees and their unions—might be partially overcome if significant resources were devoted to expanding job opportunities in public service.

prove services because of the competition of the poverty program. The state employment service system, for example, has been made somewhat more responsive to the needs of the unskilled because of the competition provided by the Job Corps programs. But the major resources have remained with the traditional institutions, and lacking significant resources of its own, the poverty program could hardly constitute a real threat. In addition, without these resources, the poor could hardly be expected to become a cohesive and effective political voice for change. The program, in fact, has often been counterproductive in this respect. Treating poor people as separate racial and ethnic groups, the program has compelled them to scramble for scarce funds—a process which has set Mexican Americans against Negroes on the West Coast and Negroes against Puerto Ricans in the East.

Thus, the heart of the poverty program, community action, has become established and has survived as a separate program outside the regular system, much as the poor themselves are outside the system. The Head Start program may bring about encouraging progress in preschool children and may establish useful links between parents and the education process, but the benefits are soon lost when children enter public schools which adhere to the old methods, and Head Start does not have the resources to compete with and impel reform of the public school system. The poverty program itself has been a significant source of employment for poor people, but it cannot compete with the rapidly expanding opportunities in state and local government employment, opportunities in which Negroes and members of other minority groups are not sharing fully. Even the notion of "maximum feasible participation" can become a trap, a means for institutionalizing the position of the poor as members of a separate community. Their having a voice in that community may be viewed by some as a small price to pay for keeping them isolated and out of sight, unable to move to other communities where real affluence and power reside.

Many of the advocates of the War on Poverty have been fully cognizant of these difficulties. They are not latter-day Dr. Coués, assuring the poor against all evidence that "every day, in every way," their lives are becoming better and better. They have been aware that without major new resources, the poverty program could not hope to achieve a large measure of success. But, aware also that the necessary resources and reform of existing institutions were not immediately forthcoming (especially in view of the massive Federal expenditures for the Vietnam war), they sought to bring about change where it seemed feasible by building new institutions and by giving the poor a voice in decisions which affected their own lives. And they viewed community action and maximum participation as a political strategy too, one that might help organize the poor into an effective lobby which could change the current political reality and thus make possible new resources and significant reform.[27]

But the political reality does not appear to have changed very much. If some of the poor have become more politically aware, they have also become more frustrated and they have not been shown a way to channel their frustrations and energies to productive ends. If the War on Poverty has made more middle class Americans aware of misery within their midst, the inflated claims which have accompanied the program may induce them to draw the wrong moral from it. They may view the program as an experiment which has failed (and which has been attended by a great deal of fraud and waste) and, unaware that the conditions for success never were present, many have concluded that the poor themselves are to blame.

Conclusion

In his last State of the Union message, Franklin D. Roosevelt concluded that the major accomplishment of the New Deal was that the nation had come to accept a "second Bill of Rights"—a bill which included the right to a useful and remunerative job; the right of each individual to earn enough to provide adequate food, clothing, and recreation for himself and his family; the right to a good education. He looked forward to further legislation that would realize these goals after the war.

Unfortunately, neither the President's diagnosis of what had been achieved nor his prediction of things to come was completely correct. New Deal legislation did establish some economic rights and it afforded legal protection to institutions such as labor unions which then were able to win economic gains on their own. But the interests of the poor in receiving government assistance to escape their condition were viewed by the Congress and the nation as a charitable dispensation rather than a right. The programs conceived during the New Deal never have been adequately funded, either to reach all people in need or to provide effective assistance to those who are reached. In deference to our Federal system, authority and responsibility for administering the programs has been so fragmented that it has been impossible to assure that the purposes of the program would be carried out. Conditions have been attached to programs which are degrading and sometimes self-defeating, and in many cases, the poor are excluded from having any part in decisions which concern them.

During the Johnson Administration, some of the gaps left by the New Deal were filled in, additional resources provided, and an effort made through the War on Poverty to give poor people a voice in the programs that affect their lives. But the resources provided by the Great Society were meager, in some cases barely compensating for inequities in the way state and local governments allocate public funds, and there has been little effort to remedy the basic defects in the way programs of economic and social assistance are administered.

In sum, government has not intervened effectively at any point in the lives of most poor people to help them escape their condition. It has not provided them with enough food, clothing, shelter, and medical care to create an environment in which growth and development are possible. It has not provided the opportunity for a good education, or enough jobs. It has not established conditions in which poor people can acquire a sense of dignity and self-confidence. The cycle of poverty and dependence continues from generation to generation unbroken.

In these circumstances, it cannot be concluded that the programs of the New Deal and its successors failed because they were fundamentally misconceived or because the poor are incapable of responding to government assistance. Paraphrasing G. K. Chesterton's observation about Christianity, it is not that they have been tried and found wanting, but rather that they have been found difficult and not tried.

5

THE POLITICS OF FAILURE

IF IT IS AGREED that the persistence of deprivation and discrimination against large numbers of Negroes and other members of minority groups stems primarily from government's failure to render effective assistance, there remains the task of interpreting government's failure. Understanding the reasons why past efforts have proved deficient and why more has not been done is important because one's interpretation of the past will strongly influence his views of what can and should be done in the future and of the tactics required to bring about change.

If, for example, the view of some spokesmen of the New Left is correct—that people are kept in poverty by a conspiracy, overt or tacit, of the "establishment" or "ruling classes," that it serves the economic self-interest of these groups to have an "underclass" in subjugation, and that government's profession of noble social goals is at best hypocritical—then the outlook is bleak indeed. For such an analysis leads either to paralyzing despair or to fantasies about revolutionary change brought about by violent action— action by an underprivileged group proportionately as small as any nation has ever known, and one with little class-consciousness and solidarity, against a ruling class deemed to be hostile and unified.

Fortunately, the factors influencing our failure to make more progress against poverty and discrimination appear to be much more complex. It should not be surprising, for example, that much of the social legislation enacted during the past three decades has been mixed in purpose. Clearly the poor do not constitute a major influence over the political process in this nation, particularly since their ranks have diminished significantly over recent years and government has adopted safeguards against mass depression. And, while historically a humanitarian impulse has run strong in the politics of the nation, the poor and the altruistic together generally do not wield a controlling influence in bringing about social change (although the passage of the Civil Rights Acts of 1964 and 1965 in response to events that touched the national conscience appear to be exceptions to this proposition). Thus, the enactment of major economic and social legislation frequently has required a coalition of forces and interests—those of the producers of housing, food, and other commodities and services, as well as potential consumers.

There would be little to complain about in legislation which stemmed from mixed motives and interests if it were sufficient to the needs of the poor and members of minority groups and if their interests were taken into account in implementing the programs. But a major problem arises when, as is frequently the case, it is the interests of special interest groups that continue to be pressed, and that are reflected disproportionately, in the administration of the programs.

Special Interests and Fragmented Programs

In large part, it is the structure of Congress that magnifies the influence of special interests in the day-to-day implementation of Federal programs. The seniority and committee systems in Congress assure that a dominant and stable role in the legislative process will be played by older legislators, generally conservative in outlook and drawn largely from the rural South (because the one-party system that has prevailed there has virtually guaranteed long and unbroken tenure to the Democrats elected). Those who rise to the top under this system range from reactionaries and racists such as Senator James Eastland who stand as obstacles to any form of social advancement to others like Senator

John Sparkman and former Senator Lister Hill whose views and motives, like the bills they sponsor, seem to be a complex mixture of dedication to the common good and responsiveness to private interests.

The position of these senior Senators and Representatives, and the necessity to return to their committees each year for new funds, assures that they, and not simply the President (to whom the Constitution entrusts the duty to "take care that the laws be faithfully executed"), will have an important role in the administration of the laws that Congress enacts. This means in turn that special interest groups—homebuilders, bankers, manufacturers, trade unions—who over the years have been able to develop cordial working relationships with influential Congressmen and the staffs of their committees, will have a strong voice not merely in the shaping of legislation to meet their needs but in the way that the legislation is carried out.

Little systematic attention has been given by researchers to the importance of these influences or to the way that Federal and state officials who administer economic and social welfare programs view their constituencies and their own roles. But general experience, such as that of the Commission on Civil Rights in quizzing such officials about the performance of their responsibilities, suggests that these factors are significant in explaining why many programs have failed to live up to their potential.

Not untypical, for example, was the testimony of Jack Tuggle, deputy director of the San Francisco office of the Federal Housing Administration and the official responsible for carrying out in the Bay Area the provisions of President Kennedy's executive order requiring nondiscrimination in federally assisted housing. Replying to questions designed to ascertain why almost five years after the issuance of the order very few Negroes lived in new subdivisions insured by FHA, Tuggle revealed a very narrow conception of his responsibilities. He said that when builders apply for mortgage insurance with the FHA, he "calls their attention" to the fact that they have signed a nondiscrimination agreement. But he did not require them to seek to reach the Negro market, or to advertise an equal opportunity policy, or even to make known to potential buyers that they were bound by the executive order.

Tuggle felt that builders doing business with FHA should not be required to pursue a vigorous equal opportunity program because their competition was not subject to such requirements. He viewed his agency primarily as a service agency to the housing industry and believed that builders following the order might be hurt and might cease to do business with the FHA.[1]

Although appointments of regional officials of the FHA are formally made by their superiors in Washington, as a practical matter many owe their positions to the support of influential Congressmen. Many such officials tend to view members of the housing industry rather than consumers as their principal constituents and to respond as much to them and to the spokesmen for the housing industry in Congress as to superiors in Washington.* It may be a measure of relative influence that although top officials of FHA and HUD made special efforts after the San Francisco hearings to inform regional staff that they expected the executive order to be enforced vigorously, Tuggle nevertheless felt free months later to restate to the press the views he had expressed at the hearing.[2]

Similar observations apply to the attitudes of many officials of the United States Employment Service. Established in 1933 under the Wagner-Peyser Act, the main mission of the Service in its early days was to assist the large numbers of unemployed people in finding jobs. The Employment Service program is operated through State Employment Security Offices. Although the salaries of staff are paid entirely with Federal funds and although administrative direction of the program is vested in a Federal agency, the Bureau of Employment Security, the employees of the offices are both in theory and practice the employees of the state.

As specified in its regulations, the major purposes of the Em-

* One commentator has observed: "An officer in the middle ranges of the administrative hierarchy accordingly looks to Congress, and particularly to members of the standing committee having special charge over his department's affairs, as well as to his executive superiors, for his cues and directives on what he should do and how he should do it. Indeed, he is likely to find he has more frequent contact with those members of Congress who have reason to interest themselves in the operation of his office than he has with the higher officialdom on the executive side of government." Kallenbach, *The American Chief Executive*, pp. 407–408. See also, Grodzins, *The American System*, pp. 260 ff.

ployment Service program are to assist unemployed workers in finding jobs and employers in securing the qualified workers they need. Ordinarily, these purposes do not come into conflict, but when they do, the tendency of the Employment Service has been to make the employer's interests paramount. In the field of race relations, these values and the Service's deference to local customs and traditions were reflected for many years in its willingness to accept racially discriminatory job orders, in refusals to cooperate with agencies seeking to remedy employment discrimination, and in segregation in its own offices. These practices persisted despite general directives from Washington prohibiting discrimination and, although progress has been made in the last couple of years, they still have not been completely eliminated.

Concern about the orientation of the Employment Service has not been limited to its civil rights policies. Recognition that the Service has functioned as fifty different entities responding to employers and to local interests and that this has not been conducive to the development of an effective national manpower policy has led several groups to recommend that the Service be "federalized." When it was concluded in the mid-1960s that a much greater national effort was needed to train and retrain people who lacked job skills or whose skills were obsolete, officials in the Federal Government realized that the Employment Service was not suited to the task, despite the fact that it had been given the responsibilities of recruitment and placement under the Manpower Development and Training Act of 1962. Accordingly, new manpower programs were established under the Office of Economic Opportunity, and the Labor Department itself has struggled to work around the Service in creating new manpower efforts.[3] Nevertheless, the Employment Service remains as the largest manpower bureaucracy possessing the greatest resources and one which operates largely immune from the changing dictates of national policy.

The Secretary of Labor has other troubles in obtaining cooperation of his bureaucracy in carrying out national policies. The Bureau of Apprenticeship and Training (BAT), one of the units responsible for implementing requirements of equal access to apprenticeships and jobs in the crafts, is staffed to a large degree by retired construction-trade union officials. These staff members not

only are receptive to the views and interests of trade union officials (the desire to keep the guild small and exclusive so that its
services will be highly recompensed and its benefits kept within
the family), they generally share them. Thus it was hardly surprising to the Civil Rights Commission to find regional BAT
officials who had done virtually nothing to enforce civil rights
regulations, and in fact, seemed only vaguely aware of their
existence.[4] The Farm Labor Service, a unit of the Bureau of Employment Security, assists in the interstate recruitment of farm
workers to assist in the harvesting of crops in situations where
sufficient local labor is not available. Although employers are required to comply with certain standards regarding housing and
health facilities for laborers in order to invoke the assistance of
the Federal agency, these provisions usually are laxly enforced
—and shameful housing and sanitation conditions prevail in many
migrant labor camps. In Indiana in 1968, a special combination of
circumstances led to more rigorous enforcement of the housing
and health standards, and Commission staff sought to explore
with officials of the Labor Service and the BES the possibility of
bringing enforcement procedures elsewhere in the Midwest into
conformity with the Indiana standards. The response of these
officials was almost completely negative; they viewed the employers, not the workers, as their principal clients and were concerned both about the expense and hardship that employers
would be put to in coming into quick compliance with the standards and about the danger that they would be prompted to
abandon the Service and seek to fill their labor needs through
other channels.

Efforts to bring this unwieldy bureaucracy under control have
not proved successful. In 1964, the Secretary of Labor established a Manpower Administration to consolidate the activities
of the BES, the BAT, and other units responsible for manpower
programs. A management consulting firm recommended that the
separate bureaus be replaced by an integrated unit organized
along functional lines. But this move was opposed by the Interstate Conference of Employment Security Directors and the
Building Trades Department of the AFL-CIO, both organizations
that have significant influence with Congressmen and Senators,
and it was not adopted.[5]

The morals to be drawn from this description of influences that affect the implementation of Federal programs should be carefully limited. It is not being suggested that the President and his chief cabinet officers are rendered impotent to carry out national policy by the exertion of private influences through powerful Congressmen. The leadership provided by the White House and cabinet officers can have a major impact upon the administration of their programs. John W. Gardner, for example, as Secretary of Health, Education, and Welfare, achieved major civil rights gains in some of the programs under his aegis at a time when little progress was made by the Secretaries of Housing and Urban Development and of Labor. Gardner did so by identifying the civil rights compliance program as a major priority, by delegating authority to an assistant supported by an adequate staff and empowered to override the objections of program heads, and by a willingness to resist Congressional pressure and run the risk that some of his programs would suffer as a consequence. In these efforts, he occasionally obtained needed support from the White House, as when President Johnson backed him in insisting that hospital administrators and physicians meet civil rights requirements as a condition for receiving benefits under the Medicare program. In effect, the President and Secretary of HEW were willing to bet that hospital administrators and doctors would sacrifice long-entrenched racial practices rather than forgo the substantial financial assistance available under Medicare. If the bet had been lost, the success of the Medicare program would have been jeopardized by nonparticipation and civil rights objectives would not have been materially advanced. But the bet was won.

The point, therefore, is not that the national executive is powerless, or that the exercise of leadership cannot make a difference, but that the executive, as the body ordinarily most responsive to the poor and members of minority groups, operates in our present governmental structure under great handicaps in representing those interests, even in the implementation of programs seemingly under executive control.

The kind of influence exercised by private interests upon the administration of Federal programs could, of course, be a two-edged sword. If groups, such as the NAACP, that represent the interests of the poor and racial minorities sought on behalf of their clients to influence the administration of Federal programs, they might generate significant counterpressures. But these groups ordinarily do not operate in this manner. They deal with legislators principally for the purpose of obtaining the enactment of social or civil rights legislation, and if they take an interest in the implementation of the laws enacted, they usually express their interest only to the President and his chief assistants. Regional and local administrators of Federal policies rarely are made the target for effective pressure by public interest groups. Nor do Congressmen committed to broad social goals often exercise significant influence in the administrative process. They frequently do engage in efforts to assure the continued funding of social programs and protect a program against legislative amendments which would dilute its social purposes. But they rarely go further into the staffing and day-to-day operations of the program. One liberal Senator did engage in a long effort, ultimately successful, to secure the appointment of an FHA director in his region who would be committed to reversing the previous policy of "red-lining" Negro slum areas, i.e., refusing to provide FHA insurance, thus leaving the area open to speculators. But such efforts by liberal Congressmen appear to be few and far between.

The problem is that such Congressmen depend principally upon civic and public interest groups to provide the intelligence that would enable them to intervene in the administrative process. And these groups do not enter the arena of administration in large measure because they do not have the resources to do so. Unlike private interest groups, they have no handsome economic return to reap from scrupulous attention to the workings of government agencies. Their ability, then, to enter the field depends greatly upon the generosity of investors who can expect little except a moral return. Despite the rising interest of foundations, labor unions, and church groups in solutions to social and civil rights problems, few resources have been forthcoming.

One further observation at this juncture: the role played by private economic interests in diluting the purposes of social programs should give some pause to those who believe that the solution to most problems is to provide governmental resources and then turn the job over to private enterprise. While the subject deserves and will receive more discussion in the context of specific proposals, it should be apparent that if the purposes of social programs have been distorted by the influence of private interests upon the agencies of government which implement the programs, there is an even greater danger that noble goals will be subverted if their achievement is entrusted directly to private interests. The various programs administered by the Department of Agriculture, perhaps more than any other in the Federal Government, entrust the achievement of their goals to private interests who share authority with government officials. They are also the programs that have served the interests of the poor—in this case poor black farmers—the worst.[6] In testimony before the Civil Rights Commission, the director of the State Extension Service in Alabama gave a candid glimpse into why this is so. Explaining the poor record of his agency in employing Negroes, he said: "We work on a cooperative basis . . . and over the years we have, and we still think this is a basically sound idea, to stay with the power structure in order to keep the lines of communication and the rent coming in . . ."[7]

The appointment of Negroes to positions of authority, he strongly implied, would come only when the local "power structure" approved.

The governmental structure employed to meet public needs has other defects apart from the way in which it facilitates the bending of programs to serve private interests. For it has become increasingly clear that the problems of poor black people in the cities cannot be treated simply as the sum of needs for more houses, more jobs, better educational facilities. If we could regard the problems thus, it might be sufficient to entrust their solution to a collection of Congressional committee fiefdoms, each responding to its own particular set of clients and interests—housing consumers as well as builders, brokers, and banks, parents and civil rights groups as well as school superintendents and teachers' unions. But when we seek to meet national needs through 200 or more "categorical" Federal programs, administered by a multiplicity of bureaucracies at the local as well as the national level, the result is chaos more often than progress. Good-faith efforts to assist people by providing them with decent low-income housing fail because they are not accompanied by needed social services such as health facilities and good schools. Shiny new school buildings in the heart of the ghetto become mirages in a wasteland of misery. Highway engineers steamroller social efforts in a community by building a freeway which isolates or seals it off.

The Model Cities program, enacted in 1966, represents a recognition of the problem and an attempt to deal with it by providing Federal rewards to cities that draw up promising plans for a concerted social and physical attack on the ills of entire neighborhoods. While the Model Cities approach is encouraging, in some respects the program is like a fighter with one hand tied behind his back. It can provide strong incentives for social planning in the small, densely concentrated areas where the poor now reside, but it cannot induce planning for cities and metropolitan areas as a whole. Affluent suburban areas are still left free to accept large government subsidies for highways, sewer lines, and other community facilities without accepting any responsibility for alleviating any portion of the poverty and discrimination that afflict the area as a whole.

Incompetence and Insensitivity

There are, of course, other important flaws in the system beyond the structural defects that magnify private interests and fragment programs that are supposed to deal with a common set of problems. Administrative incompetence is one. In city after city visited by the Commission, we encountered regional and local officials who could not articulate in plain language the purposes of the programs they were responsible for and the mission they were seeking to accomplish. It was not that these officials were unfamiliar with the details and procedures of the programs; they could and did spout statutory section numbers and administrative jargon at will. But the larger purposes of their assignments seemed to escape them completely.

In Oakland, for example, the executive director of the local housing authority, who had overall responsibility for meeting the shelter needs of people of low income, testified against all the demographic evidence that the city was "pretty well integrated."

He said that he "wouldn't know" whether minority groups had difficulty in obtaining housing in any areas of the city because "That's out of my field."[8]

In a hearing in Alabama, Commission staff asked the Defense Department's chief compliance officer for the southern region what he could do about a large contractor against whom evidence of racial discrimination had been presented. He replied:

> Well, since the facts have been called to my attention I am authorized to place that of course and would be authorized to place it prior to the facts being called to my attention on my quarterly forecast schedule. And provided I did not have directed review from outside agencies, such as preaward, and/or complaint investigation, and/or directed reviews from higher authority, we would place a man into that particular Dan River spot to conduct a compliance review.[9]

In part, the stance adopted by many bureaucrats seemed disingenuous, a means of protecting their "expertise." To exhibit a familiarity with the minutiae of the program was a way of showing that they possessed skills that could not easily be duplicated by others, while to have explained their mission in terms that an intelligent layman could understand might have been construed as a confession that their jobs were not so difficult to master after all. In part, also, the problem was a lack of skill and understanding. The salaries of many of these officials often were not nearly commensurate with their responsibilities. If society pays people much more money for making up jingles to sell toothpaste than for administering large sums of money to serve public needs, it should not be surprised that many public officials will fail to measure up to reasonable standards of competence. Whatever the reasons, it was striking to find in the Bay Area of California that by far the most impressive of the "government" witnesses were two ex-convicts who were operating a program to train poor people, including other ex-convicts, to be police, recreation, and teachers' aides. These men, who had spent most of their lives as teen-agers and adults behind bars, had a basic understanding of the mission they were seeking to accomplish; they had full empathy with their clients, and they were not inhibited by any presumed need to prove their expertise to the Commission or the public.[10]

Innovation and Imagination

If performance by government in the field is often marked by incompetence and insensitivity, the problem at higher levels in Washington frequently is a failure to innovate, an inability to design systems adequate to meet new challenges. The implementation of Title VI of the Civil Rights Act of 1964, which prohibited racial discrimination in programs receiving Federal financial assistance, provides a good illustration of the challenges to Federal administrators and the response. Since the effort involved some 200 programs, 22 Federal departments and agencies, and about $18 billion in Federal assistance, it was clear from the outset that designing an effective system of enforcement would be a major task.

There was, first of all, the need in each department to recruit a competent civil rights staff and to decide where it should best be located in the agency to assure its influence over the administration of the various programs. The problem of staff recruitment was not an easy task. The need was for people who had, or could be given, some understanding both of civil rights problems and of the system (e.g., housing, education, transportation) with which they would be required to deal. With the enactment of Title VI and other new civil rights laws in recent years, there arose a potential demand for civil rights specialists far beyond any ready source of supply. Thus, agencies were faced with the problem of finding able people and training them for a new assignment. Moreover, it was recognized that even a large staff of civil rights specialists would not be sufficient to assure the success of so huge a task of enforcement. Day-to-day administration would continue to rest in the hands of thousands of program officials whose inertia and interest in the continued "normal" flow of assistance might cause them to regard with hostility rules against segregation and other forms of discrimination that might interrupt the flow. Thus, it was important to impress upon program officials their new responsibilities and to find ways to make them more responsive to civil rights concerns.

In addition, new systems for obtaining compliance had to be devised. Traditionally, most agencies responsible for enforcing antidiscrimination laws have relied principally upon complaints as a means for detecting violations. But this technique is a poor one at best in most situations because victims of discrimination are often afraid or reluctant to complain and because the settlement of an individual complaint may allow a discriminatory system to continue operating. And it was thoroughly inadequate to deal with the problem of achieving compliance by thousands of school boards, hospitals, and builders throughout the nation. A system of compliance reporting had to be established and procedures created for self-initiated investigations designed to identify priority areas of concern and to seek out patterns of violations. It was important to devise techniques and procedures that achieved the maximum possible compliance on a voluntary basis while identifying the most important violations for intensive negotiations and the possible imposition of sanctions.

Finally, it was important for agencies to create some system for measuring their own progress in performing Title VI responsibilities. If the purpose of the law was the elimination of discrimination in all federally assisted programs, then one measure of progress would be increased participation by Negroes, Mexican Americans, and members of other minority groups in the programs. This meant devising systems for the collection of racial statistics and an effort to persuade civil rights groups, which were conditioned to regard racial data as an instrument for discrimination, that the collection of such information was an important tool for achieving compliance.

A few Federal agencies, most notably HEW, perceived the dimensions of the task and proceeded to work out compliance systems which were reasonably adequate to the need. But the great majority had little understanding of the tools needed for successful enforcement. They limped along on shoestring budgets, without perceiving the need for or requesting adequate staff and resources; they relied upon complaints rather than initiating their own investigations, and they established no system which would enable them to know how well or poorly they were doing.

The failures of these agencies should not be viewed solely in political terms. The political problems were present, of course, and may have inhibited efforts to develop the systems needed to do the job. But essentially, the qualities lacking were those of imagination, vigor, and innovation. The responsible people in many cases were well intentioned, but they simply did not know how to tackle a very difficult assignment.

Evaluation and Experimentation

The failure to create systems to measure progress toward realizing legislative goals is not limited to the field of civil rights, but affects many of the social welfare efforts of government. This reluctance to evaluate reflects more deep-rooted problems in government's response to deprivation and discrimination.

During the New Deal, Franklin Roosevelt sought to establish a framework and a philosophy for government's response to economic crises with the following words:

> The country needs, and unless I mistake its tenor, the country demands bold, persistent experimentation. It is common sense to take a method and try it. If it fails, admit it frankly and try another. But above all, try something.[11]

Roosevelt's "common sense" was very much in accord with qualities we think salient in the American character—pragmatism, experimentation, a willingness in all forms of enterprise to take risks and to admit failure. But if these qualities prevailed during the early days of the New Deal, they have long since ceased to be a hallmark of our approach to social problems.

The pattern today often runs roughly like this: Congress is persuaded with great difficulty by the executive of the need for a new approach to a particular set of social and economic problems. It enacts a new program, such as the poverty program, grudgingly, and with an implicit demand that it produce quick results or be discarded. The executive agency involved, aware of the program's jeopardy in Congress, tends to favor those aspects which appear to have a quick payoff, to highlight apparent gains, and to suppress problems, even to the extent of manipulating statistics for the purpose of casting the program in the most favorable light. Congress, in turn, is aware of the dubious quality of agency evaluations and responds by retrenching on appropriations. But since Congressional committees do not have much confidence in the information furnished by executive agencies and

ordinarily do not have resources to conduct independent apprais-
als of their own, their judgments on appropriations often are not
well considered. There is a tendency to split the difference—to
fund at low levels both programs which are promising but which
need more money to test their potential and those which have
had a fair test, have failed, and which should be discarded.*

In part, the failure to evaluate frankly and to experiment reflects the shakiness of government's commitment to solving social
problems. If a new weapons system fails or becomes outmoded
after billions of dollars are expended, it is usually treated as an
experiment and is written off as the necessary "costs of doing
business." If, on the other hand, a poverty program involves significant expenditures and does not produce tangible results, it
may be condemned as "wasteful" and "a fraud upon the taxpayers" and its failure may put in jeopardy all remotely similar efforts.

In part, too, the failure to experiment is a product of the character of Congress as an agglomeration of local interests. For example, as originally conceived, the Model Cities program was an
effort to concentrate resources in neighborhoods in no more than
fifty cities. The hope was that with such a limited focus, working
models of success could be developed that could then be applied
more generally. But it was found that the political support
needed for enactment of the law could not be mustered without
making its benefits available to the constituents of a much larger
number of Congressmen. And so, the program was broadened
to encompass about 200 cities, including, as matters turned out,

---

* My own agency, the Commission on Civil Rights, was one of the few
that had to have its authority renewed by Congress every few years. Each
time our authority was about to expire, we pleaded (unsuccessfully) for a
permanent extension. I believed in our position, because I felt our agency
was doing and would continue to do valuable work and because the renewal fight usually sapped our resources and put us at a competitive disadvantage in attracting staff with agencies that had permanent status. But I
always felt a little bit ambivalent about the issue. In the abstract, at least,
it might be helpful if every agency were required to reexamine its goals and
to justify its continued existence every few years. This, of course, would pre-
sume a review "on the merits" by a Congress which had reformed its own
procedures. As the deck is now stacked, the foes of social progress already
have an unfair advantage without the added power of reviewing an agency's
right to continued existence.

a substantial grant to a barely urban area represented by the Tennessee Congressman who controlled housing appropriations. If the funds authorized had been commensurate with the enlarged scope of the program, it might have been argued that Congress was recognizing an urgent need and was willing to take the risk of moving ahead on a full-scale effort without taking time for experimentation. But the money made available did not match the increase in the number of cities, and so a promising experiment was jeopardized by spreading and diluting resources which would have increased the chances of success.

Finally, the absence of systems for evaluating programs stems from the mixed purposes of much legislation in this area. It is apparent, for example, that we have not established as a national goal, at least not with any clarity, that all persons in this country should have a decent diet. Instead, feeding the hungry has been made a subsidiary part of laws whose principal purpose has been to establish an efficient system for disposing of surplus commodities so that farm prices would be maintained. Since the goal has not been clearly established as a matter of national policy, it is not entirely surprising that until recently the executive branch did not take the steps that would have enabled it to discover that food programs were not reaching all people who were in need and that, indeed, many thousands of people were suffering from chronic malnutrition.*

* The dawning of awareness came with the protests of black citizens in Mississippi. In 1966, a group of Negroes invaded an abandoned air force base in Greenville, Mississippi, and distributed leaflets saying that they had no jobs and were hungry and cold. In February 1967, at a stormy meeting of the Mississippi Advisory Committee to the United States Commission on Civil Rights, black citizens complained that when a number of counties switched from the commodities program to food stamps, many people were deprived of food because they did not have enough money to buy stamps. These events precipitated a visit by a team of private doctors to Mississippi and a Senate investigation. The doctors' report said in part:

> In child after child we saw: evidence of vitamin and mineral deficiencies; serious untreated skin infestation and ulcerations; eye and ear diseases, also unattended bone diseases secondary to poor food intake; . . . and finally, in boys and girls in every county we visited, obvious evidence of severe malnutrition with injury to the body's tissues—its muscles, bones, and skin as well as an associated psychological state of fatigue, listlessness, and exhaustion.

There is a movement now in Congress and the executive branch to establish a national system of "social accounting." Some proposals call for a National Council of Social Advisers, similar in structure to the Council of Economic Advisers, which would independently appraise the operations of Federal programs and compile a "social report" which the President would deliver to Congress and the nation. Through the establishment of such a system, it is hoped that agencies would be induced to set up their own social indicators to measure how well programs are meeting their goals and what additional resources or alternatives should be considered.[12] Where, for example, a Federal program calls for the elimination or reduction of adult illiteracy, a system of social accounting at a minimum would yield information on how many people learned to read and write and which of several teaching techniques proved most efficient and effective.

A system of social accounting could be helpful also in defining additional needs for data and research. While we know, for example, that the income of Negroes has increased significantly over the past decade, there is much we do not know about the factors involved in the increase. There is insufficient information on the extent to which it reflects an expanding Negro middle class rather than simply a more affluent middle class. To the extent that it reflects an expanding middle class, we do not have much data on whether the gains are across the board or largely confined to those who previously were above the poverty level, leaving the "hard-core" poor unaffected. The failure to ask and obtain answers to questions such as these means that we have very little information about the effectiveness of Federal programs.

While a system for social accounting would be helpful in meeting these needs, there is room for doubt that it would be effective without more fundamental changes in the way government deals with social issues. In the current climate, it might simply feed another trend in the Federal Government—the tendency to use

The Senate investigation discovered that such tragic conditions existed in states other than Mississippi. Remedial action has finally begun, although it is still far from complete and cannot in any case help thousands who have suffered permanent damage from malnutrition. See Citizens' Board of Inquiry into Hunger and Malnutrition, *Hunger U.S.A.*, pp. 11-13.

the need for additional research as an excuse for deferring decisions on hard policy questions. Although this may seem to run counter to the tendency to neglect to conduct research and make evaluations of programs, both are related to the failure to approach social problems in a rational, pragmatic way.

Priorities and Commitment

In the last analysis, as many have pointed out, the failure to solve problems of deprivation and discrimination reflects a lack of commitment and a skewing of national priorities, and not an absence of resources.

That resources are available to meet the needs of the poor is plain from a perusal of the Federal budget and the policy choices it reflects. When the government decides to invest major sums in the development of a commercial airplane to travel at speeds faster than sound or in particular aspects of space research, it is using tax dollars in ways which contribute little to the general expansion of economic opportunities and even less to employment opportunities for the poor. Moreover, the contrasts between subsidies to the relatively affluent and subsidies to the poor are frequently striking. Michael Harrington has pointed out, for example, that agricultural payments to one set of economic interests, the producers of cotton, were $1.8 billion over a two-year period, a sum equal to the entire yearly budget for the poverty program. In one 11-county area in Texas, it has been noted that .0001 per cent of the population collected $5.3 million in agricultural program payments, while the 37 per cent of the residents who had incomes below the poverty line received only $224,000 in food assistance.[13] Similar comparisons might be drawn using other major recipients of Federal largess such as the national maritime industry. And the curious thing is that subsidies to these large corporate interests do not stimulate fears that Federal aid will encourage idleness or economic inefficiency, cries that are frequently raised against "doles" to the poor.

The loopholes built into the Federal tax system also provide fertile material for examining our values and priorities. Studies conducted in 1969 for the purpose of proposing tax reform disclosed that there are at least 150 people with annual incomes of more than $200,000 (including 21 millionaires) who pay no income tax at all, and many more wealthy people whose tax bills are minimal.[14] If the loopholes that permit millionaires to escape taxation are properly regarded as subsidies, the contrast between government aid to the rich and to the poor again becomes striking. Similarly, the value of housing subsidies for the upper 20 per cent of income groups—through the tax deduction allowed for property taxes and mortgage payments—is about twice that of housing subsidies for the bottom 20 per cent as measured by direct housing subsidies and welfare payments.[15] (To this may be added the subsidy to middle-income people by the extension of FHA and VA credit to enable them to purchase their homes, which makes the contrast even greater.) In addition the tax laws sometimes encourage the affluent to act in ways adversely affecting the interests of the poor in order to gain monetary advantage. For example, tax provisions dealing with depreciation on residential properties encourage landlords to sell their holdings after ten years and other provisions treat major repairs as capital improvements rather than maintenance. In combination, it has been noted, these laws provide cash incentives to slum landlords to let their properties run down and then sell them off, rather than making repairs and treating the properties as stable investments.[16]

Finally, some of the priorities established for government spending not only have diverted resources that might have been used to meet the needs of the minority poor but have actually made their situation worse. The creation of a network of interstate highways, involving a Federal expenditure of $46 billion from 1957 to 1969, has in some cases resulted in the destruction or sealing off of poor communities, usually those inhabited by blacks, without providing anything to replace them.[17] Equally as important, government, in building the highway system, has facilitated the movement of jobs from the inner city to suburban areas without taking any of the measures (low-cost housing or mass transit) necessary to give poor people access to the new opportunities. Since urban renewal programs have destroyed more housing units than they have replaced, the program must be viewed as a net loss to the poor even by those who believe that the construction of middle- and high-income units enables better housing to "trickle down" to the poor. And subsidy payments to large agricultural producers have helped to accelerate the process of mechanization, driving black people off the land and to urban areas where no adequate programs have been instituted to furnish them new skills and jobs.

Conclusion

After homage has been paid to what many consider obvious—that our problems lie in establishing priorities and commitment to the goal of social justice, rather than in locating resources—what has been said that is of practical value? What guideposts are there to the future?

Certainly, the image of government that emerges from these chapters does not conform to the mold fashioned for it by ideologues of the right. It cannot be shown that government has failed because it has sought to do things for people that only they can do for themselves. Rather, the evidence demonstrates that government aid has failed to reach many of the people in the most dire need of assistance and conversely that, when assistance *has* reached people, they frequently have benefited. Nor can it be shown that the Federal Government has dictated a set of national values and policies that are wrong or self-defeating. To the contrary, in the name of federalism, the national government has allowed policies and values to be set at the state or local level, often with results disastrous to the general purposes of the program.

But if the Federal Government does not conform to the stereotype of misguided juggernaut given it by the right, neither does it conform to the labels of the far left. Government has not been an oppressor of the poor, nor the willing tool of oppressors. Even the indictment of *conscious* hypocrisy cannot be proved convincingly.* Instead, government—big, sprawling, and complex, like society itself—seems to reflect the schizophrenia that exists in its people. Within most Americans there reside attachments both to

---

* The rhetoric about justice and equality employed by many of our national leaders is not ordinarily calculated to deceive, but rather represents a weapon in the arsenal of people who are struggling within government for new programs and to justify what they have already achieved. They may be seeking reelection or a place in the history books but, on balance, their motives are altruistic.

the American credo—a society of justice and equality—and to the enhancement of one's own position, status, and material possessions. That these desires sometimes come into direct conflict is not very widely understood, because in our political system the issues are seldom posed sharply (although the current racial turmoil has tended to sharpen the issues and, in fact, to lead some groups to feel their interests more jeopardized by the drive for equality than they actually are). That the political instruments we have fashioned are better suited to maximize the gains of the already affluent than to achieve justice and equality also is not obvious to many people.

Even with the roadblocks to change built into our political system, government has produced, within the past five years, three major civil rights laws and several new programs to combat poverty—reaffirmations of the American credo and tokens of good faith, if not adequate responses to the problem. The issue, then, is whether we can reshape our political institutions so that they will give fuller expression to our positive instincts and to the interests of people whose influence is presently very limited.

To frame the question in these terms is not necessarily to be much more optimistic than those who see government as monolithic and the values of our society as corrupt. For it may be that we are not capable of summoning the qualities of creativity and initiative that are needed to renew and reshape our political institutions. It may be that the problems of governing have become so complex that we cannot solve them, that old institutions have become so firmly rooted and self-interest so rigidly defined that they cannot be changed. In short, it may be that our society and civilization have entered a phase of decline similar to that of civilizations that have preceded.

But these are not assumptions upon which those who participate in, rather than merely observe, our society can predicate any constructive action. And before one can adopt a stance of optimism or ultimate pessimism, it is necessary at least to try to determine where present policies may be leading us, to identify the conditions favorable to change and how they may be maximized, and to examine various proposals and strategies for change and try to reconcile or choose among them. These are matters we will explore in the chapters that follow.

PART THREE

Looking Forward

6

A BAD TRIP INTO THE FUTURE

PEERING INTO THE FUTURE to gain an impression of what our cities may look like ten, fifteen, or twenty years from now is an extremely risky enterprise—as the demographers and economists who do it all the time are fond of telling us. Changes in the birthrate, new departures in technology, major alterations of public policy, all may render projections into the future based on current trends far off the mark.

Nonetheless, a look even into a very cloudy crystal ball to try to determine what may happen if present policies are continued without major alteration is an exercise worth undertaking. For it is only by trying to gain a larger time perspective that we can judge the adequacy of our current and developing efforts to deal with racial and urban problems.

And when current trends, demographic, economic, and political, are projected into the future, the picture that emerges is one of continuing and heightened deprivation, racial separation, and conflict. The prospect in view is one that should be disturbing, if not horrifying, to anyone even remotely concerned about the current state of affairs.

Population Growth and Racial Separation

The basic facts are two sets of demographic trends: (1) toward a major increase in the population of urban areas, both in abso-

169

lute terms and as a proportion of the total population of the nation, and (2) toward increasing separation of blacks and whites within the metropolitan areas of the nation.

In a research report prepared for the National Commission on Urban Problems, demographers Patricia Hodge and Philip Hauser have drawn a profile of the nation's cities for the year 1985.[1] Assuming the population will grow at about the same rate that it did from 1960 to 1965, the authors deem it likely that the metropolitan areas of the nation, which held 89 million people in 1950 and almost 113 million people in 1960, will have about 178 million people in 1985.[2] This projected increase, which means that metropolitan areas will contain about as many people in 1985 as the whole nation did in 1960, reflects both natural population growth and continued migration to the cities. In 1950, 59 per cent of our citizens lived in metropolitan areas; in 1960, 63 per cent; by 1985 it is estimated that the 178 million urban residents will be 71 per cent of a total population of 252 million.

If the overall growth projected for metropolitan regions is impressive, it is the likely burgeoning of suburban areas that will have the greatest impact. This is illustrated by the following table:

Table I
Population Growth in Metropolitan Areas
1950–1985
(*numbers in millions*)

	1950		1960		1985 (*projected*)	
		%		%		%
Metropolitan Area	89	(100)	113	(100)	178	(100)
Central City	52	(59)	58	(52)	65.5	(37)
Outside Central City (suburban area)	37	(41)	55	(48)	112.5	(63)

SOURCE: Hodge and Hauser, *The Challenge of America's Metropolitan Population Outlook—1960 to 1985.*

Central cities, it should be noted, are expected to grow very slowly, with almost the entire increase in population being accounted for by cities in the South and West and the older cities in the Northeast and North Central regions remaining almost static. Suburban areas, in contrast, are likely to more than double their population in twenty-five years and will hold almost as many people in 1985 as the nation's metropolitan areas had as a whole in 1960. As a result, the central cities, once the dominant population centers, will by 1985 constitute little more than one-third of the metropolitan areas that contain them.[3]

(In using the term "suburbs" throughout this chapter, we will be describing all of the territory around a central city that is related to the city in various ways according to census criteria. Such territory frequently includes not merely concentrations of middle class homeowners but "gray areas"—industrial towns or small cities containing large numbers of workers—and rural areas with a farm labor population. Since one of our main purposes is to compare the situation of city dwellers with that of residents of relatively affluent suburban communities, to the extent that "suburban" statistical data include other types of areas it will result in understating the contrast.)

The pattern of growth projected for Negroes and other non-whites differs markedly from that of the white population.* First, since the birthrate for nonwhites has been significantly higher than that for whites, it is expected that by 1985 they will constitute a larger proportion of the total population than they do now. In 1960, nonwhites were 11 per cent of the nation; by 1985, they are expected to be 14 per cent. Second, nonwhites (particularly Negroes) are becoming urban residents at a much faster rate than whites. Even assuming that the high point of migration from the rural South to the cities has been passed and that migration will continue only at a slackened rate, the Negro population of metropolitan areas will more than double from 1960 to 1985, while whites are increasing only by 52 per cent.[4]

During this period, it is likely that Negroes will join the trek to the suburbs to a much greater extent than has been true in the past. Thus, the Hodge-Hauser report suggests that the nonwhite population of suburban areas may grow from 2.8 million in 1960 to 6.8 million in 1985, a projection which in large part reflects a

* The census figures used here treat all "nonwhites" as a single group. But since Negroes constitute 92 per cent of nonwhites, the terms will be used interchangeably.

growing Negro middle class and the relaxation of discriminatory housing practices. But the striking fact is how little even such an accelerated rate of suburbanization would alter racial patterns of residence in metropolitan areas. For, even with Negroes moving to the suburbs in relatively large numbers, the nonwhite population of central cities is expected to increase from 10.4 million to 20.1 million, while the cities lose 2.4 million white residents. And the increase in Negroes living in suburbs will be dwarfed by the enormous increase in the white suburban population.* Thus, the racial composition of metropolitan areas is likely to develop as shown in Table II.

Even this projection, which shows the nonwhite proportion of

Table II
Racial Composition of Metropolitan Areas
1960–1985

Residence and Race	1960 %	1985 (projected) %
Metropolitan Area	100	100
White	88	85
Nonwhite	12	15
Central City	100	100
White	82	69
Nonwhite	18	31
SMSA ring (suburbs)	100	100
White	95	94
Nonwhite	5	6

SOURCE: Hodge and Hauser, *The Challenge of America's Metropolitan Population Outlook—1960 to 1985.*

* See Hodge and Hauser, *op. cit.*, pp. 25-32. A recent census report seems to show a partial abatement of the trends described in the Hodge–Hauser report. It indicates an actual decline in the Negro population of central cities between 1966 and 1968. But in the absence of some convincing explanation, it cannot be assumed that we are witnessing a reversal of the trend. And in longer range terms, the census report provides support for the Hodge–Hauser projections. It notes, for example, that the Negro population of central cities grew from 9.7 million in 1960 to 11.8 million in 1968. And it also shows that despite increasing dispersal to the suburbs, Negroes have remained at about 5 per cent of the total suburban population since 1950. U.S. Bureau of the Census, *Recent Trends in Social and Economic Conditions of Negroes in the United States,* pp. 4-5.

central-city population increasing from less than one-fifth in 1960 to almost one-third in 1985, tends to understate what is likely to happen in the largest cities in the nation. For years, Negroes have migrated principally to the biggest cities and have constituted a larger proportion of the population in these areas than in cities as a whole. Thus in 1968, when Negroes were 20 per cent of the population of all central cities, they were 25 per cent of the twenty-four central cities which were located in metropolitan areas of 1 million or more people.[5] Two large cities, Washington and Newark, in 1968 had populations which were in the majority Negro. In a good many more, including Chicago, Detroit, Baltimore, Atlanta, Philadelphia, and St. Louis, Negro students were a majority of the public school enrollment. Thus, by 1985 it seems quite likely that the central cities of several of the largest metropolitan areas of the nation will be predominantly Negro in population.

What these projections mean in ultimate terms is increasing separation of black and white citizens in the cities. In 1960, 78 per cent of all nonwhites residing in metropolitan areas lived in the central city. With the projected increase in dispersal, there will be some change in this concentration, but in 1985 it is still expected that three of every four Negroes in metropolitan areas will live in the central city.[6] In contrast, in 1960, almost one-half of all whites who lived in metropolitan areas resided in the central city. By 1985, seven of every ten white people in metropolitan areas are expected to live in the suburbs.[7] Thus, by 1985 we may have traveled a long distance toward validating the basic conclusion of the Kerner Commission Report—that "our nation is moving toward two societies, one black, one white—separate and unequal."

The Movement of Jobs and People

While the projections put forward above are not immutable, they are based on trends in the movement of people and jobs which by now are well established and which tend to reinforce each other.[8] Among the most important factors are the following:

• *The movement of factories to the suburbs*—In the nineteenth and early twentieth centuries, manufacturers, dependent upon good port or rail facilities for the transportation of raw materials or finished products, were motivated to locate their plants in what was (or became) the core of the central city. But with the advent of economical truck transportation and good highways, transportation cost considerations have changed and manufacturers have been free to select sites elsewhere in metropolitan areas. At the same time, changes in technology have placed a premium on "horizontal space" (e.g., for production processes which call for continuous material-flow systems), making obsolete the kind of sites available on typical city blocks. Built-up central cities ordinarily do not have large enough sites available to meet these new production needs, and if they do the costs are usually prohibitive.

All of these factors have led to a significant decline in manufacturing in central cities and to a major increase in the suburbs. In projecting changes for the New York metropolitan region from 1954 to 1985, Raymond Vernon indicates that more than 400,000 new manufacturing jobs may develop in "inner ring" suburbs and 300,000 in "outer ring" suburbs while employment in the core (New York City and Hudson County) will remain almost static.[9]

• *The movement of people to the suburbs*—By now, the choice between city and suburbs seems to have been made definitively by most American families. They have chosen the spacious and comfortable living, better schools and services, participation in smaller units of government available in the suburbs over the superior access to jobs, cultural activities, and diversity furnished by the city. For the projections made by Hodge and Hauser to come true it is not necessary that there be a new wave of suburbanization comparable to what occurred after World War II. All that need occur is that the less built-up cities in the South and West develop in ways parallel to the older urban areas of the Northeast and Midwest and that there not be a significant countermovement of people from the suburbs back to the city. Natural population increases will take care of the rest.

If anything, the choice facing many people is becoming more weighted in favor of the suburbs with every passing year. As employment opportunities develop in suburban areas, access to jobs becomes a consideration in favor of suburban living, and for many what once was a difficult choice between competing values has become no choice at all. For others whose jobs still are located within the central city, the decline of services in the city increasingly shifts the balance toward the suburbs. And while there is no substantial evidence to suggest that desires for racial separation played any significant role in initiating the mass movement of white people to the suburbs, there is little doubt that racial tension in the cities is an element that helps accelerate the trend today. All of these factors—the movement of jobs to the suburbs, deterioration of services in the inner city, and racial turmoil— far overshadow those that might offer the prospect of a counter-movement of people from the suburbs back to the city.

Nor has there been any important change in one fundamental aspect of the movement to the suburbs: that the option is available almost exclusively to those who are affluent and white. As has been noted, during the period of greatest suburban growth, government, far from prohibiting practices of racial discrimination against middle class Negroes, actually encouraged segregation. The rules have since been altered so that discrimination is banned, but residential patterns are by now so well established that change can be expected to occur very slowly in the older suburbs. More rapid movement will be possible only where large new developments are being built, and there only if the law is enforced firmly and with an affirmative effort to reach the new Negro market.

Until, however, the economic position of black people is vastly improved, the key to opening up housing opportunity in the suburbs will not lie in the enforcement of antidiscrimination laws, but in subsidy programs which bring homes within the reach of people of low and moderate income. For more than thirty years government has provided assistance to middle class people to enable them to acquire suitable housing. It is only in the past two years that it has embarked on a similar program to provide assistance to people of low and moderate income. And, wholly apart from the question of whether the new program will receive adequate funding, there is room for real doubt about whether it will result in opening up housing opportunities outside the central city.

The doubt exists because of the persistence of controls over the use of land exercised through zoning regulations by suburban governments. These regulations, by establishing minimum lot sizes for single-family dwellings and by placing restrictions on the construction of multi-family housing, make it a practical impossibility to build homes for people of low and moderate income on much of the available land in suburbs surrounding many of our major cities. In New York, for example, it has been noted that 509 of 551 municipalities in the metropolitan region have zoning laws, and that vacant land in these 509 municipalities accounts for 3,400 square miles of the 4,500 square miles of vacant land in the region. Moreover, two-thirds of all zoned vacant land requires homes to be built on lots of one half acre or larger.[10] Land so zoned is off limits for any program designed to provide low- and moderate-cost housing.

The result is that in New York, the principal prospects for small sites for housing exist in the outer reaches of the metropolitan area, where large-lot zoning controls have not yet been imposed. But there, the remoteness of potential residences from existing and possible job locales (and the fact that controls may yet be imposed) makes it unlikely that housing will be developed for the less advantaged rather than for the affluent.

Apart from the maintenance of patterns of racial and economic class separation, the principal consequence of continuing present policies with respect to land use is that cities will continue to spread ever outward, replicating the patterns of suburban development that have taken place since World War II. In the process, land will be consumed at a tremendous rate. It has been projected that in the New York region, where 2,400 square miles of territory were developed or committed to public uses in 1960, 2,800 more miles would be so used by 1985.[11] In other words, more land would be developed or committed to development in 25 years than in the 336 years since the island of Manhattan was purchased from the Indians. But, while most people might readily agree that this is a profligate and even irrational use of land, there is little indication that this fact alone presages an imminent reversal of current land-use policies. In New York and most metropolitan areas, there is still much undeveloped land to be tamed and paved over.

While cities are spreading outward to accommodate the growth in population, changes will also be taking place in the older suburbs. Some of the less expensive housing built in these areas twenty years ago or more has begun to deteriorate or to become otherwise less desirable. Vernon has suggested that as this housing supply grows older, it will become available to lower income families, with an accompanying breakdown of zoning and building controls and with some structures being subdivided.[12] But, apart from whether this represents a desirable mode of change, it is questionable how widely low-income Negro families will share in this "filtering down" process. There exists in many cities a pent-up demand for housing among lower middle-income whites, people whose earnings fall roughly in the $6,000 to $12,000 brackets. As services in the central city deteriorate and as jobs move outward, the bonds which have tied people in this group to the city have loosened and they are impelled to seek housing elsewhere. With discriminatory housing practices likely to persist despite the enactment of fair housing laws, these whites will have an edge in the search for suitable older housing not only over poor Negroes but also over those in the same income bracket.

In sum, the forces which now motivate people to move to the suburbs and to limit access to their communities seem likely to continue to keep the mass of Negro citizens confined to slum housing and isolated from whites.

• *The movement of consumer services to the suburbs*—While the location of much economic activity is not affected significantly by shifts of population within a metropolitan area, consumer services constitute an exception to the general rule. Department stores and food chains have followed their customers to the suburbs. So have a wide variety of establishments and people dealing in professional or personal services—real estate and insurance brokers, branch banks, lawyers, doctors and dentists, barbers and hairdressers.

Such services—callings designed primarily to meet the needs of the local population rather than to sell goods and services to the rest of the world—constitute a significant share of the job market in most large cities. In New York, for example, it has been estimated that these service jobs account for about 60 per cent of total employment in the metropolitan region.[13] Their growth in the suburbs has occurred at a phenomenal rate. In 1968 shopping center sales were almost a $100 billion business and they accounted for roughly 40 per cent of all retail sales, excluding those for automobiles and gasoline.[14]

The mushrooming growth of suburban shopping centers has also begun to disturb comfortable assumptions about the continuing vitality of the central city as the hub of entertainment and cultural activities. Restaurants and nightclubs are by now a familiar sight in shopping centers. The owners of thriving franchises in professional athletics have begun to view suburbs as the logical sites for new sports arenas. Suburban newspapers and journals are thriving.

And there are signs too of the emergence of the suburbs as centers for cultural activity. Legitimate theater, ballet, and concerts are among the recent offerings at some shopping centers.[15] It is possible then to envision a time in the not-too-distant future when shopping centers will have become the focal point of community life, and contact between many suburban residents and the central city, already diminished, will almost have vanished.

Here, too, it can be seen that the trends reinforce each other. Retail establishments locate in the suburbs to follow their customers. This movement, in turn, encourages employees of these establishments to seek homes in the suburbs to have better access to their jobs. And the creation of new centers of commercial activities attracts more activity including entertainment and cultural enterprises. The suburbs thrive and the central city decays.

• *The deterioration of the central city*—The burdens major cities face in seeking to meet the needs of their citizens are enormous. The needs loom large in comparison with those of suburban jurisdictions for two major reasons: (1) a disproportionately large number of people who remain in the central city are old or poor and have need for greater outlays in services related to poverty, health, and welfare, and (2) housing and other physical facilities in older cities are rapidly becoming obsolescent.

The first problem is illustrated by the fact that while the central cities of our twelve largest metropolitan areas contain only one-eighth of the total population of the nation, they account for two-fifths of all expenditures for health and welfare that are financed from local taxes.[16] For confirmation of the second problem, one need only visit any older city and view its deteriorated housing, aged public schools, broken streets, and poor recreational facilities.[17]

Most major cities have been making conscientious efforts to deal with these problems. Municipal budgets have been rising rapidly; during the period from 1962 to 1966 the expenditures of central cities in the largest metropolitan areas increased by 27 per cent in an unsuccessful attempt to meet the backlog of accumulated needs.[18]

The basic dilemma of city governments arises from the fact that the sources available for securing revenue to meet their needs are presently very limited. If the city seeks to tax these resources to the limit in order to provide better services, it runs the risk of creating strong incentives to business enterprises and homeowners to locate elsewhere. But if the city does not make full use of its taxing powers, services will continue to deteriorate and the result may be the same—business and homeowners will be impelled to relocate in other areas. So the city is damned if it does and damned if it doesn't.

The nature of the fiscal dilemma facing cities becomes even clearer when the sources of local revenue are examined more closely. For almost all cities, the principal source of revenue is the property tax, a levy which is regressive in nature and which falls most heavily upon housing. The property tax is a significant factor in raising the cost of housing. In 1962, such taxes accounted for about 20 per cent of the total cash outlays for housing by homeowners and rent-payers in metropolitan areas.[19] The burden upon renters is even greater than upon owners; property taxes constitute 20 to 35 per cent of rent receipts for multi-family housing.[20]

In addition, it is the poor who are hardest hit. In New York City, renters in the lowest income brackets pay more than 8 per cent of their incomes for property taxes. As income increases, the proportion spent for taxes decreases so that people with earnings over $15,000 pay less than 3 per cent in property taxes.[21]

In combination, these facets of the property tax operate to raise the cost of housing significantly and to place a large portion of the existing housing supply beyond the reach of low-income families. Owners of older buildings in need of rehabilitation are deterred from making the necessary investments by the prospect that their assessments for tax purposes will be increased. And high property taxes also shrink the market for investment in new housing. Cities, then, may be tempted to meet the housing needs of their citizens by offering tax abatements to those ready to invest in rehabilitation or the development of new housing. But they do so at a cost—in order to meet the housing needs of low-income citizens, cities must decrease the revenues available to meet other immediate needs of the same people.

Property taxes are not nearly as important a factor in the costs of business and commercial activity as they are in housing. Nor is the business tax base of the city shrinking at such a fast rate as to make it an insignificant source of revenue for meeting public needs. (While manufacturing continues to move out, some central cities continue to be thriving centers of commercial activity. Enterprises which do not have a need for horizontal space continue to find advantage in locating in the central city, and major cities like New York and Los Angeles have enjoyed booms in office building.)

Nonetheless, central cities have limited flexibility in seeking greater revenue through the application of property and other local taxes to business. If economic considerations already favor the relocation of manufacturing and retail establishments outside the central city, the trend can only be accelerated by the imposition of higher local taxes. Even enterprises that have found advantage in clustering together in central business districts have the ability to take action in response to higher city taxes. Certain functions can be split off with relative ease and relocated in other areas, e.g., sewing plants in the apparel industry or the data-processing, accounting, and billing operations of an insurance company.[22]

Thus, central cities, many of which have experienced declines in assessed valuation for property tax purposes, cannot feel free to compensate for these losses simply by imposing higher tax rates on businesses which remain.[23] For this may result in further dispersal of economic activity and loss of revenue.[24]

Suburbs, of course, also face burdens in raising revenue to meet the needs of their citizens, but the contrasts between the situation of these jurisdictions and that of central cities are striking. One major factor is that most suburban governments do not have the problem of meeting the health and welfare needs of a population containing disproportionately large numbers of people who are aged or poor. Nor are they required to devote a major portion of their resources to the maintenance of police, fire, and sanitation services, which cities must provide for the benefit of commuters as well as residents. The extra expenses incurred by cities in providing these services largely account for what is usually described as the "municipal overburden"—the difference between central city and suburban costs in areas other than education. In 1965, the average expenditure to meet non-educational costs in the central cities of the thirty-seven largest metropolitan areas was $232 per person, while outside the central city, the average expenditure was $132 per person.[25] Thus, even if cities and suburbs had available to them equal resources for meeting public needs, education would suffer in the cities because the city must allocate larger parts of its budget to other services.[26]

Of course, the resources available to central cities and suburbs are not equal. Housing in the suburbs is newer and more valuable. Personal income is higher. And while the cities still retain much commercial and industrial activity, the movement of such activity to suburban areas is rapidly giving the edge to suburbs in tapping this source of revenue too.

In addition, even where suburban governments have unusually large public needs, they generally have more devices at their disposal to meet them without imposing heavy tax burdens than does the central city. It is true that newer suburbs which are growing rapidly in population often must make major investments in new schools and in other plants and facilities. But frequently they can increase the resources available to meet these needs by the use of devices such as "fiscal zoning"—i.e., zoning to attract commercial facilities which will improve the jurisdiction's tax base and decrease the tax burden of individual citizens. And the employment of other land-use controls, such as large-lot zoning, can prevent the population from growing so fast as to place a great drain on public services. These are alternatives not generally available to central cities in seeking to replace aging and obsolete facilities. Cities lack sufficient vacant land to attract major new industries and even if more land were available, they could not produce the striking improvement in tax base that a small suburban jurisdiction can bring about simply by luring one new major facility. And cities cannot as a practical matter limit their public service responsibilities by limiting the growth of population. It is too late for cities to afford this luxury; the poor are already there.

One logical way to reduce the glaring contrasts between the ability of cities and suburbs to meet public needs without imposing intolerable tax burdens would be for the state and Federal governments to contribute a greater share of needed revenues. But this, in fact, is what has been taking place over recent decades and it has not resulted in an improvement in the position of the cities. Property taxes, which once accounted for more than half the revenues used to finance public services, are now overmatched by the revenues received from various state and Federal sources, but local taxes continue to rise and services continue to deteriorate.[27] Thus, a mere continuation of the trend toward gradual assumption of responsibility by states and the Federal Government does not promise much relief for the cities.

Further, while increased reliance upon state and Federal taxes may result in more equity in the collecting of revenue (because of the more progressive character of Federal income taxes),[28] there is no assurance that it will result in equity in distribution. While Federal grants to states and localities ordinarily have an equalizing effect, the distribution of state assistance often is dictated more by political leverage than by considerations of need. So, in the past, state legislatures frequently have been more responsive to the claims of suburban areas than to the pleas of the cities. With reapportionment, the cities, far from gaining political leverage, have lost it to the suburbs.

Thus, in 1969, when Governor Rockefeller presented the New York State legislature with an austerity budget, the issue was quickly resolved into a struggle on the part of suburban representatives to maintain state aid to education against the efforts of city representatives seeking to avoid drastic cutbacks in state welfare assistance. Aid to education was maintained and major reductions were made in welfare assistance. The victory of increasingly powerful suburban legislators is a portent of the outcome of future struggles.

In sum, all of the major forces at work in the nation's cities seem to point in the same direction. Manufacturing concerns seek new locations outside the central city for sound economic reasons. Affluent people move from the city in search of more comfortable living arrangements. Retail establishments relocate in the suburbs to follow their customers. As jobs and wealthier people move out, the capacity of the central city to meet the needs of its remaining citizens, many of whom are poor or old, diminishes. The city is faced with the Hobson's choice of increasing the tax burden of its citizens or allowing services to continue to deteriorate.

There are, of course, a few countervailing forces at work. In New York and in a few other large cities there has been a boom in office building and a relatively rapid rise in white collar employment. The growth in jobs reflects both the advantages that some private corporations find in locating their headquarters in central business districts and an increase in local government services in response to a recognition of social needs. For some highly paid people, access to these central-city jobs and other benefits they see in city living have outweighed the advantages of suburbia, and this has led to small expansions of residential enclaves of affluence within the city (places like Brooklyn Heights and Riverdale in New York City).

But these small signs of vitality in central cities, even when added to other factors—the efforts at current levels of expenditure to renew central cities and the trend toward equalization of labor costs between city and suburbs—are hardly sufficient to upset the momentum of the major forces at work. Each of these great trends works to reinforce the others. People, wealth, and activity move outward, and as they do, they become magnets for more people, wealth, and activity.*

* Ten years of experience have borne out most of the major projections that Vernon made about New York City in 1958. Manufacturing jobs in the city have actually declined rather than increased modestly, as he forecast. White collar jobs have increased by about 240,000, more than the 75,000 anticipated. Middle class whites have left the city in about the numbers expected and Negroes and Puerto Ricans have migrated to New York more rapidly than predicted. For minority groups, the unfavorable shift in the character (higher skills) and location (suburbs) of jobs has occurred much more rapidly than was anticipated. See Netzer, "New York City's Mixed Economy: Ten Years Later," *The Public Interest* (Summer 1969) pp. 188 ff. Netzer analyzes the statistics presented in the Regional Plan Association's Second Regional Plan, *The Region's Growth.*

The victims are the people left behind, the minority poor who lack mobility and who remain caught in a system that is rapidly losing any capacity to respond to their needs.

Economic Consequences

During the period 1960 to 1985, the nonwhite population of central cities is expected to increase from 10.4 million to more than 20 million. The largest area of growth anticipated is in the young labor force, people between the ages of fifteen and forty-four, whose ranks are expected to increase from 4.3 million to 9.2 million. Similar if not quite as dramatic growth is projected for nonwhite youngsters under the age of fifteen, who are expected to number 7 million in 1985 as compared with 3.6 million in 1960.[29]

It is clear then that cities will have an enormous problem of absorbing new workers into the labor force. And the overriding question is whether opportunities for productive work will be available to the greatly enlarged ranks of Negroes who will be in the labor market or almost ready to enter it in 1985.

The answers to this question are by no means clear, for they depend to a large extent on what goals the Federal Government decides to pursue and what economic policies it adopts after the conclusion of the Vietnam war. They depend, too, on the resolution of issues upon which economists have long been in disagreement, e.g., whether it is possible to follow policies designed to achieve rapid economic growth and high employment without running the risk of large-scale inflation, whether automation and technological change lead almost inevitably to increased unemployment.

With all of the uncertainties, however, the sobering fact is that even those economists who take the most optimistic view—that technological change increases job opportunities and that goals of economic growth and high employment can be pursued without adverse consequences—foresee major problems in assuring employment opportunities for members of racial minorities who lack needed skills.

The major problem is finding ways for those who have been discriminated against in the past, or who lack skills and education, to keep pace with the rapid shifts in occupational distribution that have taken place since World War II. The fastest growing category, of course, has been white collar employment, particularly jobs which require professional and technical skills. White collar workers, who accounted for 35 per cent of all jobs in 1947 and 44 per cent in 1964, are expected to make up 48 per cent of the labor force in 1975. Within the white collar category, professional and technical workers, who constituted 6.6 per cent of the labor force, are expected to make up 15 per cent of all workers in 1975. At the same time, it is anticipated that blue collar employment, which was 41 per cent of the labor force in 1947 and 36 per cent in 1964, will decline to 33 per cent in 1975. This shrinking share of the labor market is accounted for largely by the category of laborers, where the jobs available will remain almost stagnant, while the rest of the labor force grows enormously.[30]

These changes in occupational distribution have been the result not simply of technology but of patterns of consumer spending that stem from increased family affluence and from needs for new services and facilities in an increasingly urban population.[31] They are likely to continue regardless of what policies we pursue. And the greatest impact will be upon Negroes, Mexican Americans, and members of other minority groups who at present are disproportionately represented in occupations where opportunities are not growing rapidly or where they are declining in absolute numbers as well as in share of the labor market, e.g., agricultural labor.

The changes can be seen most graphically in the conclusion drawn a few years ago by the National Commission on Technology, Automation, and Economic Progress that *"if nonwhites continue to hold the same proportion of jobs in each occupation as in 1964, the nonwhite unemployment rate in 1975 will be more than five times that for the labor force as a whole."*[32]

This, of course, is not likely to happen because Negroes and other minority workers are not all remaining in the same jobs they held in 1964 or in previous years but are moving slowly into the professional, technical, and other white collar categories where opportunities are growing.[33] Nevertheless, the Technology Commission's conclusion is useful because it helps us to keep in perspective the gains that may be expected from adherence to present policies. The movement of Negroes into skilled occupations is attributable in part to the whole process of urbanization, to the abatement of practices of discrimination in employment and education, to improvements in education, and to the recent recognition by some employers that they have a responsibility to provide on-the-job training and new job opportunities for unskilled people. But, despite these changes in policy, the fact remains that during the past fifteen years, through good times and bad, through recessions and booms, the rate of employment for nonwhites has remained constant at about twice that for whites.[34]

In short, using unemployment as a yardstick, present public policies designed to upgrade job opportunities for Negroes apparently are sufficient to prevent them from losing ground in the rapid redistribution of occupations, but are not sufficient to permit any ground to be gained. This does not quite amount to a standoff, for with the Negro population of central cities in the process of doubling in a twenty-five-year period, it would mean an additional 300,000 or more black people out of work by 1985, even assuming a low overall rate of unemployment.

Another way to view the problem is to assume optimistically that the nation will pursue policies designed to promote rapid economic growth and to meet major public needs and then to estimate manpower needs in major occupations and the likelihood of meeting them. One set of projections, based upon a hoped-for growth rate of 4.5 per cent a year, suggests a need for some 2 million scientists and engineers in 1975. If nonwhites are to be represented in these professions in roughly the same proportion that they are represented in the population as a whole, the study notes, there would be a need for 210,000 nonwhite scientists and engineers. This is 150,000 more than may be expected by extrapolating current trends.[35]

Where are these scientists and engineers to come from? Where will the nation train 140,000 more nonwhite elementary and secondary schoolteachers or 60,000 more professional nurses to meet goals in education and health?[36] Surely not in today's crisis-ridden public schools of the central cities or in rural high schools in the South which continue to prepare black students for non-existent careers in vocational agriculture.

Without drastic changes in public policies governing education and training, the outlook for the millions of black people who will be added to the work force by 1985 is bleak indeed. They will not be prepared for highly skilled remunerative jobs, a share of which will remain in the central city. Many, of course, are likely to find employment in less skilled white collar jobs or as production workers. In a sense, they will be entering in larger numbers into production work twenty or thirty years too late, at a time when these jobs have lost status, dignity, and social acceptability. And even in competing for these jobs, black people and members of other racial minorities will be at a real disadvantage, for they remain confined to cities while new opportunities in manufacturing and retailing increasingly arise in suburban areas that are ever more remote.

In sum, given present policies, the prospects for most Negroes in the central city in 1985 are for more unemployment, underemployment, and economic misery.

Political Consequences

If there is any silver lining in the storm clouds now gathering over the cities, some may find it in the growing political power of Negroes. Some people see in the increasing concentration of black people in cities and their rising political consciousness, a development which may have great impact in the future. In one view, the political benefits which may result from continued racial separation may even outweigh its harmful consequences.

The evidence is already at hand that Negroes, by virtue of sheer numbers and new attention to organization, are building stronger political bases in cities. Within the past few years, Negroes have been elected mayors of large cities for the first time (in Cleveland, Newark, and Gary), and the number of black Congressmen has risen from four to nine.* Concurrently, although representation is still disproportionately small, there has been an increase in the ranks of Negroes from urban areas elected to state legislatures and city councils.[37] Despite occasional setbacks, such as the defeat of a Negro mayoral candidate in Los Angeles, the prospects that this trend will continue obviously are good. In the Cleveland, Newark and Gary mayoral elections, it required a mod-

* In the 1970 elections, three more black candidates were elected to Congress. Encouragingly, all three were elected by constituencies that are majority white.

icum of white support along with fairly solid support from the black community for Negro candidates to win. As Negroes become a near majority in other large cities—Atlanta, Baltimore, St. Louis, and Detroit among others—the likelihood is that black candidates will run and be able to win, even without major help from white communities. And in the increasingly black Congressional, state assembly, and councilmanic districts of the central cities, the prospects for Negro representatives are even greater.

Some important dividends may be anticipated from the election of more Negroes to public office. As the black community gains in political strength, there will be more Negroes appointed as administrators and judges and to other public positions from which they have been excluded by local machines in the past. (The potential for change, however, is limited by the growth of the civil service system and the declining patronage powers of elected officials.) It also seems clear that forceful and intelligent Negro leaders like Mayor Carl Stokes of Cleveland, Mayor Richard Hatcher of Gary, and Congressman John Conyers of Detroit can provide a kind of effective representation on issues affecting the minority poor that is not furnished by the election of even the most committed white liberals. In addition, the election of increased numbers of Negroes to public office will have important values that are symbolic or intangible. It is likely, at least on a temporary basis, to help build confidence among Negroes in the integrity of government, to motivate young people and to stimulate community organization and efforts at community improvement.

All of this would constitute significant progress. But there is a larger and more important question, and that is whether the potential gains will be large enough to alter the current political reality. In short, can the political power that Negroes will accrue under a system of racial separation be sufficient in itself to tip the scales in favor of the major policy initiatives that are needed to prevent the grim consequences forecast earlier in this chapter?

On this overriding issue, the prognosis seems very doubtful. It is true that one area in which change is likely to occur is in the influence of Negroes and members of other minority groups in the councils of the Democratic party. In party affairs, the growing political impact of minority groups is becoming evident and it will be increasingly difficult to ignore their interests or to have them represented largely by proxy. The crucial areas for policy-making, however, are not the political parties but the Congress and the state legislatures where the influence of parties is relatively small. In these forums, where the laws are made and the funds appropriated, the most salient facts are the declining representation of the central city and the ascendancy of suburban middle-class interest—both products of the population changes described earlier.

While the patterns cannot yet be described with accuracy, it is clear that after the 1970 census, we shall see a further realignment of Congressional and state legislative districts that will reflect the diminishing population of the central city and the gains of the suburbs. These demographic trends have reduced almost to ashes the past hopes of reformers that implementation of the principle of "one man—one vote" would result in a Congress and state legislatures which would respond readily to urban interests and needs. To a limited extent, reapportionment may have benefited urban interests in the rural South, but the real beneficiaries, in both North and South, have been the residents of the suburbs.

As Robert Dixon has pointed out, "in many states, reapportionment opens the way for a new branch of coalition politics among three groups, no one of which can dominate the legislature—central city, suburban, rural–small town.[38] Thus far, except on isolated issues such as reform of divorce or abortion laws, there is little evidence of suburban and central city legislators banding together to seek laws which will meet the needs of all of the citizens of metropolitan areas. Instead the emerging pattern may well be one in which city and suburban representatives compete with each other for the lion's share of scarce revenues, as they did in New York recently in the struggle to avoid cutbacks in welfare and education expenditures. In such situations, the likely alliances are between suburban and rural–small town interests, and the natural victim is the central city.

In addition, even when they operate within the confines of the "one man—one vote" course, state legislatures still have considerable maneuvering room to draw districts in a manner which will maximize one set of interests and minimize others. For example, it can be argued with some force that the best way to assure that the interests of the Negro poor are not neglected is to draw district lines so as to make them a substantial minority in two or three districts rather than a substantial majority in one. The distribution of the voting strength of racial minorities over two or three districts may prove effective in situations where there is active rivalry between two political parties. For then an incumbent can ignore the demands of minority groups only at his peril; his opponent may be more responsive to a swing group which can vote him into office.[39] If, on the other hand, districts are drawn to be racially homogeneous, Negroes or other minorities will have the satisfaction of knowing they can always elect someone of their own race, who may then serve them well (as several legislators have) or badly (as Adam Clayton Powell has served his Harlem constituents). But the price paid for controlling influence in one area may be the loss of any effective influence in adjacent districts.

In recent years, some Negro politicians have alleged that state legislatures, acting on a political analysis contrary to the one presented here, have deliberately fragmented black voting strength so as to prevent the election of black candidates to public office. In the view of these politicians, the danger is that this trend will continue even to the point where state legislatures will be impelled to establish metropolitan governments in areas where Negroes have gained a majority of the voting strength of the central city. My own view is that if, in the past, state legislatures have sought to dilute Negro political influence by dispersing it, they acted upon an assumption that Negroes as a political group would continue to be relatively docile and apathetic and would not exercise very much leverage in districts in which they constituted minorities. As this assumption is proved wrong and black communities become more politically aware, it seems likely that political leaders who wish to limit the influence of racial minorities will do so by confining them to as few districts as possible. And if these political leaders perceive problems resulting from black control of central cities, they are more apt to deal with them by restricting the home-rule powers of the city than by establishing metropolitan governments which would inherit all of the ills of the city and the tax burdens of providing remedies.

Whichever view is correct, however, the point is that as long as dominant suburban and rural–small town factions in state legislatures see the interests of racial minorities in the cities as antagonistic to their own, they have means available for keeping minority political influence limited.

Thus, the prospect that more Negroes will soon be elected to Congress and to state legislatures does not bring with it the promise of major policy initiatives to provide aid to cities and poor people. In the Congress, the probability that many of the newly elected blacks will be more dynamic leaders than the white political machine incumbents whom they replace will hardly outweigh the loss of central-city voting strength which is taking place at the same time.* (In fact, since the sin of most white Congressmen from city districts has not been that they have voted against liberal or urban-oriented measures but that they have failed to exercise leadership, the result to be anticipated is a net loss in votes on many issues.) In the state legislatures, there is nothing to suggest that a bloc of Negro representatives will be more successful in securing a positive response to the needs of central cities than white representatives have been in the past.

The only place, then, where rising black political strength offers the prospect of control is in the central city itself. There Negro mayors and black-dominated city councils will inherit all of the problems cited earlier in this chapter—rising welfare costs, deteriorating housing, and critical needs for improved public services. With the flight of industry and affluent people to the suburbs, the new mayors and city councils will lack the financial resources to meet these pressing needs, and efforts to raise revenues by imposing higher levies on the shrinking tax base are likely to result only in further flight and loss of resources. Without massive help from the state and Federal Government, the plight of the cities will continue to worsen.

---

* On occasion, population changes and redistricting can result in an increase in liberal strength. In Cleveland, for example, Louis Stokes, a Negro Democrat, replaced Charles Vanik as the representative of a district which had become increasingly Negro in its constituency. Vanik, a strong liberal Democrat, moved to a new district which had a combined city-suburban constituency, challenged the incumbent, a conservative Republican, and won. But this hardly seems to be the emerging pattern.

In short, the new black political leaders of the cities may have formal authority without any real power to stem the tide of destruction, much less bring about meaningful change.* They are likely to be "receivers in bankruptcy," inheriting all the problems created by past neglect and mismanagement at a time when it may be too late to remedy the situation. Once it becomes apparent to the voters that black political leaders are no more able to solve the basic problems of the city than their white predecessors, the pressures on them are likely to become enormous. Unable to produce results and vulnerable to attack, these black leaders may be displaced by a new brand of leadership—one which repudiates democratic processes that have failed and opts instead for violence.

So, assuming the continuation of present policies, our city of the future, in addition to all of its other attributes, threatens to grind up those able black political leaders who are committed to reform through the democratic process.

Conclusion

Our nightmare sketch of the city of the future is almost complete. In drawing it, we have omitted entirely some aspects of urban decay such as the deterioration of the environment—the

---

* Many of the new black political leaders are painfully aware of the dilemma. In a speech in 1969, Mayor Hatcher declared, "With urban public education facing bankruptcy, with the inflation of physical blight and pollution across the landscape, with fierce competition among the poor blacks, poor browns and ethnic whites for the leavings of an affluent society, is it any wonder that we mayors of urban America find ourselves fighting for sanity?" Address by Richard G. Hatcher to the National Urban Coalition, Washington, D.C., December 10, 1969. In an earlier talk, he had said, "There is much talk about black control of the ghetto. What does that mean? I am mayor of a city of roughly 90,000 black people—but we do not control the possibilities of jobs for them, of money for their schools, or state-funded social services. These things are in the hands of the United States Steel Corporation and the County Department of Welfare, the State of Indiana and H.U.D." His hope was that the election of 50 black mayors in 50 major cities could lead a movement that would change the whole system. Address by the Hon. Richard Gordon Hatcher at the NAACP Legal Defense Fund Luncheon, New York, May 16, 1968, pp. 9-10.

pollution of our air and the poisoning of our streams. It is conceivable at least that resources may be committed to solving these problems without any corresponding commitment to deal with racial separation or economic deprivation.

Nor have we said much about the less tangible qualities of life in our future cities. In putting our portrait together, we have used the dry materials of the academicians—statistics about population increases, deteriorating buildings, shrinking tax bases, the loss of jobs and income. The sterility of life once the central city is abandoned as the meeting place for diverse groups and cultural activity and the suburbs substituted as purveyors of homogenized cultural offerings is only hinted at. The misery and impoverishment of the spirit of people who remain trapped in the central city would be difficult to describe. We have not even put forward estimates of the probable social costs of continuing present policies—in increased rates of crime and delinquency, disease and drug addiction.

Notwithstanding these omissions, perhaps enough has been said to suggest what life in the cities may be like if there is no drastic change in present policy. It may not be an overstatement to say that the specter presented is one of a nation so rich and so callous as to build a new "civilization" not upon the ashes of the old but as a wall encircling it, entombing within not only forgotten monuments or dying institutions but living people who have not been fortunate enough to escape.

It does not require a Nostradamus to make one last prediction. If present policy is not changed and the plight of most black people continues to worsen there will be no peace in the cities. Whether violence will take the form of the spontaneous reactions to police incidents that marked early disorders, the seemingly organized guerrilla activities that have occurred more recently, or will evolve into other forms is difficult to say. But as long as a flicker of hope or spirit remains in the citizen of the ghetto, he is likely to rage against his fate. And as turmoil continues and escalates, one other prospect is in view—that white society, having been blind to injustice, will respond, out of fear, to its consequence with repression as thorough and brutal as anyone can now contemplate.

7

GLIMMERS OF HOPE

IF THE GRIM FUTURE of American cities forecast in the last chapter has any validity, the search for means to prevent its coming to pass becomes urgent. Are there any forces now at work in the nation which may impel our society to intervene strongly and positively enough to overcome the inertia of present policy? Are there facets of the American character—individual and collective —that afford solid basis for the hope that predictions of disaster are simply the fantasies of men of little faith? If such positive forces exist, how can their potential for social change be maximized?

At the outset, it should be said that the reforms required to establish full citizenship for black and poor people will not be easily accomplished. Involving as they do measures (to be detailed in the next chapter) to attack the twin evils of poverty and segregation, they will clearly require a substantial reallocation of national resources and major changes in the operation of urban institutions.

It must be acknowledged, too, that the nightmare foreseen for the nation's cities if present policies continue may not be everyone's nightmare. It is surely a hell for the millions of black and poor trapped in ghettos without hope of attaining personal dignity or economic independence. It is a bad dream for planners, conservationists, and economists who have long been concerned about the aesthetic offenses of urban sprawl, the depletion of land best left in its natural state or used for recreational purposes, the exorbitant costs and wastefulness of providing community facilities for hundreds of small villages that spring up around a city. It may be a source of sorrow and anger to those (mainly middle class intellectuals) who see the cultural advantages of the central city being displaced by the sterile offerings of the mass media and suburbia.

But it is far from self-evident that the mass of middle class whites who live in metropolitan areas will be deeply distressed by any of these changes. It is true that among working and lower middle-class people who still make their homes in the central city there is widespread discontent about the decline in essential services and the increase in social disorder. But many of these people have found in their Negro neighbors a handy scapegoat for all the ills of the city, a diagnosis which hardly leads to support of positive social and economic measures; and for some the well-worn path to suburbia provides a practical means of escape.

For the more affluent whites who already populate suburbia, urban sprawl, the loss of cultural opportunities in the central city, and other problems cited by the professional critics may be scarcely bothersome or, at worst, may be viewed as the necessary, if regrettable, price of the more highly valued benefits of suburban living.

It is upon these groups—the well-off whites, most of whom live in suburbia, and the less affluent whites, most of whom still live in the cities—that our inquiry about forces for change must be primarily focussed. Today, despite all of the divergent interests, allegiances, and viewpoints that exist within and between the two groups, there appears enough consensus in views about race relations and the city to constitute a restraint upon the development of new policies involving major reform. In the near future, the relatively affluent residents of suburbia alone will constitute a clear majority of the national electorate.

Thus, these are the groups whose views will shape future urban policies. Unless there are forces at work in our society which can induce them to support new leadership and new policies, there can be no hope that change will come about through the ordinary operation of the political process.

Guilt and Conscience

A quarter of a century ago, Gunnar Myrdal based his optimism about America's ability to solve its racial problems upon the powerful hold that the American creed—our articulated ideals of justice and equality—had upon the citizens of the nation.[1]

The glaring disparities between the ideals articulated in the Declaration of Independence and the Constitution, and the institution of slavery and the practices of discrimination which followed its abolition long have troubled the consciences of a great many white Americans. It is true that consciences have been eased by studied ignorance of the plight of Negroes and by the construction of a mythology, mainly concerning presumed biological inferiority of black people, that could be used to explain the gap between profession and practice. But these rationalizations never have satisfied people for very long, Myrdal said, and as popular theories which support race prejudice are challenged and demolished, the white man's conscience becomes an ally in the Negro's fight for equality.[2]

Myrdal found—in the nation's faith in free inquiry, in its willingness to expose its worst faults, in its habit of enacting ideals and hopes into legislation—abundant evidence that professed adherence to the American creed was not sheer hypocrisy. Ideals, in America, he said "represent a social force" for change and progress.[3]

In the years since the publication of *An American Dilemma,* much has happened to substantiate its author's faith in the force of American ideals. As Myrdal foresaw, World War II, by placing the nation in armed combat with forces which propagated ideologies of racial superiority, sharpened the focus upon problems of racial injustice at home and led to reform. The series of Supreme Court decisions invalidating governmentally sanctioned segregation, the enactment of new laws and policies prohibiting discrimination in the armed forces, in private employment, in places of public accommodation, and in registration and voting, all were affirmations of the continuing hold of the American creed. Many of the measures, it is true, came about in response to demonstrations and other evidences of ferment, but the protests themselves were primarily appeals to social conscience and it was conscience more than anything else that produced the response. And if enforcement of these laws has proved far from satisfactory, they still have brought about in the past few years more improvement in the status of black people than was achieved in the century preceding.

Progress has been made, too, in stripping away the myths that permitted many Americans to rationalize the gap between ideals and practice. Mass protest has made it all but impossible for white people to maintain that, except for a handful of malcontents, Negroes are generally happy with their situation. While ghettos remain physically and psychologically remote, the reporting of television and newspapers has made clear to all but those who will not see the dreadful conditions under which most black people live. And, although the debates among academicians continue in various forms, the achievements of increasing numbers of black people in all fields of endeavor make it very difficult for white people to feel secure in notions of racial superiority.

By all accounts then, the progress of recent years would seem to have vindicated Myrdal's faith in the American people and the motive force of their ideals. But this is not what has happened. Today, few students of race relations have any real confidence that America's humanitarian ideals are guiding its people with sure, if measured, steps down a road to a society of justice and equality. Optimism has been replaced by uncertainty; the ultimate resolution of our racial struggle now seems very much in doubt.

Why should this be? In part, the answer lies in the fact that even the most perceptive observers misgauged both the depth of America's racial problems and the rapidity with which technology was changing society. It was only after the worst abuses— lynchings, mass disfranchisement, state-sanctioned caste systems— had been dealt with that an awareness began to grow that the surface had barely been scratched. Yet, as progress has been made and the myths that had sustained people have waned, the social evils still to be dealt with have become fuzzier in the minds of most white Americans.

Stated bluntly, the current reality is this: *While historically it was white racism that placed Negroes in subjugation, today our society has grown so complex in its organization and in the skills required for economic success that great numbers of black people can be kept in inferior status without recourse to active racism.* This does not mean that racism has been eradicated but only that, as the term is commonly understood—the dogma that one ethnic group is congenitally superior to another—it is on the decline and that the major problem is to deal with the current consequences of the doctrine's past ascendancy.

If this is so, if the institutions and practices that adversely affect black people today operate in more subtle fashion than in the past, if the forces responsible for perpetuating poverty and deprivation are no longer clearly identified in the minds of many white Americans, then the efficacy of conscience as an instrument for change is placed in doubt. It has been said in only partial jest that major credit for the Civil Rights Act of 1964 should be given to "Bull" Connor, police commissioner of Birmingham, who loosed the dogs and the fire hoses, and that passage of the Voting Rights Act of 1965 may be attributed in large measure to similar actions by Governor George Wallace and Sheriff Jim Clark of Selma, Alabama. The symbolic figures whose future actions might stir feelings of shame, revulsion, and conscience sufficiently to produce a new economic and social bill of rights for black people in the cities are more difficult to identify.

In short, the forces which perpetuate deprivation and inequality today are complex and largely impersonal. It is as if at birth the great mass of white infants found themselves aboard jet liners and the great mass of Negro infants found themselves aboard ox carts, each bound for the destination of a productive and materially rewarding life. The reasons why most whites are aboard one type of conveyance and most blacks aboard the other are to be found in history, recent as well as ancient, and involve specific actors and acts of discrimination. But now that the system is established, it does not require repeated acts of racism to keep it operating, but only that there be no dramatic intervention to revamp the entire system of transportation. During the course of their journey, a few whites may lose their seats on the jet liner and a number of Negroes, by dint of extraordinary effort or very good luck, may transfer from the ox cart to the jet liner, but these are exceptions which do not affect the basic rules by which the system operates.

In terms less metaphoric, it is submitted that the average white child has at his disposal, almost from the moment of birth, resources which go a long way toward guaranteeing his success. He is assured from birth of adequate nourishment, clothing, and shelter during his formative years. In addition, if his parents do not uniformly furnish emotional support, they at least transmit to him at a very early age verbal and other skills which assist his intellectual development. At school, he has the benefit not only of adequate to superior teaching but of the stimulation of fellow students from similarly advantaged homes. His community produces, usually at no great financial sacrifice to his parents, services and amenities which also assist in his development. Perhaps most important, the white child receives from his family, schools, and community not merely formal training, but a range of informal skills which will assist him throughout his life in meeting his goals and seeing that his interests are not neglected. (As D. W. Brogan, a perceptive observer of the American scene, has pointed out, the schools do not simply instruct students but also let them "instruct each other in how to live in America." And "graduation from high school is reasonable proof that a great deal has been learned about American ways of life, that lessons in practical politics, in organization, in social ease have been learned that could not have been learned in factory or office.")[4] An important part of this know-how is the cultivation from earliest youth of a network of friendships and contacts which may later be helpful in advancing his career and economic interests.

In contrast, a black child born of poor parents may lack adequate food, clothing, and shelter, perhaps even to a degree that his physical and mental growth will be impaired in infancy. With the best of will, his parents may not be able to impart to him the verbal and cognitive skills he needs to have a head start in school. In school, he is unlikely to have the sensitive and superior teaching he needs to compensate for the absence of resources in the home, in the community, and in the school itself. The community, far from providing positive services and amenities, is characterized by the lack of such services and by social disorganization, and among the most insistent influences are those (drugs, criminal activity, prostitution) which evidence wrecked lives. Needless to say, the black child in such circumstances acquires little of the political and social skill needed to help him negotiate the obstacle course of community life, and makes few, if any, contacts that will assist him in his career. And as society becomes larger and more stratified and requires the acquisition of more skills and knowledge, the escape routes available to earlier immigrants to the city—unskilled jobs and small business enterprise—are closed off.

This, it is submitted, is a reasonably accurate, if oversimplified, description of current reality, of a society more closed and less mobile in its era of greatest prosperity than when it was struggling for its economic life. But it is a view that is not shared, at least at present, by the great majority of white middle-class Americans.[5]

Whether or not they were adults during the great Depression, these citizens do not see themselves as having traveled a relatively easy road to economic security, but as having struggled in a highly competitive society to achieve a niche for themselves and their families. Having obtained a measure of security many still feel their position precarious. Far from believing that they are beneficiaries of a system which enables them to obtain public services at relatively low cost, they feel themselves overtaxed and overburdened, largely they think for the benefit of others. Since wealth as well as poverty is a relative concept, they can always find support for their views by comparing their situation to that of others, and by treating as necessities items (vacations abroad, second and third cars, entertainment costs) which only a few years ago they would have regarded as the most extravagant luxuries.

Consistent with a view that their own positions are still somewhat tenuous, most white Americans do not see themselves as agents in denying rights and benefits to anyone else. Failing to attach much significance to history and refusing to visit the sins of fathers upon sons (especially when they are the sons), they accept little responsibility for past discrimination against Negroes. "What is past is past" is the general view, and many profess not to see why Negroes, starting today, cannot achieve success by the same route others have used.

Relatively few whites, moreover, are ever confronted with situations which would force them to examine their racial beliefs and prejudices in personal terms. In some communities, issues relating to housing or schools may develop in such an inflammatory way that people are impelled to take a stand, either with the handful who are unashamedly fanning the flames of racial hatred or against them. But, more typically, issues never arise at all or, if they do, are presented in a manner which allows them to be discussed in terms that have little apparent reference to race. Thus, the potential entry of low- and moderate-income housing into a community can be debated and rejected on grounds that the cost of public services required to meet the needs of the new population would far exceed the tax revenues their homes and incomes would generate and that these are burdens a community which regards itself as already hard-pressed financially cannot afford. Educational issues can be reduced to questions of available space and problems of transportation. In employment there can be ready agreement that all who are qualified should be hired, without any real thought about how people are to become qualified or whether formal qualifications long accepted have any real relationship to the requirements of a job.

It is possible for white people to take these positions and at the same time to feel, without any conscious sense of contradiction, an attachment to the American creed of justice and equality (tempered only by observations that "after all Negroes *are* responsible for a disproportionate amount of crime and *do* constitute a large percentage of the welfare rolls"). Ultimately, then, adherence to principles of equality and justice is reduced to little more than a formal commitment—a part of the baggage of "considered opinions" that most people carry with them for use in polite conversation or in case a Gallup pollster comes to call.

The dilemma of how, in the context of the problems of today, belief in the American dream can be channeled toward practical ends was never more apparent than in the aftermath of the issuance of the Kerner Commission Report. Seeking to put the facts plainly to the American people, the Commission said:

> What white Americans have never fully understood—but what the Negro can never forget—is that white society is deeply implicated in the ghetto. White institutions created it, white institutions maintain it, and white society condones it.[6]

and further:

White racism is essentially responsible for the explosive mixture which has been accumulating in our cities since the end of World War II.[7]

Many observers welcomed these blunt statements, hoping that, other methods having failed, resort to shock treatment might awaken large segments of the public to the need for action. But Bayard Rustin, with his usual acuity, warned that the report was subject to misinterpretation which might make it politically counterproductive. The report, he said,

> . . . didn't say that Americans are racist. If it did, the only answer would be to line everybody up, all 200 million of us, line up 200,000 psychiatrists, and we'd all be on couches for the first ten years trying to understand the problem and the next ten years learning how to deal with it. All over the country people are beating their breasts crying *mea culpa*—"I'm so sorry that I am a racist"—which means, really, that they want to cop out because if racism is to be solved on an individual psychological basis, then there is little hope.

> What the Kerner Report was really saying was that the *institutions* of America brutalize not only the Negro but also whites who are not racists, and who in many communities have to use racist institutions. When it's put on that basis, we know that the fundamental problem is not sitting around examining our innards, but getting out and fighting for institutional change.[8]

In retrospect, it appears that Rustin was amply justified in his fear that a stress upon individual motives would divert attention from the need for broad economic and social programs of reform. In fact, the practical effect of popularizing the term "white racism" seems to have been to lead many white people to their own private psychiatrists' couches where, after a superficial examination of their own motives, they have pronounced themselves blameless. (A smaller number of whites have fulfilled Rustin's prediction by being only too ready to plead guilty to racism—usually, however, for the most trivial of offenses—and then copping out of organized efforts to secure institutional change.)

"White racism," then, is a charge to which few white Americans appear ready to plead guilty and the addition of a modifier—"*institutional* white racism"—does not seem to have made the concept more meaningful to large numbers of people. The dilemma, however, persists. It is true that when sufficient consensus exists to produce new laws and programs, the existence of individual prejudice can be considered a secondary concern. The new laws and programs, if vigorously implemented, produce new institutional settings and changes in behavior, and while the elimination of prejudice may come more slowly, attitudes gradually conform to behavior. But this process, familiar enough in the recent history of race relations in the South,* breaks down when individual attitudes—whether described as prejudices, rationalizations, racist beliefs, or simply a lack of understanding—operate to prevent the initial consensus on the need for new laws and programs. This is the basic situation that confronts the nation now.

All of the foregoing is not intended as a repudiation of Myrdal's faith in the power of the American creed. The evidence that he adduced in support of his belief, that Americans were committed to free inquiry, to exposing their worst faults publicly rather than suppressing them, and to enacting their hopes into legislation, is if anything stronger today than when he wrote. What *is* being suggested is that today the job of mobilizing the American conscience is more complex and difficult than it has ever been in the past. Lacking now the tangible and unambiguous symbols of racial oppression which at various times have provoked a stirring of national conscience, it is not enough simply to seek to rally people to a banner inscribed with Pogo's motto "We have met the enemy and he is us."

A major effort must be made to communicate to large numbers of people a better understanding of the contemporary facts of racial deprivation. They must be made to see how systems of government, institutions, and individual citizens, without following overtly racist rules or practices, operate to the disadvantage of black people. The more subtle rationalizations for the continu-

---

* With all of the southern resistance to school desegregation, white attitudes have changed as schools have slowly come into compliance with the law. In mid-1969, a Gallup poll reported that 46 per cent of a sample of southern white parents said they would object to sending their children to a school where half of the children are Negro. Six years earlier, 78 per cent of white parents objected. Token integration was accepted by 78 per cent of the white parents in 1969, although it had been opposed by 61 per cent in 1963. *The New York Times,* Sept. 2, 1969, pp. 1, 37.

ing gap between promise and performance must be explored and penetrated.

It is too early to say that such an effort to make conscience again a force for social change will be unsuccessful. It is not the time when one plateau has just been reached to conclude that we cannot go any higher. But neither is there much time to catch our breath. The aggravated state of race relations in the nation will not permit a leisurely process of education.

And, lastly, it is being suggested that, as Myrdal and Tocqueville before him knew, it is not enough to rely upon the American creed alone to produce justice and equality. Without it, this nation might long ago have gone the way of South Africa. But unless the desire of Americans to be moral and humanitarian in their own eyes and in the eyes of others is supported by other forces in American life, conscience is not likely to be sufficient.

Law and Order

If conscience alone will not bring progress, what of the desires of most people for an end to racial turmoil and hostility?

From the day several years ago when Chicago officials responded to rioting by meeting the demands of youth groups for sprinklers in the city streets, it became apparent that violence might be an instrument for achieving social change. Much that followed seemed to reinforce this belief in the sweet uses of adversity. In many cities Negro leaders, who never before had been able to obtain an attentive hearing at city hall, were summoned frantically in the wake of looting and destruction and asked to present remedial programs. Businessmen in particular perceived in racial disorder a threat to their economic interests and tended to respond in a constructive manner. Programs to provide training and jobs for the "hard-core" unemployed and assistance to Negro businessmen in the establishment of new enterprises were launched in many places in the name of re-establishing stability and order, with little breath wasted on appeals to justice or fairness.

All of this has placed civil rights advocates in a very uncomfortable position. Committed to achieving change, they have pleaded for a constructive public response to rioting, noting that it would be a cruel paradox if after years of failing to reward patience or redress injustice, the nation were to use violence by a few as an excuse for continued inaction. But committed also to rationality and the processes of law, they have recognized that every program undertaken in direct response to rioting tends to validate violence as an instrument of change, to make it more likely, and to undermine moderate leadership. These ambivalent feelings about disorder have not been eased by the knowledge that violence has been an element of some importance (although of debatable effectiveness) in past movements for social justice, including the struggles of labor unions for recognition and economic gains.[9]

Events, however, seem rapidly to be resolving this dilemma of liberals. For any fair balance sheet will show that the civil disorders of the past few years have resulted in far more political harm than good. Against the credit of small programs in several cities to create jobs or provide recreational facilities must be balanced the larger debit of a failure to stimulate a commitment of major resources at the national level. If riots have spoken to some civic leaders and businessmen in a language they understand, it is clear that they have not evoked the same kind of response from the public at large. Instead the political climate has grown more oppressive, and public sentiment has been rallied by candidates who advocate cutbacks in expenditures and a removal of the restraints that courts have placed upon law enforcement officers. If riots in their early stages came through to some people as spontaneous cries of anguish and despair and to others as threats to the social and economic fabric which could be averted only by remedial action, there seems little prospect that their continuation will widen the audience. Repetition dulls the sense of spontaneity and the capacity to evoke sympathy. And, with the passage of time, businessmen and others who once saw riots as a menace to the social and economic order find ways to adapt, e.g., through the pooling of insurance risks, that are less costly than fundamental reform.

Thus, advocates of peaceful change, far from agonizing over whether the existence of violence should be exploited for useful ends, must now be concerned about whether it can be overcome (since it cannot in the short run be averted) as a political barrier to change.

It is possible, of course, that the character of disorder in the cities will change—that it not only will continue but will escalate and that it will no longer be directed inward toward the destruction of property in the ghetto but outward toward people, such as white policemen, who are symbols of white oppression.

If this happens, the most predictable response by white authority is repression. Force is likely to be met by force even greater than that applied in the early days of rioting when police were largely ungoverned by riot-control procedures. Restraints upon free movement, preventive detention, and similar measures to provide security for persons and property in the white community undoubtedly would move to the top of the agenda.

It is conceivable that such an increase in violence would sharpen in the minds of many citizens the ultimate choice between repression and reform. The initiation of the steps necessary to repress disorder, it can be argued, might produce a revulsion that would add moral impetus to desires to find another way. Neglect and discrimination, after all, are easier to rationalize than brutal repression, and few Americans would be comfortable with the image of themselves as citizens of a garrison state.

But the possibility that conscience would be reasserted as a force for change in such aggravated circumstances seems far too conjectural. Fear and irrationality, already prevalent in many cities, would be running still higher. There would be even less disposition than there is now to examine root causes or to initiate long-range reforms.

Economic Necessity

Similarly, it is probably wishful thinking to suppose that change may be impelled by a belief that the economic well-being of all citizens is dependent on the elimination of poverty and discrimination.

True, it can be and has been argued persuasively that developing the potential of people now disadvantaged would add significantly to the nation's economic wealth. It also has been shown in various ways that the social costs we pay now for correctional institutions, welfare payments, and the like are in the long run far greater than the investments in human resources necessary to educate, train, and develop the potential of disadvantaged people and to avert crime, disease, and dependency.

These are rational arguments that ought to be well received in a society that places great stock in cost-benefit analysis. But such analysis is helpful only *after* a basic commitment has been made to attack deprivation and discrimination (by demonstrating that the nation can afford to invest the necessary resources). It shows little promise of helping us to arrive at the necessary commitment.

For what cannot be shown is that the maintenance of the status quo threatens in any serious way the economic well-being of the great majority of citizens. In a society where the majority is so affluent that new needs are constantly being fabricated, it is hard to demonstrate that the continued poverty of a relative few could menace the economic structure. In a society where technological advances can be used to reduce needs for additional labor to produce goods and services, it would be hard to show that the enforced idleness of a few jeopardizes satisfaction of the wants of the many. Even those temporary shortages of manpower, in fields such as health and education, that affect the well-off as well as the poor may be overcome without providing skills and employment for great numbers of the disadvantaged.

It is quite conceivable then that the nation's economy will continue to grow and prosper while a small but significant number of people either remain unemployed or work for low wages at marginally useful jobs.

Other Interests

If, as seems likely, neither the fundamental need for peace and order nor that for economic security is a sure guarantor of major reform, the questions become a good deal more difficult. Are there other needs and interests which are being threatened by what is happening in cities and which, although less tangible and immediate, are important enough to bring about change? Are the measures needed to eliminate the poverty and isolation of black people irreconcilable with what affluent whites consider to be their vital interests? May developments in technology contribute to a redefinition of interest in ways which will permit a reconciliation of goals? Are facets of character which have been identified as typically American—e.g., optimism, perennial dissatisfaction with the status quo, a willingness to experiment with change —likely to lead to reform?

The City as a Center of Culture and Diversity

One of the more imponderable questions in our inquiry is whether people who live in metropolitan areas value the city sufficiently as a center of culture and diversity that they would be ready to support action to arrest and reverse its deterioration. The evidence on this issue, to say the least, is ambiguous.

On one side is the dubious place that cities occupy in the history and values of the nation. From the time of Jefferson a dominant element in political and religious thought has regarded large cities with suspicion and mistrust, at best a necessary evil. Although American cities, by virtue of sheer numbers, gradually became an important part of the political process, unlike their European counterparts they never have dominated the political life of the nation. And while it has always been useful for politicians with national aspirations to stress their humble origins, the assets have been log cabins, not city slums.

During their periods of greatest growth, cities were reviled as places of vice and corruption by critics who found few saving graces. Today, when cities are in decline, much of the criticism again implies that the evil is the city itself rather than what men have permitted to happen to it.

Nor is there much evidence that any large number of urban dwellers form permanent attachments to the city. Gans, in his study of residents of Levittown, N. J., found that few regretted their move from city to suburbs and almost no one planned to return. Those who said they missed the city were concerned primarily about diminished contact with friends and relatives in their old neighborhoods.[10] While the sights, sounds, and smells of the city, the variety of peoples, foods, and customs, the clashing and interaction of all these elements, may still be celebrated in song and story, they do not appear to have a hold on many who formerly were among the cast of characters.

It would be wrong, however, to dismiss too easily the values that people have found in cities. Brogan has pointed out that urbanization in this country has not resulted in the establishment of one or two great centers and many provinces but in a great many regional centers.[11] Despite their drab sameness in appearance (with exceptions like Washington, San Francisco, Boston, New York, and Chicago), individual cities are in many ways autonomous entities, sustained by the pride of citizens in local institutions such as symphony orchestras, museums, universities, baseball and football teams. Despite the insistent pressures of the mass media, many cities remain their own molders of opinion and taste, refusing to accept complete direction from any national source. Although many cities have gone rapidly downhill since Brogan wrote more than a decade ago, civic pride still seems a sustaining force. People still think of and identify themselves as hailing from Cleveland or Philadelphia rather than the sylvan suburb they may actually call home, and they still boast of local institutions with which they may have little contact. Moreover, it is possible that the cities hold values not only for those elderly who are too set in their ways to move, but for young people who have grown up in suburbs. One of the elements in the prevalent unrest among students is a rejection of suburban life, and, for some at least, a new interest in the city. It is too early to say whether for many this interest will survive the strong drawing power of suburbia, once they reach the stage of marriage and the raising of a family, but at the moment it does offer some hope for the revitalization of the city.

All of this may be a slender reed upon which to predicate an urban renaissance. It is theoretically possible, for example, that some cities might decide to renew their inner cores as centers for cultural life without determining to alleviate the poverty and isolation of the people who live there. This, after all, was the basic thrust of the urban renewal program during the 1950s and early 1960s. But the experience of urban renewal has contained some valuable lessons for everyone. If poor and black people do not yet have the political power to compel affirmative reforms, they at least have acquired, through bitter experience, skills which enable them to exercise a veto power. In many cities it is no longer feasible for planners to carry out their schemes for highways, public facilities, or middle-income housing without negotiating with the communities most directly affected. Few communities are ready to accede to programs whose benefits are not direct, tangible, and almost immediate. And increasing numbers of officials are beginning to get the message that even if they succeed in moving the bulldozers in, it is really not possible to renew a city without renewing the hopes and spirit of its people.

It is conceivable, too, that faced with difficult political problems, government planners may skirt the central city entirely in maintaining and renewing the institutions that give a city its distinctive character. If a few cities are concerned about keeping culture downtown and making it more relevant to the immediately surrounding communities, others are planning or talking about theaters, museums, and sports arenas to be located in the suburbs, generally near the beltways that now encircle many cities. But, while such plans may be the forerunners of completely transformed patterns of urban life, there still remains some room for doubt. If civic pride and feelings of autonomy still have a hold on people, it is difficult to see how they can be maintained in cities without a vital center. And if optimism and a reluctance to concede defeat are indeed a part of the American character, people may be impelled to do something about the rotting core of a city which will continue to stamp its character no matter what is done in the suburbs.

Disaffection of the Lower Middle Class

Civic pride and optimism, an attachment to some of the values of the city, may then be one force that can be made to work for desirable change. In a very different sense, the disaffection of many white people who remain in the city may be another.

For it has become increasingly clear that it is not only Negroes and poor people who are disadvantaged by the present structure of urban life. Others, frequently described as the "lower middle class," have grievances which are also deeply felt. In general, they are factory workers, clerks, civil servants and their families, whose incomes range roughly from $6,000 to $12,000, and who, willingly or not, still retain ethnic identifications as Italians, Poles, Irish, etc. They number as many as 80 million citizens, and although a good many reside in suburbs, the bulk are still to be found in the city.

The situation of many of these white city dwellers is not totally dissimilar from that of blacks. They suffer from poor municipal services—overcrowded schools, inadequate trash collection, and few opportunities for recreation. They ride the same antiquated buses and trains and breathe the same foul air. If the threat of crime is not as severe in their neighborhoods as in the poverty areas, it is real enough. If their economic situation permits them a few more of the amenities of life, it is often achieved only at the cost of much effort—long hours and second jobs.

Most important, they, like black people, are prone to feel that they have somehow missed out on the keys to the good life. Many did not have the resources to attend college in a period when scholarship aid was scarce. And, without the knowledge and skills that are now so important to advancement and mobility, they have little to look forward to in life. As Adam Walinsky has written:

> So he faces the future, this young man, with 30 years of working life ahead of him; 30 years in which the educational requirements for economic and social advancement will rapidly grow beyond his wildest dreams; 30 years to go to the plant, and to watch television; 30 years of "day that follows day, with death the only goal."[12]

At present, the handiest targets for these accumulated discontents are Negroes and any local official or politician who has shown sympathy for the plight of the black and the poor. A white worker who feels himself caught in the squeeze of high taxes is likely to focus on rising welfare costs which, he believes, maintain at living standards nearly as high as his own people who are unwilling to work. Worried about the immediate threat of crime, he is not very indulgent of complex sociological analysis of its causes and long-range solutions. If he is a production worker, he may be concerned about potential competition from black work- ers in a time when jobs may not be as plentiful. If he is a police- man, a fireman, or a local merchant, he sees himself as a scape- goat and target for all the grievances of black people. Perhaps most galling of all, the lower middle-class white may see Negroes as the recipients of special privileges which were not available to him. Negroes, he may note, are being admitted to colleges through the relaxation of standards that may have kept him out and with scholarship aid that he could not obtain.

In the day-to-day expressions of these frustrations there is ample material for anyone wishing to document charges of rac- ism. The practical manifestation has been the defeat of a number of liberal politicians who have exhibited concern about poverty and discrimination, by candidates who advocate a "get tough" policy and whose campaign utterances thinly veil an appeal to racial bias. In the persistence of these discontents lies an even greater threat of rising racial tensions and open conflict.

But, if the existence of deeply felt grievances by moderate- income whites is an unstabilizing element that threatens to ag- gravate conditions in the cities, it is at least possible that it may be a force for positive change. For, if the situation were to be seen clearly by white city dwellers, they would understand that the responsibility for their problems does not rest either with black people or liberal mayors and that remedies are not to be found in opposing efforts to alleviate poverty. White people in the cities are in fact victims along with Negroes of a system of allocating public services that favors the affluent. The remedy for this situation is not to be found in a competition among neigh- borhoods and ethnic groups for the inadequate resources that are available within the city, but in more equitable systems of raising and distributing revenues in metropolitan areas.

Moreover, lower middle-income whites in the cities are correct in their feelings that it is they who have been asked to shoulder almost the entire burden of social change. When efforts are made to improve education by achieving better racial balance in the schools, the focus is frequently on lower middle-class areas where people already are insecure about the quality of their children's education. When efforts are made to find sites outside the ghetto for low-income housing, the target areas are not usually affluent parts of the city or suburbs but moderate-income neighborhoods already burdened by inadequate services. The remedy for this situation, however, lies not in opposing all such efforts but in the advocacy of measures that will ensure that whatever burdens are involved will be distributed equitably throughout metropolitan areas.

And, lastly, if the tight limitations on their mobility and that of their children are to be removed, it will not be by denying opportunities to the black and poor, but by allocating additional resources and providing new kinds of education and training for all.

Suggestions of this kind are subject to the accusation that they are nothing more than nostalgic longings for a bygone age of populism. But it is not necessary to presuppose a deep affinity between blacks and whites of limited income to believe that they have common interests which may be channeled toward common remedies.* What must be assumed is that the racial antagonisms that exist in the cities are not so ingrained that rational and pragmatic appeals for support of solutions that are mutually beneficial will inevitably be resisted. (On this question social science has not had a great deal to contribute and conclusions must be drawn, in large measure, from the observer's own subjective experience.[13] My own conclusion, from the perspective of having grown up in working class neighborhoods in New York City, is that most people are motivated by positive yearnings for security and respect and by decent instincts that far outweigh feelings of racial hatred and expressions of cruelty. But the longer people are required to function in an environment in which no one's goals can be satisfied, the more likely it is that fear and hatred will gain the upper hand.)

In the end, the question whether the disaffection of white city dwellers can be channeled toward positive change is likely to depend upon the incalculable factor of political leadership. In

* There is little evidence that many white people have any real understanding or empathy for the situation of Negroes. Despite the educational efforts of writers and television commentators, many whites would be likely to agree with the sentiment of a bar patron who told Pete Hamill: "If I hear that 400-years-of-slavery bit one more time, I'll go outta my mind." Hamill, "The Revolt of the White Lower Middle Class," *New York* (April 14, 1969), p. 26.

his last campaign, Robert Kennedy exhibited a concern and identification with the problems of the black poor and the white worker that enabled him to draw substantial support from both groups. No one can tell whether he would have been successful in translating that support into a working consensus for new initiatives and programs. But it is surely not an idle dream to retain the faith that someone else might.

Suburban Alienation and "Community Control"

The disaffection of white city dwellers is now so prevalent and openly expressed that it is difficult to ignore. While there is little tangible evidence of comparable dissatisfaction with the status quo among the more affluent residents of suburbia, here too there are stirrings that eventually may prove significant.

Social scientists are in disagreement about the importance of desires for community participation and control as a factor in the burgeoning growth of suburbs. For Robert Wood, much of the phenomenon of suburban growth is explained by the American people's attachment to an ideal of "grass-roots democracy"—a belief in the small political unit as the purest expression of popular will—that is among the oldest and strongest of our traditions.[14] From the earliest days of the republic, political philosophers, Jefferson and Tocqueville among them, exalted the values of small independent town governments as a form of organization which promoted reason, goodwill, self-identity, and a sharing of common interests and objectives. With industrialization and the growth of cities came forms of organization that were antithetical to the ideal. City government was viewed as too big and often corrupt, unresponsive to the needs of its citizens and as promoting conflict and feelings of personal impotence. Thus, in Wood's view, when the coming of the automobile and a prosperous economy made mass suburbs possible, one of the most important motivating forces was the desire of people to recreate the presumed values of small-town life.[15]

In contrast, Gans in his study of the residents of Levittown concluded that their move to the suburbs was prompted by much more tangible and practical considerations. The goals sought by most people, he found, were home ownership, more spacious housing, and the kind of privacy facilitated by a free-standing house. Few, he said, were seeking roots in the suburbs or a sense of community or civic participation.[16]

Whatever the initial attractions may be, it is clear that once established, suburban communities have been strongly resistant to change. Over the years, they have withstood many efforts at consolidation and reorganization—efforts based on arguments that the profusion of small separate units of government has made for inefficient services and higher costs to taxpayers. That these rational arguments have been rejected is testimony that the concepts of participation and community control have become meaningful to many suburban residents. The concepts, however, are ones uniquely adapted to the conditions of modern life. One key element of control is the ability of a community to keep itself homogeneous in exactly the way it wants. In Wood's words:

> They [suburban residents] can, by zoning, covenants, selective industrial development, taxation and informal patterns of segregation, literally choose their own fellow citizens. Because they do not have to reproduce all parts of a self-contained economic system and admit clerks, craftsmen and laborers within their bounds, a degree of homogeneity can be achieved that was not possible before. The central city becomes a receptacle for all the functions the suburban dweller does not care to support.[17]

In this definition of community control is wrapped all of the values of status and homogeneity that together constitute the most formidable barrier to equal opportunity for the black and the poor. But though the barrier remains strong, the underpinnings of community control are being placed under stress by factors which eventually may help to undermine the whole structure.

One such factor is the growing complexity of governing, which increasingly renders notions of individual participation and direct access to governmental decision-making an illusion. As Wood and others have pointed out, problems in fields such as finance and public health have become so technical that more and more they are entrusted to professionals. Even issues usually thought to be within the ken of the individual citizen, such as honesty in government, land development, and taxes, are not really within his control.[18] As elected officials and technicians assume more authority and responsibility, it becomes less easy for the average suburban citizen to maintain the illusion that he really exerts much influence on the conduct of local affairs.

Nor is it possible any longer for suburban residents to feel secure in a belief that they are citizens of communities that are economically self-reliant and independent. With the mounting costs of public services, suburbs, like other local units of government, have come to rely heavily on subsidies provided by states and the Federal Government. It is true, of course, that suburbs have wielded enough political influence to prevent their "outside" benefactors from imposing conditions or setting local priorities, and that they may be able to prevent such intrusions for years to come. But with the loss of self-sufficiency, the walls of suburban isolation are breached and there is at least a recognition that broader kinds of participation are necessary even for the conduct of local affairs.

The ceding of local control to technicians and politicians and reliance upon Federal and state subsidies are no longer new developments, and many suburbanites seem to have withstood them with their feelings of community control relatively intact. But there is a more recent development—the upheaval of the cities—which (while its impact is still too new to be assessed) may yet force an examination and redefinition of the concepts of "community" and "control."

As long as the cities and their inhabitants were quiescent, citizens of suburbia could derive a sense of satisfaction and personal competence from control of their communities, without questioning how significant such control was in the larger setting of American society. But with cities in turmoil, with established values and institutions being questioned not only by the black and poor but by their own children, affluent whites can hardly maintain the illusion that they are masters of their environment. There are signs that they too have begun to share feelings of alienation and to sense that as society is now organized, they too are powerless to control the currents that swirl around them.

It is possible, of course, that the insecurities induced by national and world turmoil may lead only to a further withdrawal into suburban isolation. A decade ago, Wood noted that the growing complexity of society had reinforced rather than diminished the attachment of the suburban resident to his small community:

> With so many demands on his attention, with so many inscrutable developments taking place on the larger stage of human affairs, men need more than ever, it seems, a place where problems are concrete and familiar, where abstractions are unnecessary and where "people take what they can without surrendering their way of life."[19]

But it is also possible that the current upheaval may lead people in a different direction. In a few suburban communities around the nation, citizens have reacted to their new perceptions of racial problems by reaching a hand across the border—to assume some responsibility for the education of children in the inner city, to accept some part of the burden of providing adequate shelter for people of low income. They have been motivated not merely by a sense of moral duty, but by a need to be "relevant," to feel that they have some influence in events of more transcending importance than, say, a new swimming pool for Whitehaven.

There is, then, the bare promise that from these feelings there may evolve new definitions of community, new forms of political organization of cities in which suburban citizens would accept some of the costs of dealing with poverty and racial discrimination in return for a share of control over a larger environment. The road to establishing new modes of metropolitan cooperation undoubtedly would be treacherous. Accustomed to obtaining the best of any bargain, white suburbanites are apt initially to place greater stress upon obtaining control than upon assuming responsibility; metropolitan police forces, for example, are likely to have more appeal for many than regional school systems. Yet if one may dare hope that suburban man will see it in his interest to reexamine his traditional beliefs about community, it would signal a new political maturity—a willingness to deal with complexity and conflict and to accept risks—that would hold enormous potential for good.

Technology and Education

In assessing the possibility that seemingly settled definitions of self-interest may be reexamined, the potential impact of technological change and of new concepts in education should not be ignored. As several commentators have pointed out, we are in the midst of a technological revolution which may make possible the development of new kinds of cities, the outlines of which are now only dimly seen.[20] Among the changes in urban institutions that technology may help to bring about are some which affluent people may regard as being in their own self-interest and which at the same time would produce a better life for the minority poor.

The most promising possibilities in this direction lie in the field of education. As long as the limits of educational opportunity are defined by "neighborhood" schools, small in size, serving limited geographical areas, and containing the traditional "egg crate" classrooms, conflict between the interests of black and white, affluent and poor, seems inevitable. Researchers may conclude that racial and economic integration of children in such schools will benefit the disadvantaged without harming advantaged students,* but affluent white parents either do not believe it or are unwilling to take any kind of risk. Thus they successfully resist "bussing" programs and permit integration to occur only when adherence to the concept of neighborhood schools compels it, which generally means at the high school level. When Negro and white students first meet at this level, having been segregated throughout their formative years, the potential for racial tension and conflict is considerable, and when conflict occurs it reinforces the fears and resistance of parents. And when school systems remain segregated and must compete for scarce resources, any claim by one group to a greater share is naturally viewed by the other as detrimental to its interests. In the context, then, of present educational facilities and systems, few solutions appear which all groups would regard as mutually beneficial.

---

* See *Equality of Educational Opportunity*, U.S. Office of Education, Department of HEW, pp. 21-23. This survey of students, teachers, and schools, the largest of its kind ever conducted, concluded that the socioeconomic composition of a student body had an important influence upon the achievement of disadvantaged students. But, while disadvantaged students might benefit from schooling with more advantaged children, the advantaged children did not suffer. The report said that even where a white student from a home that is strongly and effectively supportive of education is put in a school where *most* children do not come from such homes, his achievement will be little different than if he were in a school composed of other advantaged children.

But educators have begun to question seriously whether the present system serves anybody's needs very well.[21] Recognizing that children of the same age may differ widely in their levels of achievement and that the same child may progress much more rapidly in one subject than in another, educators have sought more flexible means of grouping and grading children than are presently employed in most schools. Recognizing, too, that some school activities are most appropriately conducted in large groups and others in small groups with as much individual attention as possible, educators have introduced the concepts of team teaching and flexible classroom space. The increasing stress upon the value of attention to the individual needs of children has also led some educators to view the computer as a potentially invaluable aid to teaching. A computer designed to be operated by an individual child can be programmed to present problems of increasing difficulty in subjects such as reading or arithmetic. It can keep instantaneous track of each student's work, provide higher-level materials as his skill increases, and analyze his work so that teachers and school officials may maintain a daily check on his progress. And it has the virtue of infinite patience in permitting a child time to master problems which may be difficult for him.*

These reforms are appropriately, and sometimes necessarily, carried out in facilities that are different from and larger than those which now exist. Few primary or secondary school plants now permit the expansion or contraction of classroom size. Computers as aids to instruction would be economical only if they served large numbers of children.

Larger and more flexible facilities are also indicated by other educational needs. As preparation for mastery of today's world becomes more complex and as we recognize the ability of children to learn at very rapid rates, the needs of schools for new materials become apparent. Libraries for elementary school stu-

* In one such effort—at the Brentwood School in East Palo Alto, Calif.— one hundred first-grade students spent a half hour each day learning either arithmetic or reading with the help of a computer. Each student worked at an individual computer-desk, consisting of a typewriter keyboard, a microphone and speaker, and a television screen. Problems appeared on the screen and the student responded by typing the answer, answering audibly, or marking the screen.

dents, audiovisual materials, and relatively advanced scientific equipment begin to be perceived as essential needs rather than as luxuries. So, too, as we recognize that children can beneficially pursue specialized interests at an early age, do other needs become apparent—needs for teachers of language, music, and art (as well as for teachers skilled in overcoming the special learning and emotional handicaps that some children have). The services of these specialists, the materials and facilities newly identified as needs, can be provided most efficiently and economically in schools that can accommodate substantial numbers of children.

To meet all of these needs, educators have begun to plan a new type of school facility, generally described as an education park. In one form appropriate for larger cities, for example, the proposals would assemble on one campus several elementary schools and a lesser number of junior and senior high schools to serve a population of 10,000 or more students.* Although such a facility would be far larger in total size than individual neighborhood schools, the plans call for the park to be divided into sub-units, organized in a manner which would avert problems of uniformity and impersonality.

Proposals for the development of education parks offer the strong prospect of reconciling interests that now appear to be irreconcilable. Although one of the major advantages of the park would be the opportunity it offers for racial and class integration, it would also offer the promise of education improved in more tangible ways for all children. Most important, by providing the means for teachers to give attention to the individual needs of students and for students to progress as rapidly as their individual capacities allow, the new schools should allay concerns that more advantaged children will be held back by the presence of disadvantaged students.

---

* Plans generally contemplate a cluster of small school buildings around a central facility, with the central unit housing special services and facilities such as libraries, lecture halls, science laboratories, health and counseling centers. One type of education park now operating is the Nova School, in Fort Lauderdale, Fla. Other plans are in various stages of development in Syracuse, N.Y., Pittsburgh and Philadelphia, Pa., Berkeley and Sausalito, Calif., and other cities.

Among other advantages of these new types of educational facilities is the opportunity for a more meaningful kind of participation by parents and other members of the community as well as by teachers. Although community control of local schools is dearly prized in the suburbs and has become the subject of hot controversy in the inner cities, it is submitted that with schools organized into very small units, there are few choices of any consequence that the community can make, even when it is given a voice. In contrast, when a school has as many resources as are envisioned for an education park, a local board and community could have the opportunity to exercise influence on questions of resource allocation more significant than where a new school should be located or whether a budget increase should go for new textbooks or for a cafeteria. As educator Dan Lortie has noted, education parks can be a stimulant to diversity and choice:

> As in the city, a denser population leads to greater variety in human relationships and greater diversity in the creation and flow of ideas. Cities, not villages, spawn civilizations; choice among alternatives and cultural riches occurs where ideas and persons mix freely in diverse relationship. Thus the educational complexes, if properly used, could produce a higher culture within the school.[22]

It is not being suggested in all of this discussion that advances in technology and new educational concepts will *inevitably* result in improvements in race relations or in the education of the black poor. Some suburban communities may decide, for example, that many of the educational innovations noted can be had without enlarging the size of schools and that they are willing to sustain the additional costs and inefficiency in order to maintain their exclusivity. Even if it is determined to enlarge the size of schools to achieve economies of scale, suburban communities may decide that this is best done by cooperative arrangements with their affluent neighbors rather than with central-city school districts.

What *is* being said is that if the will exists to improve opportunities for the disadvantaged and to better race relations, technology and innovative thinking may help us to overcome hurdles which now seem large or insuperable.

Economic Gain and Shifting Interests

Earlier in this chapter it was noted that no convincing case could be made that the economic well-being of the mass of citizens requires affirmative solutions to the problem of racial deprivation. But if this is so, it is also true that there is no immutable economic interest in maintaining black people in a subordinate status. The few who derive direct financial gain from the practices which keep Negroes powerless and dependent are generally marginal operators, such as slumlords, real estate speculators, and ghetto merchants, whose influence in the body politic matches their tenuous economic status. And while many receive indirect benefits from practices of racial subordination (in the absence of job competition and in the inequitable distribution of services, for example), as long as the nation has the capacity for economic growth, there is the prospect that these practices can be ended without producing major conflicts of economic interest.

In this relatively neutral economic situation there is broad scope for political initiative. And in a society as complex and pluralistic as our own, there is the potential that even small changes in policy may produce realignments of economic forces which in turn may lead to more significant results.

Recent policy developments in the field of housing provide an illustration of this process and of its promise. Until quite recently, whatever impetus there was behind efforts to meet the needs of people of low income for adequate shelter came principally from people motivated by altruism. The lagging pace of the public housing program provided testimony to the fact that good intentions were not enough. In early 1968, however, the Johnson Administration presented to the Congress a housing package which contained some new elements. In addition to continuing and expanding existing programs, the bill proposed two major new programs to subsidize home ownership and the rental of private housing by people of low and moderate income. In each case, the legislation allowed for respectable profits for builders who would construct homes eligible for the new subsidies. And with little fanfare, the Administration also proposed to eliminate the veto power that previous legislation had given suburban governments over the location of low- and moderate-income housing within their borders.

That the Housing and Urban Development Act of 1968 passed the Congress with relative ease can be attributed in part to the support of builders who recognized its potential for providing a new market and new profits. But enactment of the law did not remove all of the obstacles to the development of these new markets. While suburban governments no longer had a direct veto power over proposals to locate low-income housing within their borders, they still retained in local zoning controls what amounted to the same thing. As long as zoning boards had authority to prescribe minimum lot sizes and floor areas and maximum densities, they could effectively prevent builders from constructing houses that would be eligible for Federal subsidy.

The reaction of the housing industry to this remaining barrier was interesting. Through their trade association, the National Association of Home Builders, the builders urged that Federal restraints be placed upon the power of suburban governments to use zoning controls as a bar to low-cost housing. Attacking the fairness of permitting suburbs to pick and choose among Federal subsidy programs, the builders said that assistance should not be made available for the construction of highways or other facilities that suburbs regarded as desirable unless they were also willing to meet their responsibilities for providing shelter to low-income people.

Previously, this kind of forceful Federal action had been urged only by a few civil rights advocates (including a handful of builders) and had been rejected by many people as too radical. Clearly, the proposal's newly attained respectability among conservative homebuilders was made possible only by providing economic incentives for them to embrace it.

It is still too early to tell whether the enlistment of new forces in the battle against exclusion of the poor through land-use controls will result in victories. Nor is it possible to say that the development of similar strategies in other areas will pay sure dividends in meeting the needs of the black and the poor.

But it is a hopeful sign to observe that ideological principles that have been a barrier to progress are not etched in concrete, that our society is still fluid enough to permit realignments and redefinitions of interest, and that with imaginative planning some of the special interests that have so often worked against the needs of disadvantaged minorities may be enlisted as their allies.

Conclusion

To sum up, no neat balance sheet can be drawn to weigh the probabilities of social change. No data fed into a computer will tell us whether we are capable of renewing ourselves and our society.

We have said with Myrdal that belief in the American creed of justice and equality can be a powerful force for social change. But with the abatement of some of the most blatant racist practices, achieving the understanding of injustice that is necessary to mobilize conscience has become an extraordinarily difficult job.

Observing that conscience can be effective as a catalyst only when allied with other interests and values, we have concluded pessimistically that self-interest narrowly defined need not impel affluent white Americans to respond affirmatively to the needs of the black and the poor. Proof is already at hand that the economic well-being of the mass of citizens is not jeopardized by the continued poverty and degradation of a relatively small minority. And there is more than a suspicion that threatened disorder is more apt to be met by repression mixed with half-measures designed to appease than by fundamental reform.

But this pessimism must be tempered by a recognition that there are broader if less definable interests and values that are menaced by continued injustice and neglect. Whatever values the cities have as centers of choice, culture, and diversity can hardly be preserved without a genuine effort to provide opportunity for their inhabitants. While it cannot be said that these values are widely or deeply held, there is some encouraging evidence that more people are beginning to respond as the threat to the city becomes clearer. There is, moreover, strong evidence of dissatisfaction with the status quo on the part of groups other than those most disadvantaged. Working people, who stand between the affluent and the poor, are rightly aggrieved that they are joint victims with the Negro of urban neglect and that they alone are asked to shoulder the burden of the few small steps toward social change that are undertaken. Many privileged young people, while lacking prescriptions, are dissatisfied with the current order not simply because it visits injustice upon minorities but because it threatens their own concepts of a rewarding life. And even among the affluent in suburbia there are signs of discontent—the bare beginnings of a recognition that communities built upon the premise that the problems of the world should be excluded rather than mastered cannot provide real satisfaction or security.

There is in this prevalent discontent and alienation a very real danger of heightened racial conflict, of nihilism, and of a devaluation of the rule of law. But there is a promise too—that if the right kind of political leadership emerges, discontent can be channeled toward a restructuring of urban society in ways that will reconcile interests and better satisfy the needs of all.

For, if we have concluded that narrow self-interest does not compel the majority to seek solutions to problems of poverty and discrimination, it is equally the case that no rational interest bars the way to a solution. It is true, of course, that needed investments to provide jobs, training and economic security, and to improve education and housing will require a substantial reallocation of resources. But (as will be shown in the next chapter) this can be accomplished without imposing a Spartan existence upon affluent citizens.

Nor would the opening of access to jobs, housing, education, and other services throughout metropolitan areas jeopardize the fundamental desires that have motivated the suburban migration. These, it is generally agreed, have been desires for more comfortable living space and privacy, and for a cleaner, healthier, and more attractive environment for raising a family—drives which have prompted outward migrations not just in contemporary America, but throughout history in urban communities everywhere.[23] As recently as thirty years ago when poverty was still widespread and affluence limited to a relative few, it might have been impossible to accommodate within the same community the interests of the poor in better housing, schools, and services, and the interests that led the affluent to seek refuge in suburbia. But now the situation is almost reversed, and there is no reason why a policy of providing access to suburban communities, if combined with policies of renewing the central city and of establishing new towns and cities to accommodate growing populations, would entail a sacrifice of basic interests in living space, privacy, and a healthy environment.

If, however, opening access to suburban communities can be reconciled with these tangible interests, it would clearly clash with another dominant theme of suburban life, the drive for social status. A realistic policy of providing opportunities for Negroes and poor people throughout metropolitan areas would not insist upon total racial and economic integration. Dealing necessarily with communities that already exist, it would obviously permit a good deal of economic segregation in housing arrangements. It would recognize, too, that even with strong enforcement of fair housing laws, some self-segregation along racial and ethnic lines in housing and in social contacts would inevitably persist. But any meaningful policy of providing choice and access inevitably would entail a sharing of public services, most importantly the public schools. It would also require political integration of community life—a willingness of all groups to meet on a basis of equality, to give all interests a fair hearing, and to reach community decisions by a process which takes into account the need of all.

For this to happen, a large number of Americans would have to be ready to forgo the rewards of social status they receive from living in communities that are racially and economically exclusive. They would have to begin to overcome the irrational fears and mistrust that have been bred by years of racial isolation. They would have to be prepared to take the risk that satisfactory substitutes for social status could be found in the achievements of new kinds of communities where problems are met rather than evaded.

Lastly, we have noted that if the will to change otherwise exists, technology and the profit motive, which so often have been used as swords against the black and the poor, could well become tools that would help to serve their needs.

And so, in the end, we return to all of the contradictions which have marked our history and the American character.

Tocqueville chronicled in detail the brutality of the white settler toward the American Indian and, while predicting the end

of slavery, foresaw continuing subordination of the black man.
Yet he was still able to summarize as follows the beliefs and
principles that held the United States together:

> They have all a lively faith in the perfectibility of man, they
> judge that the diffusion of knowledge must necessarily be advan-
> tageous, and the consequences of ignorance fatal; they all con-
> sider society as a body in a state of improvement, humanity as a
> changing scene, in which nothing is, or ought to be, permanent;
> and they admit that what appears to them today to be good, may
> be superseded by something better tomorrow.[24]

Myrdal, who exposed himself and his readers fully to the evils
of the caste system in the South, was still able to conclude:

> Behind all outward dissimilarities, behind their contradictory
> valuations, rationalizations, vested interests, group allegiances and
> animosities, behind fears and defense constructions, behind the
> role they play in life and the mask they wear, people are all
> much alike on a fundamental level. And they are all good peo-
> ple. They want to be rational and just. They all plead to their
> conscience that they meant well even when things went wrong.
> Social study is concerned with explaining why all these potentially
> and intentionally good people so often make life a hell for them-
> selves and each other when they live together, whether in a fam-
> ily, a community, a nation or a world. The fault is certainly not
> with becoming organized *per se*. In their formal organizations,
> as we have seen, people invest their highest ideals. These insti-
> tutions regularly direct the individual toward more cooperation
> and justice than he would be inclined to observe as an isolated
> private person. The fault is, rather, that our structures of organ-
> izations are too imperfect, each by itself, and badly integrated
> into a social whole.
> . . . With all we know today, there should be the possibility to
> build a nation and a world where people's great propensities for
> sympathy and cooperation would not be so thwarted.[25]

America is in countless respects both a better and a worse
place than it was when Tocqueville wrote in the 1830s and when
Myrdal wrote in 1944. Perhaps all that can be said with certainty
is that, for the first time, all of our problems are out in the open
and we must now decide either to realize the American dream
or abandon it; the aggravated state of relations between the races
will permit no intermediate course.

8

STRATEGIES FOR CHANGE:
TOGETHER *AND* AUTONOMOUS

HOPES THAT THIS COUNTRY will act effectively to eliminate racial deprivation and urban decay must be qualified by a recognition that there is now scant evidence that the majority of Americans is committed to seeing the problems solved. The decline of the cities and the conditions under which many black and poor people live may be widely deplored, but there is as yet little support for remedies that would require major new commitments of resources and significant changes in American institutions.

To make matters worse, prospects for generating the political will necessary for major reform are dimmed by the fact that the ranks of those who advocate change are torn by disagreement over means and ends. This dissension, perhaps greater than at any time in recent history, extends even to a definition of the broad objectives to be sought by disturbing the status quo.

Participation v. Separation

In general, the goal shared by the largest number of activists and reformers may be loosely defined as securing for black people and members of other minorities the opportunity "to participate fully in the mainstream of American society." This goal envisions somehow arriving at the point where those who have been deprived and discriminated against will have the full range of choice now available to most people in our society.

Free choice is the key. It means that individuals and families would have the economic, political, and psychological resources to be self-sufficient, to exercise a large measure of control over their own lives, to select their own priorities and styles of life. The objective is not equality of results or mathematical equality in the distribution of resources, but rather the elimination of poverty and of disparities that are racially based. It calls not for the destruction of a system based on competition but for its reformation so that all people will have the opportunity to develop to their full capacities and compete for society's rewards.

But the goal of full participation in American society, even as broadly defined, is not accepted by all advocates of change. It is rejected by people (not easily categorized politically but who consider themselves on the radical left) who argue in substance that our society is so corrupt that it is not worth joining. America, they say, is aggressive and imperialistic abroad, acquisitive, venal, and exploitative at home. The values of its people, as exemplified by middle class suburbia, are overly materialistic, culturally uniform and sterile, and generally distorted. Following this line of analysis, some radicals conclude that to provide black people with the opportunity to participate in the American system as it is now is to offer them nothing of value. Negroes, they argue, would be better off pursuing their own separate lines of development, organizing their communities for radical change, and shunning contact with the bulk of white society, at least until the day when it is so radically restructured as to be worthy of black participation.

It is difficult to come to grips in any practical way with these radical arguments because they constitute less a political program for change than the most deeply pessimistic view of American society. Most who adhere to it do not offer alternative objectives other than the toppling of the old order, or any strategy for achieving their goals other than the vague prospect of violent revolution at some remote point in the future. Nonetheless, some observations on the radical ideology as it relates to problems of racial deprivation may be pertinent.

It is important to note that many of the proponents of racial separatism as an end rather than a means are affluent whites, although it is true that they receive some support from a few separatist black groups. While these affluent whites and militant blacks contemptuously reject the goal of integration as paternalistic because they feel that it requires Negroes to conform to the values of white society, they engage in an even more blatant form of paternalism themselves. For, convinced as they are that their own values are morally superior, they are quite prepared to ignore the expressed desires of the great majority of black people to be a part of this society and to share in its rewards.

Time and again public opinion polls have demonstrated that a substantial majority of Negroes would prefer to live and work with whites and to have their children go to integrated schools.[1] For some, these preferences reflect a practical view that integration is the only way to obtain better schools and community facilities, while others are prompted by a belief that integration will bring about more harmonious race relations. The polls show, too, that most Negroes share the middle class strivings of white Americans; parents, for example, would like to own their own homes in the suburbs for the privacy it would provide and for the more spacious and healthy environment it would make available to their children. And, while the pull of separatism is stronger among the young, they, too, reject separatist goals and opt for integration and participation.[2]

The rationalizations employed by the radicals—that Negroes who express these conventional aspirations are "Uncle Toms" or "house niggers," or at best the innocent victims of brainwashing and exploitation—are not sufficient to mask the patronizing attitude that their own values are the only correct ones. In fact, most Negroes have concluded that there is nothing contradictory about being integrated into American society and having a sense of one's identity as a black man and pride in one's culture and traditions.[3]

At a Black Power conference in 1968, one delegate replied to separatist arguments simply and bluntly:

> Don't buy this bullshit that just because you might want some clean air and green grass for your kids, that makes you an imitation white man. Dig it, we ain't no more native to the ghetto than

the white man is native to America—fact is, if it weren't for him, we'd be back in Africa where we'd have more fresh air, open space, and green grass than anyone in the world.[4]

And Negro leaders, such as the late Martin Luther King and Charles Evers, whose personal courage and devotion to their followers are unquestioned, have consistently affirmed the goal of becoming equal participants in American society with all its faults.[5]

It is not terribly surprising that affluent white separatists should choose to ignore this main thrust of black opinion. For many, a belief in separatism is nothing so much as a means for working out personal problems. Dissatisfied with the emptiness of their own lives and apparently ridden with guilt, they choose to see the Negro as a kind of "noble savage" uncorrupted by the values of Western society. Nothing seems to satisfy their needs for punishment so well as the revelation of their own unconscious "racism" (manifested in such profound ways as their use of the term "flesh-colored Band-Aid") and nothing satisfies their need for absolution so well as winning the attention of a militant black man. To recognize Negroes more simply as Americans afflicted with the same material desires and imperfections as themselves would spoil both the illusion and any possibility of gratification.

There can be little doubt, too, that the practical effect of the radical argument that full and equal participation by black people must be preceded by a drastic change in the whole structure of American society would be to make the struggle for equal rights longer and far more arduous. The radicals would answer that this is unavoidable because any gains made by Negroes under present circumstances would be illusory and devoid of real meaning. But people who live in relative comfort should recognize that they assume a great moral responsibility in suggesting that black citizens must continue to suffer in ghetto poverty until the millennium comes. Before advocating such sacrifice on the part of others, they should be terribly sure of the correctness of their analysis.

Lastly, the radical position discounts the possibility that gains won in the struggle for Negro equality and participation might themselves have a profound impact upon other American values. A respectable case can be made for the proposition that much of the current concern about poverty, the environment, and about American values and morals was sparked by the civil rights struggle of the 1950s and early 1960s and the national stirring of conscience it impelled. If energies were now to be channeled toward a broader effort to achieve racial justice in cities, we might begin to develop communities in which black people were full participants. The mere existence of these communities, it is reasonable to assume, would help bring about a desirable transformation of other values. As Ralph Ellison wrote in 1944:

> In Negro culture there is much of value for America as a whole. What is needed are Negroes to take it and create of it "the uncreated consciousness of their race." In doing so they will do far more, they'll help create a more human American.[6]

More than a quarter of a century later the consciousness Ellison spoke of is being developed and its potential for creating "a more human American" is more than faintly discernible, but only if we are prepared to establish a single society.

This hopeful kind of analysis may, in the jargon of the political scientists, be "incrementalism"; if so, the most should be made of it.

Ghetto Enrichment v. Ghetto Dispersal

Because it addresses itself to arguments made outside the ordinary realm of political debate, much of the preceding discussion is theoretical. Not that the radicals have not had a major impact upon the political climate. Their wholesale attacks upon established institutions, particularly when accompanied by violence, have provoked an emotional backlash which at least in the short run has diminished the prospect for legislative and political reform. And by joining the radical right in embracing conspiratorial theories of government and of institutions such as universities and the media they have undermined faith in the only instrumentalities for reform that presently exist and have contributed to a general loss of confidence and paralysis of the will. Despite all this, since the radicals usually eschew involvement in the ordinary arenas of legislative, political, or community action, it is very difficult to come to grips with them on specific and concrete issues.

But if the debate between "revolutionaries" and "reformers" is often amorphous, there is a more tangible division among the reformers themselves. For, even among those who adhere to the goal of black participation in "the American mainstream" and who retain faith, however wavering, in the efficacy of the ordinary and peaceful channels for reform, there is a fundamental dispute over the specific measures for achieving their common objectives. In broad terms the two camps may be described as consisting of people who advocate dispersal of the ghetto and those who advocate enrichment or development of the ghetto.[7]

Proponents of ghetto dispersal place major emphasis on policies designed to bring black people into predominantly white institutions and communities. Thus, they favor measures to give Negroes access to jobs, housing, schools, and services located throughout metropolitan areas rather than just in the central city. Proponents of ghetto enrichment, while differing from the *radicals* in that they do not view separatism as an ultimate goal, do believe that meaningful participation by black people in American society will be possible only after Negroes have improved their positions sufficiently to enable them to meet whites on equal terms. Thus, they see separate development as a kind of "way station" on the road to full participation, and they give priority to such measures as incentives to industry to locate and provide employment in ghetto areas, support for the development of black owned businesses, and community control of schools and other institutions in the central city.

The divisions between advocates of ghetto dispersal and ghetto enrichment are not as deep as the schism between both groups and those who reject the goal of full and equal participation. Both dispersal and enrichment people are basically committed to change through peaceful political action. There is also a broad measure of agreement on the need for, and magnitude of, economic and social investments that are consistent with both strategies, e.g., the substitution of some form of income maintenance program for the present welfare system.

But there is division and mistrust between the two camps as well. Negroes who advocate dispersal are sometimes accused of being "Uncle Toms," of wanting to attach themselves to the existing order for personal profit. Whites who espouse a dispersal strategy are often viewed as paternalistic—people who want integration, but only on terms in which whites remain dominant and Negroes continue to occupy a subordinate role. On the other hand, whites who advocate a ghetto enrichment strategy are accused of offering palliatives to Negroes in order to keep them separate. And Negroes who support enrichment are sometimes suspected of seeking to capitalize politically or financially on a captive black constituency or market. And, apart from *ad hominem* attacks which become all the more bitter when they are regarded as being "in the family," there has been a strong tendency toward polarization and a view that the two positions are mutually exclusive.

Defects of an Enrichment Strategy

If either of the two strategies can be said to have the upper hand at a time when few initiatives have been undertaken to solve problems of racial deprivation and urban decay, it is the position that major emphasis should be placed upon solving problems within the confines of the ghetto. For a ghetto enrichment strategy, however costly it may be, runs with the tide by aligning its advocates at least for a period of time with those who seek to preserve the existing segregated structure of the city. Since ghetto enrichment seems the most likely course to be adopted if there is any deviation from present policies and since a decision to make major investments in ghetto areas would push the possibilities of dispersal or integration even further into the future than they now may be, the assumptions of such a strategy and its prospects for success should be examined with particular care.

(1) One of the critical assumptions of the proponents of ghetto enrichment is that the measures they advocate are politically far more feasible than dispersal or integration remedies, at least on a short-term basis. In arguing this point, ghetto development people often engage in a considerable revision of contemporary history. The *New Republic*, for example, some time ago ran a series

of articles by Richard Cloward and Joseph Alsop, the gist of which was that racial integration had been national policy for a decade and that the Federal Government's insistence upon it had not only been ineffective but had prevented the nation from meeting the "real needs" of the black and poor, e.g., by slowing the production of low-income housing, and diverting attention away from the need for massive assistance to education.[8]

The articles constituted the worst species of "newthink." While Alsop argued that in "every major northern city" known to him efforts to achieve school desegregation had resulted in a flight of whites to the suburbs and resegregation, the fact is that there were few such efforts in the North in the 1950s and 1960s. Except for the legal prohibition of southern segregation laws, there was *no* national policy of integration and very few communities undertook such policies on their own. While Cloward and an associate argued that the needs for decent housing might have been met if the Federal Government had not insisted on integration, actually the Federal Government had no hesitancy about subsidizing massive high-rise public housing developments built exclusively for Negroes in northern cities and, in some cases, even tolerated overt practices of segregation in low-income housing. In reality, the migration of whites to suburbs took place in many cities where there was no "threat of integration" or where there was only a small minority population, for reasons largely unrelated to race. And the inadequacy of government assistance to the black and poor stemmed not from an insistence upon integration, but from neglect and the absence of any political consensus supporting a major commitment of resources.[9]

None of this, of course, blinks the fact that ordinarily integration is politically a very difficult remedy to achieve. Efforts, for example, to secure a greater measure of integration in the public schools through state legislation or local action have stirred great controversy and have rarely been successful except in cases where the courts have required it. The relevant question, however, is not whether integration is presently a politically feasible remedy, but whether it is *any less feasible* than an effective alternative remedy of enrichment.

In the case of schools, for example, the issue is whether integration is less attainable politically than an effective system of "compensatory" education designed to make up for the deficiencies of a disadvantaged and segregated environment. This is a question that the advocates of enrichment have dodged assiduously. They have conceded, often grudgingly, that existing programs of compensatory education involving expenditures of an additional $100 or $200 for each disadvantaged child have rarely produced meaningful improvements in achievement. But while the implication is that if more money were spent the results would be different, the proponents of compensatory education have not been ready to spell out what the elements and costs of an effective program would be. A few years ago former U.S. Education Commissioner Harold Howe outlined his concepts of an effective program of compensatory education:

> If it is to be genuine compensatory education—education that makes up for the failings of the home and for an entire heritage of failure and self-doubt—we are probably talking about massive per-pupil expenditures, about providing a great variety of special services ranging from health and psychological care to remedial education efforts. We are talking about remaking the relationship between the school and the home, and between the school and employment opportunity. We are talking about identifying and appointing that essential person who is in such short supply—the inspiring elementary school principal. We are talking about arrangements for retraining most teachers and for putting a city's best and most experienced instructors in its ghetto schools, which now get more than their share of uncertified, inexperienced, temporary teachers. We are talking about new curricular materials, scme untried and some yet to be developed, as well as about revised methods of instruction.[10]

While no one can say with certainty what the costs of such a genuine remedial program would be, some estimates have ranged from 6 billion to 10 or 12 billion dollars a year more than is currently being allocated for education.[11]

If this is the kind of program that advocates of compensatory education have in mind, it would be difficult for them to demonstrate that it is more politically realistic than efforts to achieve integration. It would require a reversal of 180 degrees from the current situation in which many state legislatures and school boards treat ghetto schools as stepchildren to one in which they would be willing to allocate far greater resources to black schools in the inner city than presently are allocated to white schools in the suburbs. It is questionable, to say the least, that with many white city and suburban residents feeling concerned about the quality of education offered their own children, substantial political support could be mustered for a program requiring major expenditures whose potential benefits would accrue only to children in the ghetto.

It should also be clear that even if the political hurdles involved in the commitment of such large and unequal expenditures could be overcome, the benefits of a compensatory program are not likely to be available in the short run. The thousands of new teachers needed, the training and retraining of teachers to equip them to deal with the problems of disadvantaged students, the development of new curricula would not come overnight even if programs were initiated on a crash basis now.

It is not being suggested, of course, that if integrated schools were pursued as an alternative course of action, they would provide a bargain-basement remedy. It is true that, since experience indicates that an economically and racially heterogeneous student body is a key to learning, many of the remedial programs required for children who fall behind in segregated schools might never become necessary. And certainly, integrated schools would render unnecessary the expensive and usually ineffectual "compensatory" efforts to simulate a less impoverished educational environment. But many of the investments contemplated for a program of "genuine compensation," such as those for the training of teachers and the development of new curricula, would be needed in integrated as well as in segregated schools. And, despite economies of scale, the capital costs of building education parks which would facilitate integration in metropolitan areas (as outlined in Chapter 7) are not likely to be lower than those required for replacing segregated schools in cities and suburbs as they become obsolete.[12]

The *key political difference* is that, in contrast to a program providing segregated compensatory education, an integration program offers the prospect of improving the quality of education for white as well as Negro children. All children would benefit from a program that promised educational innovation and more attention to the individual needs of students through flexible classrooms and team teaching, more counseling and specialized services, improved libraries and laboratory facilities. True, many affluent suburban communities have already embarked on such efforts. But if the Federal Government were to assume a greater share of the responsibility for education, the financing of improvements through general revenues would ease the burden that many communities are now seeking to meet through the inefficient device of raising property taxes and floating more bond issues. Until national political leadership is exercised in behalf of a program embodying school integration and improvements in the quality of education for all children, no one can say whether the necessary support will be forthcoming. At a minimum, however, it seems no less promising than an effort to achieve a drastic shift of educational resources from white to black children on a segregated basis.

Similar observations may also be made about the political feasibility of other ghetto development programs that contemplate separate facilities and services for black residents. Efforts, for example, to supply better health services and recreation facilities to citizens of the ghetto may be clearly defensible on grounds that the need is greatest there and that simple justice dictates an effort to make up for past neglect. But white city residents who also suffer from inadequate services and facilities are not likely to view matters the same way. Here again, an effort to meet public needs on a segregated basis seems more likely to aggravate than to alleviate political problems. It almost guarantees a continuation and widening of the schism between black citizens and lower middle-class whites—a schism that has already produced political paralysis and great racial tensions in the cities.

(2) Even if it were assumed that ghetto development strategies were at least as politically feasible as dispersal remedies, important questions would remain. The chief issues are whether the specific remedies proposed are efficient in terms of the results that particular investments can be expected to yield and, in some cases, whether at any level of investment the measures advocated are likely to be effective.

Substantial doubts of this kind have already been raised about the likelihood of producing significant educational improvements through enrichment programs as long as public schools remain segregated by race and class. Equally serious questions may be raised about the potential effectiveness of the measures for economic improvement advocated as part of a ghetto development strategy.

These measures fall into two categories: proposals to increase the number of industrial jobs available in ghetto areas and steps to foster black ownership of business enterprises.

The proponents of action to increase the number of industrial jobs in the inner city usually recognize that all of the economic trends are running against them. For some years, manufacturers have been closing old plants in the inner city and relocating in suburban areas for a variety of sound economic reasons—higher land costs in the ghetto, inability to assemble enough land to accommodate their need for horizontal space, complex city building codes that raise costs even higher, readier access to markets in suburban locations, higher insurance rates in the ghetto, the unattractiveness of inner city areas to a firm's managers and technicians.[13] To counteract all of these factors, champions of ghetto development urge that the Federal Government provide financial inducements for industrial enterprises to locate in ghetto areas. The candid purpose of such inducements would be to compensate manufacturers for acting against their economic interests.

It should be clearly understood that such a program of financial incentives would not in any sense constitute a *job creation* program. Federal assistance would not add any new jobs to the market; instead existing jobs and others that would develop in due course without government aid would be made more accessible to Negro residents of the inner city. A key issue, then, is whether it is more efficient to solve this problem of accessibility by moving jobs to people or by moving people to the jobs through the provision of better housing opportunity in the suburban areas where industrial job opportunities are increasingly to be found.* Neither

---

* Either approach would need to be supplemented by efforts to improve transportation facilities for those low- and moderate-income workers who would continue to live far from their jobs. But no one has suggested that better transportation can serve as a substitute strategy for moving jobs or people. The problems of urban transportation systems are simply too massive for that approach to work.

program would meet the overall need for additional jobs. Each would have to be supplemented by skill training programs which would be roughly equivalent in cost regardless of which strategy was adopted. A program of providing new housing opportunities for people of low and moderate income near the site of suburban jobs would, of course, involve major expenditures. But unless the proponents of ghetto development were willing to see the continuance of intolerable housing conditions, their program of incentives to industry would have to be accompanied by substantial expenditures to provide better shelter for the poor in the ghetto. And, given the high costs of land in central cities and of rehabilitation, there is every reason to believe that such an effort would be at least as expensive as a program to provide new housing in suburban areas.[14]

Thus, the real difference in costs between a ghetto development and a ghetto dispersal program in providing access to industrial jobs would be the major expense involved in inducing manufacturers to locate in the inner city. These extra costs of following a ghetto development strategy would be in the nature of a "bribe" to industrialists and would provide no direct benefit to the disadvantaged black workers.

In addition to the inefficiency of a financial incentive program, there is also reason to doubt its effectiveness. Existing ventures by major corporations in inner city areas have not proved profitable. The Aero-Jet Corporation which opened a plant in Watts, IBM which located an installation in the Bedford-Stuyvesant area of Brooklyn, and other similar ventures have suffered significant losses in their early years of operation.[15] As Thomas Watson, president of IBM, said of the decision to locate a plant in Bedford-Stuyvesant, "a slum is normally the last place you would want to invest." IBM made its decision because "a very large company has a responsibility to society as well as to its employees and stockholders."[16]

Recognizing that few businessmen take such a broad view of their social responsibility, the major legislative proposal in this field, a bill introduced by the late Senator Robert Kennedy a few years ago, would furnish tax incentives of 7 per cent and 10 per cent on plant and equipment and a 125 per cent deduction for wages paid to low-income workers. A preliminary analysis of the results to be anticipated under the Kennedy bill found that over a ten-year period some 250,000 jobs might be located in ghetto areas at a cost of about $500 million.[17] But the analysis concluded that even with the substantial tax inducements offered by the legislation, only a small number of industries could be expected to have a greater return in the inner city than in suburban areas. And most of these were low-skill industries already located in the cities, some in ghettos.

Moreover, the use of tax incentives as the form of government assistance to industry could create additional problems. A few industries which had already decided that it would be profitable to locate in ghetto areas could take advantage of the tax incentives anyway and thus receive a windfall. Also, to the extent that tax incentives could provide a spur, they would have to be general, including the abatement of local as well as Federal taxes. Otherwise, local taxes might largely offset the advantage to business offered by a Federal tax break. But if local government provided a tax abatement, it would lose revenues needed to support other services vital to the inner city. Some of these problems might be overcome by substituting economic development grants to cities for tax incentives to businesses, but the fundamental limitation of industry incentive plans would remain.[18]

The second pillar of the economic strategy of ghetto development proponents is the fostering of black entrepreneurship. Recognizing that Negroes have been discriminated against in the past in efforts to begin their own enterprises and that they are substantially underrepresented in the business world today, ghetto development proponents advocate a great expansion in government credit and technical assistance to facilitate minority business ownership. Such a program of government assistance in the view of its partisans would not only facilitate the establishment of black-owned businesses, but would "repatriate" some of the profits that white store owners now take out of the ghetto and would expand job opportunities for Negro employees.

Unfortunately, prospects for the establishment of successful minority business enterprises on any large scale are dimmed by the contemporary facts of economic life. New retail businesses, even when well financed and competently run, generally stand little chance of competing successfully against the chains, a fact attested to by the very high rate of business failures. Relatively few industrial firms have been founded in recent years and the prospects for new enterprises except, perhaps, in a few specialized areas are not good.

Nor is it likely that the other objectives of a black entrepreneurship program will be achieved even if a number of successful businesses are started. While the notion of stemming the outflow of capital from the ghetto by replacing white store owners with Negro owners may have some appeal, it appears relatively insignificant in the light of findings that the net profits of white store owners in the ghetto are usually small, often 4 per cent or less.[19] And experience thus far with black-run enterprises does not suggest that they are likely to become fruitful sources of Negro employment. In New York, two development corporations begun in Bedford-Stuyvesant under the leadership of the late Robert Kennedy in the first few years invested about $1 million to establish 22 black-owned firms whose average potential is only 16 employees each.[20]

There are a number of variations on the basic proposals for financial and technical assistance to stimulate black-owned businesses. Some ghetto development advocates, repelled by the implications of "black capitalism," have suggested alternative schemes designed to assure cooperative ownership or other forms of community involvement. But these proposals are subject to the same basic economic limitations as the black capitalism plans. Some also introduce additional complications and problems. For example, a CORE-initiated legislative proposal envisions the establishment of community development corporations that would devote part of the profits from successful enterprises to welfare and other community services. Implicit in the plan is the highly dubious principle that the fulfillment of public needs should be made to depend upon the success of private enterprise.

All of the doubts raised here are not meant to suggest that there is no future in efforts to foster black business enterprise. There are, in fact, a number of promising ventures, the most promising being those that are not bound by artificial restraints imposed by some brands of black power ideology. In Philadelphia, for example, Reverend Leon Sullivan has added to his already considerable success in training disadvantaged workers by establishing a black-owned shopping center, "Progress Plaza."[21] The center has been designed and located not simply to serve black residents of the ghetto but white customers as well. Similarly, the prospects for some kinds of franchise operations, such as automobile dealerships, may be favorable because the franchise holder can start with the advantage of a well-known brand name and the backing and know-how that can be provided by an established company. So, too, the handful of Negro construction contractors around the nation undoubtedly can benefit from foundation and government programs to help them meet bonding requirements and acquire additional technical and business skills. Excluded and discriminated against in the past, these contractors have managed to survive and with some help could even prosper if there were an upswing in the building industry. (There is, it may be added, bitter irony in the fact that some of the most vocal advocates of ghetto development tend to overlook opportunities for helping black men who already are in business. For example, when the insurance industry implemented its much-heralded $1 billion commitment to ghetto projects—a limited-risk project at best since it dealt almost exclusively in government-guaranteed loans—it did not channel business through the people who know the ghetto best, Negro realtors and mortgage bankers, but through the correspondent banks it usually deals with.)

But, while favorable results may be anticipated from specifically targeted efforts to aid the development of black-owned businesses, the potential gains must be kept in perspective. If the ghetto were to be treated as an underdeveloped country—as it sometimes is in rhetoric—the results of such efforts might be considered respectable when compared with the progress of other underdeveloped nations. But the objective is much larger— to eliminate the disparities that separate blacks from whites in *this* affluent nation. In meeting this goal the gains that may be made by stimulating black-owned businesses in the ghetto are paltry when compared with efforts under a "dispersal" strategy to assure that black people win a place as executives, managers, technicians, and professionals in business enterprises across the land which have in the past excluded them. As economist Andrew Brimmer has said:

> . . . no matter how much investment may be made in plants and other job-creating enterprises in the ghetto, the vast majority of the Negro population will have to find employment in exactly

those firms in which the vast majority of the total labor force is employed: the large national manufacturing corporations, the nationwide commercial and transportation enterprises, the large financial institutions, and those government agencies serving the community as a whole.[22]

Accomplishing this objective is the real task.

What then may be said of the potential effectiveness of a ghetto enrichment or development strategy that aims at improving the positions of Negroes sufficiently to enable them to meet whites on equal terms? In recent years, particularly since the advent of the "War on Poverty," many useful projects have been initiated in ghetto communities—to organize tenant, credit, and consumers unions, to begin the education process at an early age and to involve parents, to establish the legal rights of the poor. Almost all have been "self-help" projects, at least in the sense that while government funds and outside resources were required, the poor were involved in improving their own lot. Where successful, such efforts have materially assisted the black poor, e.g., by reducing exploitation or improving skills, and, equally important, have provided them with some solid evidence that they need not be immobilized by feelings of powerlessness and self-doubt.

But impressive as some community action projects have been, they do not add up to a strategy for achieving parity with whites. Such a strategy must be based on accrual of the real elements of power—knowledge and skills, economic resources and political authority. Here, as we have seen, ghetto enrichment programs are sadly deficient. Plans to strengthen education within the confines of the ghetto do not appear promising. Ghetto economic development proposals cannot generate enough jobs or income to make them successful. The most likely positive outcome of continued segregation in the cities is the accession of Negroes to political office. But, as noted in Chapter 6, if continuing racial hostility is assumed, winning political control may prove a hollow victory; black political leaders may simply become receivers in bankruptcy of gutted cities. Even if hostility is not assumed, the political route in itself would not constitute a viable strategy. The trend of urban politics in most cities has been toward the increasing dispersal of influence and authority.[23] Political authority no longer furnishes very much control over jobs or other economic resources. Nor does the formal authority it provides over such institutions as public schools furnish any real leverage. The hope of making public schools a going concern would depend upon the cooperation of those who already command economic resources and these are people whose stake in the public school system is diminishing rapidly as they send their own children to private and suburban schools.

It is doubtful, moreover, whether the continued racial concentration of black people in the cities is of real benefit in the struggle for meaningful political influence and control. We have previously suggested that Negroes might exercise more influence over state and Federal policy if they were represented in numbers in several districts throughout a metropolitan area rather than confined in a few wards in the central city.[24] Other important arenas in the struggle for influence are labor unions, organized religion, and professional and business associations. In none of these can it be demonstrated that Negroes are helped by being isolated geographically; in fact it is likely that they are hampered.

In sum, then, although a ghetto enrichment strategy may ameliorate the conditions under which some black people live, there is little hope that it will be effective in eliminating the critical economic, educational, and political disparities that now separate the races. To achieve this objective, remedies outside the ghetto must be sought.

(3) A final assumption of ghetto enrichment proponents is that their strategy will ultimately lead to a single society, marked by racial understanding and harmony as well as by justice and equality. In brief, they argue that while black leaders pursue plans to improve ghetto communities, white reformers can profitably occupy their time working to reduce racism in their own ranks. In this view there is little to be lost by temporary abandonment of the goal of integration, for it is assumed that after blacks better their status and whites alleviate prejudice, everything will come together.

This hypothesis can be valid only if the other assumptions about a ghetto development strategy—that it is politically feasible and will prove effective—are also true. And apart from the doubts already expressed about political feasibility and effectiveness, there are independent reasons for questioning the view that continued separation may be a road to racial harmony.

Experience has demonstrated time and again that racial separation and racial mistrust are mutually reinforcing processes. It is the whites and Negroes who grow up in isolation who wind up fearing, mistrusting, and hating members of the other racial group. Their fears are nurtured by ignorance and they usually assume not only racial differences but differences in beliefs and values. Because of these fears, they strongly prefer continued segregation and resist efforts at integration.[25] Conversely, improvements in racial understanding almost always occur only when the barriers of segregation are broken down. Each breech in the wall—whether ending segregation in the armed forces or in factories and offices—has been attended by awkwardness and even conflict, but eventually acceptance and better understanding have been the results.

For some, the validity of these observations may be obscured by the racial tensions that now exist in desegregated schools and other institutions. But almost always, conflict is traceable to the reservoir of fears and mistrust built up by years of isolation before contact occurred, and also to the fact that many ostensibly desegregated institutions have not in truth established conditions under which whites and blacks can meet on equal terms. Further, despite the prevalence of conflict and tension, with each small victory for integration the ranks of people, black and white, who have been able to rid themselves of most of their racial prejudices have increased. And it is only because of the smaller triumphs over segregation laws and discrimination against middle class Negroes, that we have been able to confront the more difficult issues of racial practices and discrimination against the black poor.

So, here again, advocates of separate development are urging a course of action that will not achieve the objectives they espouse. White reformers cannot dispel the racial fears and hostilities of suburban communities by dealing with them in the abstract but only by providing practical experience and contact. Whatever may happen in the ghetto, all of the evidence suggests that as long as the walls of separation are maintained and isolation continues to grow, race relations will continue to deteriorate.

Defects of a Dispersal Strategy

Unlike most proponents of ghetto enrichment, advocates of a dispersal strategy have not taken an "either/or" position. While in the past, efforts to secure new economic and social programs have often been subordinated to legislative and judicial attacks on segregation, no one today argues that attention should be focussed almost exclusively on the latter types of measures. High on the priority list of almost any advocate of ghetto dispersal are increased funds for job training, transformation of welfare into an income-maintenance system, more resources for education and health care. Nonetheless, adherence by dispersal proponents to the goal of integration is still often dogmatic in character, with insufficient attention devoted to the real objectives to be sought or the major problems that must be overcome to achieve them.

One huge problem, of course, is the magnitude of the policy changes required to overcome current demographic trends toward massive segregation. In Chapter 6 it was noted that even with a slackened rate of migration of Negroes from rural areas to central cities and even with an increase in the rate of migration of Negroes from central cities to suburbs, the black population of central cities is expected to grow by about 9.7 million people between 1960 and 1985. Let us suppose, somewhat arbitrarily, that the goal set under a dispersal strategy was to have the 9.7 million increase take place in suburban areas rather than in the central city. This would mean that the Negro population of suburbia would be some 16.5 million people in 1985 instead of the 6.8 million now projected. It would also mean that Negroes would be about 12.5 per cent of the total population of suburban areas rather than the 6 per cent now estimated on the assumption that there will be no major policy change. (Actually, they would probably constitute a somewhat larger proportion, since any policy of increasing the housing opportunities for black families in the suburbs would sensibly be accompanied by policies designed to stem the tide of middle class whites from the central cities and to attract some back to the city.)

The goal would be modest enough. It would be to assure that a significant number of Negroes have access to a share of the

jobs and better services that will be available in increasingly affluent suburban communities. It would also be designed to ensure
that the black population of ghetto areas does not increase, probably a minimum condition if cities are not to become more in-
tolerably overcrowded than they already are and if there is to be
an opportunity to revitalize and integrate the city.

Yet modest as the goal is, it would require an average suburban migration of about 388,000 black citizens each year. This is
more than ten times both the rate of migration that occurred
during the 1960s and the slightly expanded rate that is expected
if no major policy changes take place during the 1970s.

It is clear that even if a massive program of providing new
housing in the suburbs and redevelopment in the central cities
were begun now it would be extraordinarily difficult to meet the
goal set for 1985. Of course, the objectives of a dispersal strategy
—providing access to jobs, schools, and services—can be partially
achieved by measures that can be implemented in advance of
vast new housing programs. Access to better-quality integrated
schools can be attained for many thousands of children by expanding present programs that permit children who live in the
city to attend schools in the suburbs. Access to suburban jobs
can be provided for black residents of the inner city by improvements in mass transit facilities specifically designed to achieve
this end. And, as stepped-up job-training programs, upgrading
of existing jobs, and access to new employment opportunities
outside the central city produce improvements in income for
Negroes, many will be able to buy homes outside the ghetto without waiting for subsidized low-income housing. Notwithstanding
all of this, the conclusion seems inescapable that no combination
of dispersal and non-ghetto enrichment programs is likely to be
sufficient in itself to end the ghetto as we know it for many years.
Major efforts will still have to be made to provide opportunities
for people where they now are.

A second set of problems is associated with the need to think
through carefully the question of how a dispersal strategy can be
made to work. As the term itself implies, a policy of dispersing
the ghetto is not necessarily synonymous with racially integrated
patterns of residence. In fact, it must be recognized that even if
fair housing laws are firmly enforced and subsidies for low-in-

come housing are geared to promote economic and racial integration, it will be a long time before there is any substantial degree of residential integration in settled suburban communities.

This is not necessarily a fatal defect, for, even in segregated suburban neighborhoods, black people may still reap the advantages of having access to good jobs, good schools, good services, and a better environment. But the prospect that there will continue to be a good deal of separation in residential patterns does point up the fact that dispersal is hardly an automatic cure. In the suburban rings of many large cities, there are now pockets of poverty inhabited largely by black people. Although sometimes geographically less remote from jobs and other advantages, these Negro citizens are often no better off than denizens of big city ghettos. And in a sense they may be said to be worse off, since their isolation in small numbers makes it difficult even for their voices to be heard in protest. A dispersal policy which might result simply in a proliferation of such small, isolated communities hardly would provide an effective remedy.

To this it may be responded that any dispersal strategy worthy of the name would work a vast improvement in the situation of black people in suburban areas. It would guarantee access to jobs and to integrated schools and provide the training and remedial help needed to make these opportunities effective. Still, doubts persist. In the suburban communities where Negroes would locate under a dispersal strategy they would inevitably be a numerical minority (as they are in metropolitan areas and in the nation) and, at least at the beginning, a relatively powerless minority.* Ultimately, of course, the hope of a dispersal strategy

* Downs maintains that the only way in the short run to obtain stable integration is to assure whites that they will remain the dominant majority. He bases his view on a belief that most people seek an environment in which their own cultural values will be dominant and that whites resist Negro entry into their communities in large part because they think Negroes adhere to a different value system. Accordingly, the only way he sees to undermine this belief is to seek integration on terms that do not threaten whites so that they can learn gradually that race is not a critical factor in cultural dominance. Downs, *op. cit. supra* note 7, pp. 1338-1341. Downs' thesis should be qualified by the observation that there are neighborhoods in the nation in which Negroes constitute a majority or a very substantial minority and which show signs of being stably integrated, at least in the

is that providing access to jobs, schools, and a decent environment will enable people to acquire the knowledge, skills, economic resources, and political know-how to overcome their powerless condition. Ultimately, too, the affluent white majority, through exposure and contact, will learn to deal with Negroes on terms of equality, and to avoid subtle as well as overt forms of discrimination. But this is over the long haul. In the interim, there is a real danger that black people in suburban communities may find their interests on many matters subordinated to the interests of the white majority. In some areas, such as resistance to the needs that Negroes perceive for changes in curriculum and special programs in desegregated schools, the exercise of white dominance may impair the effectiveness of dispersal remedies.

There is no magic cure for this problem simply because there is no way to decree social equality and an end to white prejudice overnight. But there may be ways to mitigate it. Recognition that early contacts between affluent whites and less advantaged blacks will not be on equal terms suggests that steps be taken to protect the interests of the new black community. This may mean not simply that a dispersal strategy should be accompanied by job training, remedial education programs, social services, and other non-ghetto enrichment programs, but also by a transference of some of the community action techniques that have proved effective under the poverty program. These would include the establishment of legal service and neighborhood action organizations to assert the rights of the less advantaged community in the councils of suburban government (just as they have done in the inner city) and the formation of tenant and consumer unions and cooperatives to represent and strengthen the interests of the community on particular problems. This approach, of course, would increase the likelihood that initial conflicts between blacks and whites in suburbia would be marked by some degree of abrasiveness and conflict. But this would be greatly preferable both to allowing the customary relationships of dominance–subordination

---

sense that both white and black families are still moving in. But these neighborhoods are very few in number and tend to be homogeneous in terms of class. See Sudman, Bradburn, and Gockel, "The Extent and Characteristics of Racially Integrated Housing in the United States," 42 *University of Chicago Business Journal* 50 ff.

to go unchallenged in a new setting and to following a course of separate ghetto development in the vain hope that someday in the indefinite future whites and blacks may be able to meet on equal terms.

Guidelines for Remedy

Out of the preceding analysis, there emerge a few points which may provide useful guidelines in approaching specific formulas for change.

(1) Perhaps the most obvious point is that the strategies of ghetto enrichment or development and of dispersal or integration cannot be viewed in "either/or" terms. Neither strategy, if pursued alone, is capable of producing the results its adherents seek. Effective ghetto development requires a vast expansion and reallocation of public resources with almost all new assistance directed to the black poor. In political terms, the likelihood of such a course of action being adopted would be very small even if other groups in the population did not have public needs that are not now being met. Even if they were politically feasible the economic and educational remedies put forward by ghetto development proponents would not promise timely or effective help for any significant number of people. And, in any case, even if politically feasible and economically and educationally viable, a ghetto development strategy would entail many more years of racial isolation—a sure prescription for continued fears and mistrust and for a deterioration in the already bad state of relations between the races.

A ghetto dispersal or integration strategy, on the other hand, could not achieve its goal except over the course of several decades. In addition, a dispersal program of providing access to better jobs, schools, housing, and services, even when combined with enrichment programs of job training and remedial education, may not be sufficient in the short run to alter the subordinate status of disadvantaged Negro citizens. To deal with these problems, major assistance will be required to aid those who remain in the ghetto, and some of the techniques of community and political action in the inner city will have to be imported to new black neighborhoods in the suburbs.

In short, the only practical and sensible strategy is one that combines elements of ghetto enrichment and development with a program designed to disperse the ghetto and provide access to jobs, schools, housing, and services on an integrated basis.

(2) A corollary though perhaps less obvious point is that it is a fallacy to think of ghetto enrichment as the only short-range strategy and ghetto dispersal or integration only as a long-term remedy. Short-term and long-term goals must be established in each sphere; otherwise it is likely that enrichment programs will prove insufficient and that dispersal and integration will never be reached.

In education, for example, a short-term integration goal would be to achieve a significant expansion of programs under which inner city and suburban schoolchildren attend public schools together. In Boston, Mass., Rochester, N.Y., Hartford and New Haven, Conn., voluntary programs have been adopted to enroll in neighboring suburban school systems Negro students who had been attending segregated ghetto schools. In each case, the central city system pays transportation and tuition costs (sometimes with the assistance of a foundation), supportive and remedial services have been provided as needed, and special care has been taken to make the adjustment for the city children smooth and to facilitate the development of friendships.

These efforts at metropolitan cooperation have been criticized as "token" since they involve at most several hundred Negro children in each city. Critics also contend that the programs are paternalistic because they involve only black children traveling to suburbia and not white children attending schools in ghetto areas.

But all remedies that can be implemented on a short-term basis are subject to attack on grounds that they are piecemeal and unsatisfactory in other respects. If every proposal had to meet the stringent test of providing a complete solution, nothing would be attempted.

The important fact about these metropolitan school programs is that they have yielded gratifying results: black children who have participated have improved their achievement scores, white children have progressed at a normal rate, the adjustment of both groups has been good, and in some communities it has been reported that the contact provided with Negro youngsters and their parents has lessened the resistance of white adults to racial change.[26] Given these heartening results, there is every reason to expand the programs. In cities where they have been instituted, the numbers of black children participating might be increased from the hundreds to the thousands by soliciting the cooperation of suburban communities not yet involved and by adding to the enrollment in suburban districts that already are participating. And similar programs can be begun in other large cities.

All of this will not, of course, make a major dent in the racial isolation that persists and is growing in the public school systems of major cities. It will not detract from the need to identify and expand the most promising programs of enrichment and compensation for disadvantaged children who remain in the inner city. These may include programs to begin the educational process at a very early age and to involve parents in it, and to help those who have already experienced failure in the schools by placing more resources in remedial reading efforts that have produced results and by expanding new initiatives such as the "street academies" in Harlem that have had a measure of success in motivating dropouts to continue their education.

Even in combination, short-run efforts at integration and enrichment will still be piecemeal and unsatisfactory. But they can accomplish much. Successful programs of integration will not only benefit the thousands of children involved but will pave the way for a much larger measure of integration by overcoming the fears and resistance of white parents. Successful programs of enrichment or compensation can help dispel the mood of utter hopelessness that pervades the public school system. Taken together, they can build some momentum toward the day when longer-range and more lasting solutions (new educational facilities which permit both a large measure of integration and utilization of the best techniques for meeting the individual needs of students, the coming of age of a new generation of teachers better equipped to motivate and teach disadvantaged children) can be put into effect.

(3) Once it is recognized that the only workable strategy is one that combines elements of ghetto dispersal and ghetto de-

velopment, means must be found to rationalize and reconcile the programs that have been advanced in each area.

One rough but critical test that must be applied to ghetto development programs is whether they will defeat prospects for integration and participation by entrenching the ghetto for many years to come. Many enrichment or development efforts present no problem in this regard. For example, large-scale investments to improve the quality of teaching in ghetto schools and to reduce the pupil-teacher ratio, in addition to being desirable and necessary, do not interfere in any way with efforts to achieve integration.

But a decision to make a major investment in building new school plants in the ghetto would constitute a devastating defeat for proponents of a dispersal strategy. Once made, the prospects for obtaining resources to provide educational opportunity outside the ghetto would be reduced almost to the vanishing point. The same may be said of a decision to continue or expand the policy of building mass institutional public housing in the ghetto. And a program of attracting to the ghetto industrial plants offering low-skill jobs would, if successful, have the same kind of impact, because it would channel energies into preparing people for these jobs rather than the broader opportunities available in a metropolitan job market.

Adoption of policies of this type would be the height of folly. In the apt phrase supplied by Kenneth Clark, it would be a recipe for "embalming the ghetto." Life might be made slightly more comfortable for some ghetto occupants and a few might be provided with the means to escape to a better life, but the great majority would be sealed inside, their status as second-class citizens assured for the foreseeable future.

Fortunately, application of a test of effectiveness leads to the same conclusions about the inadvisability of pursuing these kinds of ghetto development remedies. There has been enough experience with building segregated schools and huge public housing projects for anyone to conclude that these are costly and largely ineffective investments for which alternatives must be found. Application of economic criteria to determine the best "business" uses of scarce inner city land will result in a judgment that ordinarily it makes far more sense to devote such land to the construction of a medical center or a state office building than to an industrial plant. And such a judgment would be consistent with a policy of providing more varied and useful job opportunities than could be achieved by focussing only upon an expansion of industrial jobs in the ghetto. Similarly, the only kind of an entrepreneurship program that makes economic sense is one that would enable black businessmen to compete in the broader market rather than just for Negro patronage in the ghetto.

Lastly, sufficient energy and attention devoted to reconciling ghetto dispersal and enrichment strategies may permit not only the development of parallel programs of action that do not impede each other, but also unified approaches that combine the best elements of each program. For example, on the face of it, few objectives seem as irreconcilable as those of achieving integrated schools and of achieving a greater role for black parents in the running of the public schools. But whether the goals are actually in conflict depends upon the true intent of efforts to secure greater community participation. One group of proponents of school decentralization and community participation sees the effort as part of a larger campaign for black people to capture control of their own institutions. In franker moments, these advocates come close to admitting that the schools are merely pawns in a larger game and that they do not measure the success of their efforts by whether there are improvements in the academic performance of black children. If political control of the ghetto is the objective of community participation measures, they clearly are irreconcilable with integrated schools. But such an objective should be rejected as requiring the sacrifice of the interests of children no less surely than present educational practices of neglect and discrimination.

There are, however, others who state a legitimate and indeed a compelling case for decentralization and increased participation by poor parents. They trace the school system's failure to respond to the needs of ghetto children to the fact that it is not accountable to parents and the community. While affluent suburban communities have been able to exercise the leverage necessary to bring about educational improvements, parents in the ghetto have had no voice in educational affairs. By giving them a voice, by bringing school administrators closer to the community, it is suggested that parents can be given a real stake in the education of their children and school systems can be made more responsive.

Stated in these terms, there is nothing necessarily inconsistent in the goals of integration and a decentralized school system in which the community has a greater role. It all depends on how the community is defined. In Rochester, for example, Negro parents who lived in the inner city but whose children were attending suburban schools told the Commission on Civil Rights that they had never before had as much influence in educational affairs. Thus, if the community is defined broadly enough, solutions may be found that encompass both integration and a decentralized system which allows broad scope for parent initiative and innovation.

Such an effort is being made in the Boston area. With foundation assistance, a new school has been established in the Roxbury-Dorchester area and placed under the jurisdiction of state education authorities rather than the central city bureaucracy. Although designed principally to serve the needs of low-income black children, the school has achieved a measure of racial and economic integration by attracting middle-class white students from a wide area. At the same time, parents, both black and white, have been given an important role in the school's decision-making process. While it is still too early to assess results, this is precisely the kind of unified approach that should be expanded and tried elsewhere.[27]

(4) Finally, wherever possible, efforts should be made to shape remedies in a manner designed to attract broad political support by appealing to the positive self-interest of urban whites as well as to humanitarian instincts.

We have suggested that measures to provide educational opportunity for Negro children may draw wider support if made part of a single program to improve the quality of education for all children. While such a program would be costly, it can be made less burdensome to taxpayers if financed through Federal income taxes than by the present method of relying heavily upon regressive and inefficient local property taxes. So, too, if remedies are framed properly, it should be possible to impress upon less affluent white city dwellers that the most sensible way to deal with their concerns is to make the alleviation of poverty and discrimination a metropolitan responsibility and to open up opportunity throughout the area.

Similarly, we have suggested that there are appropriate incentives that may be offered to private industry to enlist business support for remedial action. So, for example, Federal subsidies for the construction of low- and moderate-income housing can give the building industry an incentive to join in the battle against suburban zoning laws. Anthony Downs has provided other illustrations of how business interests may be appealed to in a positive manner.[28]

Needless to say, making this approach work will not prove easy. But it is far more satisfactory than the appeal to negative interests that marks much of the present discussion of urban and race problems. What is being said widely and not very subtly is in effect: "We must provide some assistance to Negroes so that they will stay in the ghetto and not be violent." This appeal, as we have tried to show, is defective on two counts: it is morally wrong and it will not work. An approach based upon a mixture of moral concern and an appeal to more positive self-interest just might prove to be workable as well.

9

ELEMENTS OF A PROGRAM

IF THE NATION is at last to come to grips with its problems of deprivation and discrimination, it is clear that solutions must be sought in all of our institutions and at every level of American life—in states and cities as well as in the Federal Government, in business and industry, labor unions, universities, the church, community organizations, and in the action of individuals. But as we have sought to demonstrate throughout this book, the *sine qua non* of any successful program is action by the national government. Our political system is so structured that those who are poor and discriminated against generally have a better chance of being heard by their national leaders than by any other level of government, and—even if this were not so—only the national government has the wherewithal to respond to their needs.

While the success of any national program depends ultimately upon the efforts of local governments, organizations, and citizens in communities throughout the nation, only the Federal government can establish the conditions that will make it possible for local efforts to be effective. In this section, then, we confine ourselves largely to a specification of some of the critical actions that must be taken collectively by citizens of the nation through their representatives as the first steps in the larger struggle against poverty and discrimination.

It should also be noted that while our focus has been on the cities, any program to assist people in the cities must reach far beyond present urban boundaries. For example, even if it were possible to move immediately to expand economic opportunity in central cities, such a step taken in isolation would be self-defeating, for it would undoubtedly precipitate a greatly increased migration of poor people from rural areas to the cities. Accordingly, many commentators have urged that the Federal Government embark on a conscious policy of influencing national urban growth, in large part by stimulating economic development in non-metropolitan areas, particularly in the South. Although still on a relatively small scale, such economic development is taking place, but black people are often excluded from its planning and from a fair share of the jobs and other economic benefits that result.[1] The critical task of the Federal Government is to put an end to these discriminatory practices both in existing economic development efforts and those that may result from expanded government assistance. Otherwise, the establishment of a "national urban growth policy" will prove a hollow victory indeed, one that will defeat the desires of a great many black people to remain in the South and that will widen the racial gap.

Similarly, programs that involve investments in human resources can only be effective if they are placed on a national basis. As long as the South continues to lag far behind the rest of the nation in the education of black children (and whites as well), major problems will remain in seeking to provide opportunity for migrants to the cities. So, in addition to direct actions to meet the crisis in urban education, the national response must include efforts to bring education in the poorest rural states of the South up to a minimum level of performance.

The need for a national urban policy is further illustrated by the inevitable growth of new towns and communities. Recognizing the population pressures on the cities, private developers have already embarked on the planning and construction of whole new communities, some contemplating populations of 100,000 or more. With the Housing Act of 1968, the Federal Government entered the field of assisting new town development and as such developments proliferate and become more ambitious, government involvement will surely become more extensive. Until now, few new town planners have taken steps to assure that opportunities will be provided for members of minority groups. Only Columbia, a community being built between Washington and Baltimore, has a substantial number of black families, and even there the opportunities are largely confined to those who have achieved middle class status. Thus, if these communities are not to become new islands of privilege and affluence much like the suburbs, the Federal Government must require that homes and jobs be made available for people whose incomes are low and who are members of minority groups.

In short, then, solutions to what we call urban problems are dependent upon the establishment of conditions of equality and opportunity in the nation as a whole.

Lastly, it should be added that only if a *concerted* attack upon poverty and discrimination is mounted is there a real chance of success. In this chapter, we focus upon measures to provide employment and economic security, equal educational opportunity and decent housing in a suitable environment. These are the critical points where effective government intervention can make a real difference in the life of an individual and can break the cycle of dependency and poverty that threatens to make this a nation with a permanent underclass. But measures in these areas can hardly be separated from others—e.g., to improve the administration of justice and provide physical security for city residents, to extend and improve the delivery of health care services to all citizens—that are also essential if cities are to become places where people can live in harmony. Certainly, priorities must be established, but ultimately an investment of adequate resources in all that is deemed important will prove less costly than a continuation of the piecemeal approaches of the past.

Employment and Economic Security

Two basic approaches are necessary to deal with the poverty and deprivation that still are the lot of many citizens and that afflict black city-dwellers with disproportionate severity. One approach is to deal much more effectively with all of the impediments that still bar some people from productive employment—

barriers such as racial discrimination, a lack of training and education, the inaccessibility of jobs. The second is to make up for income deficiencies through direct cash payments to the poor; more specifically to replace the present public assistance program with one that provides more adequate assistance and reaches all people who are in need.

Of the two approaches, the second is far more controversial because it is bound to conflict at certain points with the American work ethic and because, while both approaches are costly, the second calls more directly for a redistribution of wealth from the more affluent to the poor. But an employment-oriented strategy alone is not sufficient because it will take several years before many people benefit from it and, in any event, cannot help people who are unable to work. And, apart from these simple moral considerations, it must be recognized that a direct cash subsidy program is necessary if employment-oriented measures are ever to be effective. For the child who is born to poverty and who grows up without adequate food or medical care, all of the schooling and training an employment-oriented approach can offer may not be enough.

The current discussion about what structures and mechanisms should be established to reform the welfare system involves many complexities.[2] Without attempting to grapple with all of these, the following are suggested as the essential elements of an effort to replace present welfare programs with an income maintenance system that is more humane and effective. Such a system should:

• *Establish a national standard of assistance and full Federal financing.* A person's right to the necessities of life should not continue to depend upon the accident of his place of residence and upon the variations in the wealth and social conscience of the governing bodies of fifty states. A national standard of assistance would also remove whatever incentive the present system may now provide for people to migrate to areas where assistance levels are relatively high—what some people regard as mindless national migration policies that draw people to large industrial cities in the North without providing them with the opportunity for employment.

• *Establish a level of assistance not below the official definition of poverty.* The current poverty standard is about $3,500 for a family of four. If children are expected to have a reasonable chance in life, this would seem to be the minimum that is required. It is in fact well below government definitions of the minimum budget required for the *well-being* of a family. To some extent, this deficiency would be compensated for by the continuation of subsidies for medical care and housing for the poor. (Housing assistance in the form of interest-rate subsidies and rent supplements must be continued even after an income maintenance program is enacted so that the housing industry will have an incentive to build decent low-cost dwellings; otherwise much of the increased income to the poor might be absorbed in higher rents charged by slumlords.)

The Nixon Administration's welfare reform proposal would provide a guarantee of only $1,600 a year for a family of four. In addition to the obvious inadequacy of such a proposal, the cost savings that it appears to achieve are in some measure illusory. While the cost to the Federal Government would be much lower than what is proposed here, the overall difference in cost to taxpayers would not be so striking, since the Nixon proposal contemplates that the many states that now provide more than $1,600 a year would continue to supplement Federal payments under the new system. The Nixon plan thus also suffers from the defect of allowing continuing differentials in the payments made by states.

• *Be broad enough in coverage to include those who are excluded by the present welfare system—principally the working poor and families of the employable poor.* There is little argument to be made for a policy of denying assistance to people who work but whose services are not valued highly enough by employers or by society to pay them more than a poverty wage. While increases in the minimum wage and extension of the law to employees who are now excluded would tend to accomplish much the same objective, it is not a satisfactory substitute. Almost everyone agrees that at some point raises in the minimum wage become self-defeating by resulting in the displacement of marginal workers.[3]

Nor can the denial of assistance to dependents of an unemployed adult be justified, even in cases where the adult has not made every effort to secure a job. The Nixon Administration's proposal seems to embody a conflicting philosophy since it requires that even mothers of school-age children make themselves available for employment as a condition of receiving assistance. But as a practical matter, there may be little difference in the way it actually operates. Since the bill does not contemplate a major training program or the creation of jobs for untrained mothers or the establishment of the thousands of day-care centers necessary to care for their children, few mothers are likely to be denied assistance on grounds that they wrongfully refused employment. But there is a danger that by vesting discretion in local officials to determine eligibility, the Nixon program would permit the same kinds of abuses of authority that have taken place under the current welfare system. An income maintenance program, such as a negative income tax, which makes lack of sufficient income the only qualification for assistance, would be much simpler to operate and would eliminate the need for a vast bureaucracy whose function it is to investigate the affairs of the poor to determine whether they are "deserving." The advantage of simpler and less expensive operation and of eliminating the possibilities for administrative abuse may well outweigh the danger that such a system would unjustly reward large numbers of idlers.

• *Remove the disincentives to work built into the present welfare system.* The major argument against guaranteeing income in the manner suggested above is that it would violate the Puritan ethic by encouraging idleness. Much the same argument was made, of course, against the social welfare measures enacted into law during the New Deal, and the experience of more than three decades has demonstrated that the fears were unwarranted. Moreover, under any conceivable system of income maintenance, people who do not work would have little enough income and would still lack the status and respect that are so important in our society and that can be attained only by having gainful employment. To the extent, however, that a problem exists, it can be mitigated by changing the present system which thoroughly discourages work by taking back almost all of the earnings of those receiving welfare payments. Any new system should encourage work by taxing earned income at a rate substantially less than 100 per cent—in other words, by subsidizing the work-

ing poor but to a lesser degree than those who have no income.*
If, under such a system, a schedule were established allowing
benefits to be paid at a declining rate to the near-poor, it would
also eliminate the unfairness and social abrasiveness of the present system that sometimes results in welfare payments that almost
equal the salaries of low-paid working people.

An income maintenance program of the kind described would
be extremely expensive. With initial costs ranging as high as
$15 to $20 billion a year, it would require the allocation of more
resources than any other initiative to be taken against poverty,
segregation, and urban decay.[4] But it is very difficult to see how
programs of education and training can be effective unless they
are built on a base of minimum security that only an income
maintenance program can provide. And, as employment-oriented
measures begin to be effective, the costs of income maintenance
will decline. In the long run, adopting an income maintenance
program should prove far less expensive than simply continuing
an ineffectual welfare system under which poverty has been
handed down from generation to generation.

The major objective of the second approach to problems of
poverty and deprivation should be to secure the employment of
disadvantaged workers in greatly increased numbers in both the
private and public sectors of the economy. To accomplish this,
a series of initiatives are needed in both sectors to remove the
impediments that now bar many people from productive employment.

One of the chief barriers stressed throughout this book is the
physical inaccessibility of suburban jobs to people who live in
the central city. This problem can be solved in the long run by
changes in government housing policy that result in the con-

* Preliminary results of an income maintenance experiment sponsored by
the Office of Economic Opportunity in New Jersey are encouraging in this
regard. Two groups of poor people were selected, one to receive guaranteed
levels of income support with varying kinds of work incentives and the other
to receive no payments. In a preliminary report to President Nixon, OEO
concluded, "There is no evidence that work effort declined among those receiving income support payments. On the contrary, there is an indication
that the work efforts of participants receiving payments increased relative to
the work effort of those not receiving payments." See *The New York Times,*
Feb. 19, 1970, p. 38.

struction of homes for families of low and moderate income in suburban communities. But even in advance of the time when new housing policies can become fully effective, there are interim steps that can be taken to mitigate the problem. One principal step would be to establish as a matter of national policy that private employers in the suburbs shall not be permitted to justify poor compliance with equal employment laws by arguing that minority group members do not reside in the immediate labor market area. Rather, these firms should be required to seek job applicants aggressively throughout the wider metropolitan market. Instead of permitting employers to plead that workers who live long distances from the job often have poor attendance records, government should insist that suburban firms use their influence in the communities in which they are located to break down practices of racial discrimination and restraints against the construction of low-income housing. Major employers have significant leverage when they are in the process of deciding whether to locate an installation in a particular area, and they should be required to exercise this leverage on behalf of urgent public needs just as they already do as a matter of course on behalf of their own private interests. Even after they are already in a community, these firms as major taxpayers may still be able to exert considerable influence to see that the housing needs of their employees and applicants are met.

There should hardly be a need to add that the Federal Government ought to follow a like policy with respect to its own operations. But in recent years, the government, like private industry, increasingly has located installations in suburban areas, and in doing so has paid scant attention to the impact of these moves upon members of its work force. Once a clear policy is adopted, Federal agencies, too, should be able to exercise real influence in securing housing for their workers in suburban communities.

At the same time, the Federal Government and state governments as well should take care that their policies in locating installations do not add unduly to the job drain taking place in many central cities. A balanced policy of site selection should be adopted and one of the major criteria ought to be location in the central city of government enterprises that will be economic assets to the city and that will provide training and job opportunities for Negroes and other central-city residents in white collar fields. In this way, site selection policies can become an instrument for helping to revitalize the city while housing and job opportunities are being opened in suburbia.

A program of the kind described, combined with improvements in mass transit facilities specifically designed to make suburban jobs more accessible to inner city residents, could go a long way toward eliminating geographical job barriers even in advance of residential dispersal.

While jobs are being made more accessible, a strengthening of civil rights laws and enforcement is also needed to break down the remaining *racial barriers to employment*. One important way for the Federal Government to strengthen civil rights laws would be to make the sanctions already available credible by demonstrating a willingness to employ them when needed. Only by showing that it is prepared to bring lawsuits and to hold up a project until employers and unions have made every effort to recruit minority employees can the government induce the most recalcitrant segments of industry, e.g., the construction trades, to abandon their racial practices. A second aspect of a strengthened civil rights program would be the devotion of more attention and resources to the problems involved in upgrading minority employees who are already on the job. In many industries and businesses outside the South, Negroes have been employed for many years, but racial practices have restricted their ability to advance. Opening up opportunities for advancement often entails dealing with job practices that have become encrusted with tradition and complex adjustments of seniority systems in an effort to assure that justice is done for all concerned. In addition, efforts must be made to modify the unnecessary use of formal qualifications, such as the possession of a high school diploma, and of written tests as requirements for promotion as well as initial entry. In this endeavor, government can profitably enlist the assistance of enlightened businessmen who have modified their practices without ill effects to help persuade personnel officers who still fear to do so.

A third key facet of the strengthening of civil rights policy is the extension of Federal equal employment laws and sanctions

267 ELEMENTS OF A PROGRAM

to state and local employment. While minority groups are in general better represented in public than in private employment, there are many geographical areas and governmental departments where Negroes, Mexican Americans, Puerto Ricans, and members of other minorities are employed only in token numbers or excluded altogether. Since state and local government is the fastest growing field of employment, a vigorously enforced fair practices policy could make a major contribution toward meeting the economic needs of people who have been discriminated against.

Another keystone of an employment-oriented strategy is a greatly increased effort to meet the needs of the disadvantaged for *job training*. Since the Federal Government assumed a responsibility for assisting in job training and retraining only a few years ago, it is much easier at this stage to point out defects in what has been done than it is to prescribe the elements of a successful program. One clear need, however, is to expand substantially the scope of training efforts. Although current and reliable statistics are difficult to obtain, one estimate is that over the course of seven years fewer than 500,000 poor people have completed federally-assisted training programs and been placed in jobs.[5] As indicated in Chapter 4, this is far below the training effort that has been undertaken in some European countries and far short of what is needed to deal with the problems of the unskilled and unemployed in this country. Enough has been learned and achieved in training programs here to warrant confidence that an expanded effort on more than a pilot basis would be worthwhile.

Among the difficult policy issues that arise in planning training programs is the question of how responsibility should be allocated between government and private industry for the many tasks involved in a successful effort. One policy change worthy of consideration is the assignment of virtually all responsibility for direct job preparation to private industry. Attempts by government to teach specific job skills through institutional programs have often fallen short because they were unrelated to the current specific needs of industry and because without a definite job in view it has sometimes proven hard to motivate trainees. Relieving government of this responsibility would enable it to focus more clearly on the equally formidable tasks of trying to cure particular kinds of job disabilities such as the lack of basic literacy skills, alcoholism, and drug addiction, and of preparing people for public employment.

Among those who believe that private industry should assume increased responsibility for job training, a debate has been going on about what kinds of government assistance or incentives should be offered to induce employers to do the job. It is submitted here that rather than mount a new and costly program of financial aid, government should make the training of disadvantaged workers a specific obligation of private industry to be performed with little or no financial recompense. Training the disadvantaged is, after all, in the interests of private employers in meeting increasing shortages of skilled labor as well as in the larger public interests of economic justice and domestic peace in which industry should feel some stake. While there is every reason to believe that private employers would honor an obligation hammered out in discussion between government and industry, it could be enforced by making a firm's training performance a criterion in bidding on government contracts. Where individual employers were too small to conduct their own training programs efficiently, they could do so collectively through their trade associations.*

All of the measures advocated thus far—improving access to employment, strengthening civil rights laws, and expanding training efforts—would not add substantially to the numbers of jobs now available. A further essential element of any employment-oriented strategy is *the creation of new jobs in both the public and private sector*. The greatest prospects for adding to the supply of jobs available are in the government sector where the need for public servants is so large as to assure that a job creation program will not be simply an exercise in "make-work" assignments.

One approach is the restructuring of existing jobs to provide roles for disadvantaged workers. The new careers program has

* It is recognized that if this course were adopted most businesses would pass the costs of training on to the consumer. But, since the public expenditures required to deal with deprivation and discrimination are very large, it is important to shift some costs to the private sector. And in job training, as in the case of remedying industrial pollution, it does not seem inappropriate for consumers to share the burden.

already demonstrated that developing such positions as teachers' aides and health, recreation, welfare, and law enforcement assistants can not only provide useful work for disadvantaged workers but may free the professional to perform his mission better by relieving him of time-consuming ministerial duties. There are limitations to the new career approach. Attempts to extend it frequently encounter the opposition of civil service organizations with vested interests in the status quo. And, despite efforts to provide mobility, such positions do not always offer promising careers for the young. Nevertheless, an expanded effort to restructure public jobs could result in new opportunities for many people seeking to enter the labor market.

In addition, government initiatives to deal with major public needs—for improved delivery of health care services, for steps to control pollution, for low- and moderate-cost housing—can, if properly planned, result in many thousands of new employment opportunities for disadvantaged workers. Nor will advances in technology necessarily be a deterrent. As computers take over routine tasks, new positions will become available for people trained for such jobs as program analysts. If a breakthrough is made in the industrial production of housing units, a whole new field will open up for production workers. The Commission on Technology, Automation and Economic Progress has proposed an initial effort to create 500,000 new public service jobs at a cost of about $2 billion—a recommendation which seems modest and attainable in light of its estimate that there is a potential of more than 5 million new jobs in meeting the nation's social needs.[6]

The employment-oriented measures discussed thus far hardly exhaust the list of those that may be profitably undertaken. As indicated previously, such a list would also include, among other things, selective measures to assist minority-owned business and a program to aid the establishment of day-care centers to enable mothers to enter the labor market. A comprehensive employment-oriented program will, of course, be expensive. But experience has already demonstrated that it is far more effective in enabling people to get off the public assistance rolls and become self-sustaining than all of the political rhetoric, sermonizing, and restrictive welfare provisions we have tried thus far.

Lastly, it should be noted that a combined strategy of income maintenance and employment-oriented measures can be effective only in the context of fiscal and monetary policies which maintain the nation's economic growth. In fact, when the nation's economy is growing and the labor market is tight, some of the steps advocated, such as increased training for the disadvantaged and the relaxation of formal job requirements, are implemented to a degree by private industry without much government prodding. At the same time, adoption of many of the employment-oriented steps proposed—such as increased training for the disadvantaged and the restructuring of jobs—would make it possible to reduce unemployment without depriving other workers of jobs or adding to inflationary pressures.[7]

Education

In the preceding discussion of an employment strategy, the most important of all employment-oriented measures was omitted —the establishment of equality of opportunity in a totally improved system of public education. For whatever is done to train people or to make jobs more accessible or to create new kinds of public service employment, the major opportunities in the years to come will be for highly trained professionals and managers—for educators, engineers, scientists, physicians, and lawyers. If these opportunities are not opened to the children of the poor and the black, we will not have closed the gap that now separates white and black America. And for these children to have the opportunity to develop to their full capacities, nothing less than fundamental reform of our educational system will be sufficient.

In Chapters 7 and 8, we set forth many of the elements of a program to establish true equality of opportunity. Among the many things that must be done, it was suggested that the critical task of the Federal Government is to bring about a *change in the school environment* that now makes learning difficult and sometimes impossible. The best evidence compiled by educators has made it abundantly clear that interaction among students is a basic factor in the educational process and that when disadvantaged children are lumped together in ghetto schools their chances for learning are severely impaired. The same evidence and all of the lessons of history teach us that the impact upon the aspirations of children of isolating them by race in public schools cannot be counteracted by pretending that such segregation has no significance or by trying to compensate for it.

Accordingly, the first crucial step in establishing a suitable educational environment is the enactment by Congress of *a law making the racial integration of public schools national policy*. To implement this new national policy, each state should be required to devise a plan for ending racial isolation in its schools.

The states are the units of government upon whom responsibility is appropriately placed. It would be unwise for the Federal Government to attempt to prescribe any single solution or set of solutions for the nation. Many local governments, particularly big cities with substantial minority populations, do not have the means to eliminate racial segregation in their public schools. States, on the other hand, have assumed the responsibility of providing public education to all of their citizens and of establishing the basic conditions under which it is offered. They possess the authority and means for securing cooperation among local units, if necessary by consolidating or reorganizing school districts or by providing for appropriate joint arrangements between them. In framing plans, each state should be required to give full account to the desires of local education authorities and of parents, teachers, and students in the affected communities, but the ultimate responsibility should remain with the state.

Each state should have very wide latitude in devising plans to bring it into conformity with national policy. In some communities, where the minority population is small, school integration can be achieved by using any one of a variety of formulas (already successfully employed in some places) that do not require major changes in existing educational arrangements.[8] In cities with large numbers of black people, states may choose to meet their obligations in part by securing the construction of low-cost housing in suburban areas (as outlined in the next section), thus providing the opportunity for school integration. But, in addition to these measures, some states undoubtedly would want to avail themselves of an opportunity to achieve integration by building new and larger school facilities—education parks—in which it would be possible to improve the quality of education offered to all children.

As a second step, then, *a new Federal law should include programs of substantial financial assistance for the construction of these new facilities and improvements in the quality of education in all schools.* As previously noted, the building of such new schools would make possible a number of innovations that educators believe would permit more attention to the individual needs of students—flexible classrooms to facilitate team teaching and nongraded instruction, computer-assisted instruction, libraries, and language laboratories.

Such a Federal program, it is submitted, would establish the basic conditions for equalizing and improving educational opportunity. It would not, however, provide any guarantee that major changes needed in American education would actually take place. Education authorities in this country have proved far more adept at designing the hardware for change than at providing the substance that would make it useful. They have already shown, for example, that they can build modern flexible classrooms and then fail to instruct teachers in the team teaching techniques that are needed to help children. They have shown also that they can design sophisticated computer and other teaching aids and then fail to furnish educational materials any better than the primitive textbooks now used in many schools. Most important, while integrated and improved schools are of great importance, they provide no assurance that the children who attend them will be instructed by teachers who can engage their interest, who expect much of them and are able to help them fulfill these expectations.

All of these problems point to another central need in the educational process—*a drastic upgrading of the quality of the teaching profession.* This is a need that cannot be met solely by the enactment of new laws. It requires a major increase in the salary scales of elementary and secondary school teachers to place them on a par with other professionals and thus to make it possible for teaching to attract more of the most able college graduates. It requires major changes in civil service rules so that pay can be based on merit and the mastering of difficult teaching challenges rather than on longevity, and so that the ablest teachers are not drawn inevitably to administration because of the

273 ELEMENTS OF A PROGRAM

greater rewards involved (although there is also a great need for able teachers to be involved in administration). It requires other changes of values within the education hierarchy, so that talented people will be induced to turn their talents to devising useful materials and curricula rather than just to research. It requires changes in teacher training and a relaxation of rigid requirements for certification.

Many of these things can happen only if a minor revolution occurs in the ranks of the guilds of superintendents, principals, teachers, and the other organizations that together make up the education establishment. These groups must be impelled, in the interest of putting an end to educational failure, to reexamine long-held positions that have come to be regarded as vested interests. While the Federal Government cannot compel the necessary changes in educational values, there is much that it can do to influence and encourage them. It is certain that if educational needs are to be met, the Federal share of total public school expenditures, now only about 8 per cent, will rise significantly within the next few years. With these increased national expenditures, the Office of Education will have both an opportunity and an obligation to invest in vital and neglected areas of educational reform such as teacher training, curriculum development, preschool education, and effective techniques for teaching reading, and to apply rigorous tests of educational effectiveness to projects undertaken with Federal assistance (something it has not done with Title I of the Elementary and Secondary Education Act of 1965).[9]

Whether or not this is done will depend to a large extent upon the leadership furnished by the President and his Commissioner of Education. They will have to resist efforts in Congress to turn educational reform laws into pork barrel legislation and efforts by the educational establishment to staff Federal offices with representatives of their own interests. This may be difficult, but it is not impossible. During the Kennedy and Johnson Administrations, the Office of Education was infused with new blood and new ideas. There is, everywhere in the nation, including the Congress, new leadership for educational change. By giving responsibility and authority to this new generation of educators, the national Administration can accelerate the pace of reform.

In the general despair about the current state of public education, there are dangers as well as opportunities. For example, some educators, viewing the massive bureaucracies of big-city school systems as immovable, propose to improve education by dismantling the public school system. They would do so by placing funds for education directly in the hands of the consumer, enabling him to select his own schools—public or private. Presumably, this would spawn a host of new private school enterprises, introduce competition into the field of education, and provide a much wider range of choice to parents and students. In the wistful hope for panaceas, the perils of such an approach broadly applied should not be overlooked. It cannot be assumed that most of the organizations that would enter the education field under this kind of plan would make the interests of children paramount or that they would be better equipped to manage schools. Nor can it be assumed that low-income parents—whose children are supposed to be the prime beneficiaries of such a system—would have enough information to make wise choices. And a fragmentation of the public school system would run the risk of destroying any possibility that mass education could serve as a healer of social divisions—a function never more vital than now when the nation is torn by racial, class, and economic divisions.

A far more prudent course of action would be for government to encourage the kinds of competition that might strengthen rather than impair public education. Efforts like the Ford-assisted Boston project discussed in Chapter 8, conducted within the ambit of the public school system but freed from the restraints of bureaucracy, can, if successful, impel the system to change. Similarly, the talents of business in providing preparation for vocational and technical careers and the resources of universities can be enlisted in efforts that give them a far greater role than they now have, without abdicating all responsibility to them.

In addition, the most important objectives of those who advocate competitive schools could be accomplished if government insisted that existing private and parochial schools assume a greater share of the responsibility for educating disadvantaged children. The basis and need for government action to formulate rules of equal opportunity are clear. Although some token efforts have been made, most private schools in the cities still are largely segregated. Yet few such schools could survive without government assistance in the form of tax exemptions and more direct subsidies (and the pressures for increasing aid are great despite constitutional requirements of the separation of church and state). It is entirely reasonable for government to insist that a condition of any public assistance be the assumption of some responsibility for extending opportunity to children who are most in need. Those few parents who want racial exclusivity badly enough to forgo any public aid and who are affluent enough to afford it would still be free to continue as before.

One last rule of any national education program should be that *Federal assistance must be conditioned on each state's willingness to eliminate the gross inequities that now exist in the financing of public schools.* It makes no sense for the Federal Government to continue its present practice of accepting the consequences of a property tax system in which the wealthy get well-equipped schools with a small tax effort while the poor pay more and get less, and then trying ineffectually to compensate with Federal tax money. Of course, if national legislation requires each state to eliminate racial isolation in public schools, the plans, of necessity, will include some equalization of school financing. It is possible, too, that the movement in some states for state government to assume the full responsibility for financing public schools will spread, or that the Supreme Court will ultimately sustain the constitutional challenges to inequitable financing that are now pending in the courts. However it is established, the basic principle should be that equal tax efforts in school districts must produce equal revenues. Building on this base of equity, the Federal Government can then add funds to meet the special needs of students to the extent that states and localities are not already doing so.

In sum, it is submitted that while the needs for change are enormous, they can be met without either nationalizing the public school system or dismantling it. The most urgent task of the Federal Government is to set down a basic requirement of equality of opportunity and the means, e.g., racial integration, equitable financing, to accomplish it. The Federal Government must then furnish the additional resources required to improve the quality of education and establish priorities that will direct the resources to the most important and neglected areas of reform.

Under such an approach, local initiative, far from being stifled, will be liberated. If, as a nation, we can agree upon a fundamental rule of fairness and can furnish the needed resources, it may be possible to give real meaning to the concepts of "diversity" and "choice," words enshrined in the history of public education but now a mockery for so many.

Housing and the Environment

The two most urgent objectives of a national housing policy for the cities are to provide a sufficient supply of decent dwellings within the reach of people of low and moderate income, so that they may escape the deplorable conditions under which many now live, and to provide opportunities for black people and other minorities outside the inner city ghettos in which they are now isolated.

The Housing and Urban Development Act of 1968 (along with civil rights laws and court decisions) established a goal adequate to the need—the construction of 6 million units for low- and moderate-income families in this decade—and created many of the mechanisms needed to reach it. But serious obstacles remain, the most formidable being the retention in the hands of thousands of small governments of zoning and land-use controls that can be employed to thwart the construction of homes for the poor and members of racial minorities. The task of the Federal Government must be to find a means to remove these impediments to the fulfillment of the humane objectives of national policy without preventing the continued use of controls for legitimate and beneficial purposes.

To accomplish this, the Congress should enact *a law requiring each state to devise a plan to meet the needs of people of low and moderate income for decent shelter by the construction of suitable housing available without racial restrictions throughout every metropolitan area.*

As with our education proposals, states should be accorded

very wide latitude in determining how best to meet this basic condition of national policy. They could, for example, select the major agency responsible for carrying out policy from a variety of available choices. Some states might decide to create an urban development corporation similar to the one already established in New York State with authority to override local zoning and building restrictions, acquire land and dispose of it for planned private development. Others might provide for the organization of regional authorities—either with direct planning and zoning powers or with power to review and override the decisions of local units within the jurisdiction.

Nor would it be necessary for the Federal Government to stipulate more than a few minimum conditions for determining the adequacy of the state plan. One such provision should be that housing constructed under the plan must be reasonably accessible to places of employment. A second should be that in the formulation of an overall plan there must be the widest possible consultation, not simply with all of the governmental units involved, but with citizens' groups including representatives of the poor and racial minorities.

Beyond these kinds of minimal conditions, there should be a good deal of flexibility. For example, while one urban planner has suggested that in modifying suburban zoning barriers the number of low-income units in each individual suburb should not exceed 5 per cent of the total housing supply to avoid concentration, this should not be required by Federal law.[10] Such a provision might be objected to as requiring too great a scattering of needed social services or too much dilution of black political power. A plan under which some suburban communities assumed a large responsibility for furnishing housing might meet the basic national policy equally as well and be more satisfactory to all concerned. To the extent that such a plan resulted in an unequal distribution of the fiscal burden of assisting the poor, it might impel the state to regionalize the property tax base in metropolitan areas and to provide for a more equitable distribution of revenue. In any event, the wide variety of conditions in different states and metropolitan areas suggests that these are matters best resolved at the state and local levels, so long as there is compliance with the fundamental objective of according everyone the opportunity to obtain decent shelter and to have a range of choice as to where to live.

While the Federal Government should keep to a minimum the number of conditions it imposes upon states, it can, through the types of housing subsidies it offers, help to channel development in desirable directions. For example, full funding of the rent supplement program and of the provisions of the 1968 Act that furnish interest rate subsidies for home ownership and rentals can foster the development of housing that will be economically and racially integrated.* Unlike the public housing program, these programs encourage private developers to build dwellings attractive to middle-income families who can occupy them with little or no government assistance along with lower income families who receive a Federal subsidy. At the same time, the national policy suggested here would necessitate a change in the remaining provisions of Federal law that still permit suburban governments to veto the construction of low- and moderate-income housing within their borders. Rent supplements should be made available wherever builders and renters can come together, regardless of whether a local government approves. Local public housing agencies should have authority to operate in entire metropolitan areas, not just in the central cities. Otherwise, states will not be able to carry out an obligation to provide housing opportunities throughout the metropolitan region.

It is anticipated that almost all states and local governments would act in good faith to comply with a clearly defined national policy of extending housing opportunities for all people throughout metropolitan areas. Nevertheless, the Federal Government should be prepared to enforce its policy against any state or local jurisdiction that refuses to submit or carry out an appropriate plan. If a state defaults on its obligation, local governments in a metropolitan area should be given the opportunity to submit their own plan. If both state and local governments refuse to comply, the Federal Government should enforce the law by withholding from the offending jurisdictions most forms of Federal assistance, including not only grants for sewer and water lines

---

* Unless an income maintenance program is adopted, it would also be necessary to expand the programs so that they can serve the poorest families in need of assistance, many of whom are now excluded.

but transportation subsidies and government contracts. Such an enforcement policy would be tough but fair: a community that closed its doors to the poor would not be compelled to open them, but neither would it have the privilege of continuing to receive public subsidies that go largely to the affluent while refusing to assume any public responsibility for contributing to the solution of the nation's most urgent problems. (An alternative approach cited by the Kaiser Commission for securing achievement of the goals of national policy would be for the Federal Government to stand ready to act as the "houser of last resort."[11] Where state and local governments refused to act, the Federal Government would have authority to acquire land directly, superseding local zoning ordinances, and to sponsor the development of subsidized housing.)

While the Federal Government should be prepared to enforce its policies firmly, it should also extend assistance, beyond that already available in subsidized housing programs, to help communities in carrying out their obligations. Increased aid should be available to construct the public utilities and other facilities needed to accommodate new settlers in suburban areas. The Model Cities approach should be specifically applied in areas where a significant volume of new housing is being provided for the poor—a step that will benefit local governments by having the Federal Government assume a larger share of costs and that will also facilitate the needed coordination of social services. And particular attention and assistance should be devoted to programs —such as the training of tenants to assume responsibility for the management of developments—that promise to give people a stake in their new communities and a sense of confidence that they can succeed.

Beyond the development of a national system for overcoming the barriers posed by land-use controls, other kinds of action are needed to help achieve the objectives of national policy. If a large volume of decent housing is to be produced and a good portion of it placed within the reach of low- and moderate-income families without extremely high subsidies, a variety of problems must be solved. One critical problem is to find means to assure that the flow of private capital to the housing market is protected from fluctuations in the economy. During recent periods of inflation, when monetary restraints have been employed to curb spending, it has been quite difficult for housing to compete for funds. Money that does come into the housing market is available only at very burdensome rates of interest. One consequence is that subsidy programs that operate by making up the difference between the market rate of interest and a 1 per cent rate can provide much less housing when the going rate is 9 per cent than when it is 5 per cent. To cope with this, the Kaiser Commission has proposed the issuance of a new form of obligation guaranteed by the government and designed to attract investment funds from endowment and pension funds, individual investors, and other sources that do not traditionally enter the housing market.[12]

Similarly, through research and assistance, government should spur efforts to make technological breakthroughs in the industrial production of housing. To insure that these efforts will not be in vain, government must decide upon some means for replacing the maze of local building codes with uniform standards so as to make possible the production of standardized housing components. It must also find ways to deal with the inefficiencies of a fragmented housing industry by inducing cooperative efforts among builders and helping them to assemble land for large-scale projects. As previously noted, government must greatly increase its training efforts and break down union restrictions on access to the building trades if a sufficient supply of manpower is to be assured. And it should also provide incentives for state governments to rely more upon state and local income taxes and less upon property taxes as sources of revenue, thus easing the inequitable burden that the latter impose upon less affluent renters and homeowners.

To achieve the second goal of national policy—that housing shall be made available without racial restrictions—*stronger sanctions should be supplied for the enforcement of the Federal fair housing legislation.* At present, the law may be enforced only through litigation brought by the Department of Justice or by private parties, frequently a long and cumbersome procedure. Better results would be achieved if, in addition to these remedies, the Department of Housing and Urban Development were given authority to issue cease-and-desist orders and if the agency demonstrated a greater readiness to employ authority it already has to withhold benefits from discriminators. Equally as important, the energies of other Federal agencies that assist and regulate the housing industry should be enlisted in the drive against discrimination. Without seeking new laws, President Nixon can direct the Federal Home Loan Bank Board and other agencies that supervise financial institutions to see that these institutions do not themselves discriminate in lending money and that they obtain assurances of nondiscrimination from builders to whom they make funds available.

Once it is demonstrated that government is both willing and able to open up housing opportunities throughout metropolitan areas, it should be possible to take effective measures to *revitalize central cities*. There is nothing inherently evil or unworkable in the concept of urban renewal. Its great failure has been that, unaccompanied by programs to meet the housing needs of slum residents, it has made their lives worse, not better. As this is remedied, the basic conditions for successful renewal programs will be established. Slum clearance areas can become the sites of mixed-income housing, meeting the needs of those residents who wish to remain as well as attracting more affluent families. Salvageable houses in older neighborhoods can be rehabilitated and the communities themselves made attractive to people who still hold high the urban values of the past. The nonhousing aims of urban renewal can include not simply commercial enterprises but the establishment of new colleges and universities, health facilities and cultural centers designed to reclaim the central city as a magnet for all the citizens of the metropolis. There are already enough successful illustrations of each kind of endeavor to demonstrate that the goals are not unrealistic. The difference is that they will not represent islands of affluence surrounded by blight and decay, but part of a total strategy for revitalizing the city.

A final key element in a strategy to meet urban housing needs is *a government program to assist the development of new cities and towns*. Such a program would hardly constitute a short-range solution since the completion of any new community of significant size with its own jobs and economic base may take a decade or more. But the important place of new communities is suggested by one group of urban planners who have recommended an objective of building 10 new cities of one million people each and 100 new towns of 100,000 each—a program, they point out, that will accommodate only 20 per cent of the 100 million increase in population that is expected by the end of the century.[13]

New communities, moreover, present a rather special opportunity to provide the poor and black with access to better jobs, schools, and housing, and to improve race relations. As Harold Fleming has noted, social change ordinarily comes more easily in a new institution than in old, established situations.[14] For this opportunity to be realized, however, the ground rules must be made clear from the outset. *A condition of any Federal assistance to new community development must be that the community will assume a proportionate share of the responsibility for meeting the housing needs of the poor on an unsegregated basis.* (This is hinted at but not spelled out in the present law which speaks of "a proper balance of housing for families of low and moderate income.") Otherwise, there is a real danger that new communities, like many suburbs, will become enclaves of affluence, contributing to the problems of the cities rather than to their solution.

As in the fields of economic security and education, the costs of a housing program genuinely designed to meet the need would be very substantial. One commentator has calculated that it would require the expenditure of $26 billion over the course of the next decade to provide adequate subsidies for the 6 million families in need of assistance to obtain better housing.[15] This figure for housing subsidies would be significantly reduced if the incomes of the poor were upgraded through the income maintenance and job programs proposed earlier. But this reduction would be overshadowed by other costs that would accompany housing subsidies—expenditures for upgrading public services and the environment in the suburban areas where new housing would be built, for urban renewal and for new community development—all of which the Federal Government would contribute to substantially. In addition, the job of bringing about in a decade the needed institutional and technological change of a housing industry that has lagged far behind the times is a monumental one.

But while the task is formidable, it should not prove impossible. What is required, as Downs has noted, is that the share of the gross national product invested in housing rise from its present proportion of 3.3 per cent to about 5 per cent.[16] This is a percentage that the nation has achieved in the past and one that is certainly not out of line in any rational scheme of priorities. The investments needed may also be balanced against the financial and social costs of dealing with ill health and the other consequences of slum housing, and against the "sprawl tax"—the wasteful expenditures for overextended transportation and community facilities—that is the price paid for a lack of planning and for zoning controls unrestrained by any concept of the public interest. And, while the institutional and technological problems should not be underestimated, mastering them should hardly be beyond the reach of a nation which fulfilled its promise of placing a man on the moon in less than a decade. What is required, of course, is the commitment to do the job.

Can We Afford It?

A rough estimate of the price tag for carrying out the preceding proposals in education, housing, employment, and economic security is that it would add some $45 to $50 billion in expenditures to the present annual Federal budget of about $200 billion. Thus, it is reasonable to ask whether—even if the necessary commitment to change can otherwise be obtained—the nation and its taxpayers are affluent enough to pay the price.

One partial answer is that in some small measure the projected increase in expenditures does not reflect a rise in total government spending but only in expenditures by the Federal Government. In other words, to the extent that a recommended annual increase of $6 to $10 billion in Federal spending for education reflects our view that the national government should assume a greater share of the total responsibility for financing public schools, it would mean simply a shifting—not an increase—of the burden on the taxpayer. But this is hardly a satisfactory answer, for a reallocation of financial responsibility from state and local governments to the Federal Government accounts for only a small part of the projected increase. It also will be far outweighed by demands for additional measures to meet other aspects of the urban crisis—

measures that will require greatly increased expenditures by all levels of government.

One such demand is for more resources to improve the administration of justice. Despite all the campaign rhetoric of the President and his Attorney General, there is a growing realization in the Nixon Administration that efforts to overturn court decisions protecting civil liberties and to institute repressive measures such as preventive detention, even if successful, are not likely to result in a significant abatement of the crime rate. To have any hope of stemming crime, there must be (in addition to measures attacking its roots) an increase in the number of local law enforcement officers and improvements in their professional training and salaries; efforts to deal with judicial delays by expanding the numbers of judges and court personnel and improving court procedures and facilities; an upgrading of correction facilities and a genuine effort to make rehabilitation more than a catchword, something that will require many more professionally trained people and more halfway houses, work-release programs, counseling services, centers for the treatment of narcotics addiction and alcoholism. All of this will require an expansion of the law enforcement assistance programs recently begun and more expenditures by both Federal and state governments.

Similarly, the belated recognition of the pressing needs to create viable systems of mass transit in the cities and to attack pollution of the environment means an increase in Federal assistance under programs recently begun in these areas. And it is also inevitable that aid to higher education will increase at all levels of government if the need for trained manpower is to be met and if the dream of extending full opportunity to young people throughout the nation is to be preserved. All of these are legitimate, indeed urgent claims upon government that, together with the housing, education, employment, and economic security programs previously proposed, could raise annual Federal expenditures by $75 billion or more.

Where is the money to come from? There are three major possibilities: (1) a reallocation of national priorities that would reduce expenditures for defense and other programs and apply savings to an attack upon poverty and racial deprivation; (2) a determination to use the "fiscal dividend"—the additional Federal revenue generated by normal economic growth less the unavoidable expansion in Federal expenditure stemming from rising wages and prices—for these purposes;[17] (3) a determination to increase revenues by raising taxes.

The most promising area of savings in the present Federal budget is, of course, a reduction in the massive amounts now spent for national defense. It has been estimated that some $20 billion of the more than $70 billion annual defense budget represents the cost of the Vietnam war.[18] But an end to the war is not likely to result in a $20 billion reduction in expenditures since military needs that have been deferred along with general increases in costs are likely to claim a significant portion. Any real hope for a significant decrease in the military share of the total budget must rest upon a determination not to undertake major new weapons' system programs, to stretch out those already being financed, and to reduce the size of the armed forces. Fortunately, respected defense experts whose views are not predicated on an assumption of Soviet benevolence are saying that these things can and indeed must be done in the interest of national security.[19] Accordingly, a successful conclusion to the effort begun in the Senate in 1969 to impart some rationality to military strategy could liberate several billion dollars for domestic spending. Smaller amounts could also be made available through a determination to cut spending on domestic programs that benefit only small special-interest groups or that are worthwhile but should be accorded low priority. So, for example, farm price supports could be reduced by placing a ceiling on the amounts payable to any single farmer, subsidies to the maritime industry could be cut substantially, the decision to build a supersonic airplane reversed, and spending for the space program kept at a minimum level by revising its objectives and moving back the target dates for their achievement.

The second source of funds for the programs proposed is the fiscal dividend, the growth in revenues that existing tax rates will yield in a prosperous economy (adjusted for increased costs). Assuming a generally high rate of employment and economic growth, it is anticipated that Federal receipts will rise quite rapidly, growing by about $60 billion between 1970 and 1974.[20] A part of this increase will go to higher prices and wages and another significant part almost inevitably will be devoted to improving social security and Medicare benefits. Nevertheless, if care is taken to assure that the dividend is not dissipated on nonessential programs, a substantial portion of it could be made available for the major remedial efforts proposed.

Whatever may be done, however, to increase resources through reductions in defense and nonessential domestic spending and through careful management of the fiscal dividend, it seems clear that the needs of the '70s cannot be met without increasing taxes. It will be objected that this would place an intolerable burden on many American taxpayers. But whether this is indeed the case may be seriously questioned.

Of this nation's total expenditures, about 30 per cent is spent in the public sector (roughly 20 per cent by the Federal Government and 10 per cent by state and local governments) and 70 per cent in the private sector.[21] The proportion of national income devoted to public needs is far less than that of many other industrialized countries (and on domestic needs the gap is even greater since the United States spends a disproportionately high sum on military security).[22] It has been estimated that this nation could add some $40 billion in tax revenues to its budget and still not exceed the tax burden borne by the citizens of some European nations. And there is no economic impediment to a decision to devote more of this nation's enormous affluence to public rather than private needs.[23]

Nor is there any reason for more than a small share of the burden of increased taxes to be borne by people in the middle and lower income ranges (a share less than commensurate with the benefits they would derive from the programs that additional taxes would finance). The greatest burden should fall upon people with incomes of $25,000 or more. In fact, a good deal of revenue could be raised without increasing general tax rates, simply by closing some of the glaring loopholes that benefit affluent people. While a small start in this direction was made by the Tax Reform Act of 1969, inequities favoring the wealthy still exist in the treatment of capital gains and interest and dividend income, in special concessions to the oil, gas, and other mineral industries, in the exemptions accorded interest on state and municipal bonds, and in other areas as well.[24]

All of this may seem utopian in view of the traditionally strong resistance to increased taxes. But there has not yet been a test of what can be achieved through the exercise of strong political leadership. Surely, nothing but harm is accomplished by a President who one day attributes inflation to expenditures for welfare and education and the next urges costly new weapons' systems and money for the construction of a plane that will fly faster than the speed of sound. But what would happen if the choices were put more clearly? Would consumers prefer to see millions of their dollars spent on advertising designed to convince them that there is a difference in toothpastes or soaps that they know does not exist or on programs to feed, clothe, and educate poor children? Do most travelers really want to pay for "gourmet" dinners served on airplanes or would they prefer to pay for efforts to make their cities livable? Would businessmen respond favorably if urged to consider how many minority employees they could train out of funds saved from the cancellation of a conference in the Caribbean?

It may be that the American people are unwilling to make the same kinds of sacrifices to deal with deprivation and the disintegration of their cities that they were willing to make when the threat was external in the 1940s. But we shall never know until they are asked to make the choice.

Local Control and the Federal System

Apart from the fact that they are costly, the programs outlined in this chapter are likely to be objected to on grounds that they entail a significant enlargement in the exercise of Federal authority. Such protests will certainly come from conservatives who traditionally have found advantage in basing their opposition to social legislation on the seemingly neutral theory that national power should be strictly limited. Increasingly, however, concerns about the exercise of Federal authority are being expressed by other groups—by young people who distrust big institutions in any form, and by some black leaders who seek Federal dollars but whose notions of "self-determination" imply at least a disinterest in any form of national regulation. And beyond the con-

cerns of specific groups, there exist at all levels of society pervasive feelings of powerlessness and alienation—a quiet rebellion
against the complexity and size of modern society and yearnings
for a return to a simpler time—that give great appeal to generalized calls for "community control."

Insofar as these legitimate concerns find expression in a distrust of (or disinterest in) the use of national authority to cope
with major social problems, they stem from a misanalysis of the
reasons for governmental failure and a refusal to come to grips
with the hard questions of how these problems can be solved. As
we have argued throughout, in recent times the national government has failed to cope with racial deprivation, poverty, and
urban decay, not because it has acted strongly and repressively in
the wrong direction but because its efforts in the right direction
have been too weak. Remedial efforts have faltered not because
authority has been centralized in an arbitrary Washington bureaucracy but because authority to make basic policy decisions
has been delegated to state and local governments unresponsive
to the rights and interests of minority groups. Nor has anyone
who is worried about an undue concentration of power in the
national government been able to suggest what entity other than
the Federal Government can be made capable of restraining the
unbridled growth of private economic power and of protecting
the rights and interests of racial minorities and the poor.

Nevertheless, in a different but very important sense, the concerns that many people share about overcentralization and the
absence of community control are quite justified. In response
to the abdication of responsibility by state and local governments,
the Federal Government has been compelled to take action in a
great many areas. It has done so through the enactment of a large
number of categorical aid programs, each administered by a bureaucracy of its own. While the programs have failed to lay down
the basic rules of fair and equal participation, they have encouraged a mass of administrative regulation often applied uniformly throughout the nation and not easily adapted to local
conditions. Often uncoordinated and conflicting, these programs
virtually preclude the kind of rational planning that is needed to
serve the needs of communities. And except where the programs
are administered by people with great sensitivity and intelli-

gence, the possibility of innovation and diversity at the local level is stifled.

The dilemma then is very real. The overriding social problems of our times can be dealt with only if the fundamental policy decisions are made in Washington. Yet as long as we maintain a federal system, the effective operation of government demands an end to state and local units that are weak, inefficient, responsive principally to special interests, and largely devoid of talent and resources. The resolution of the dilemma, it is submitted, lies in the exercise of national authority in a manner that strengthens state and local government and encourages the exercise of community initiative and discretion within the broad limits of clearly articulated national policy. *What is needed is a set of national ground rules establishing the basic conditions of justice and equality under which local government can be made to work for everyone.*

This, we believe, is the thrust of the programs advanced in this chapter. Although the proposals are numerous, the basic changes and conditions they impose are only two:

(1) *The proposals would ensure that the interests of the poor and of racial minorities in an adequate diet, decent shelter, health care, and the other necessities of life would be treated as matters of right rather than of privilege.* The power of states and local governments to refuse entirely to make benefits available to their citizens or to hedge them in with humiliating and self-defeating conditions would be eliminated.

With all the rhetoric about "black power" and "community control," it is only through an economic and social bill of rights that the poor will be empowered with the opportunity to make something of their lives. Certainly, more is needed than a guaranteed income (as has been indicated in some detail), but without it all talk of power or control becomes a tragic joke.

(2) *The proposals would ensure that the political subdivisions in which community decisions are made would not be homogeneous jurisdictions composed almost exclusively of the rich or the poor, of white citizens or black citizens.* In doing so, they would establish freedom of choice and mobility for all people in the city.

The absence of such diversity and choice lies at the heart of the failure of the existing urban system. As long as it exists, the black, the poor, and the near poor in the central city will continue to struggle ineffectually over control of inadequate resources. In suburbia, affluent citizens may continue to derive some satisfaction from control over their own communities but increasingly they will be threatened by their inability to make any constructive contribution to solving the massive problems of the inner city. They may try to insulate themselves from the threat (cowering behind their picture windows as some are already doing) or they may take the offensive with repressive measures. Neither approach is likely to meet anyone's definition of the good life.

What must be fervently hoped is that there is a better way to give meaning to the time-honored concepts of grass-roots democracy and community control in the context of today's complex, sprawling, technological society. This cannot be done by trying to reconstruct romantic images from the past or to find a modern-day equivalent of the old town hall. Almost everyone today is a member of numerous communities serving different needs, not all of them geographically locatable.

It is this fact of life that deters us from trying our hand at the political scientists' exercise of constructing a model of workable urban government. It would not be difficult to conclude that what is needed is some form of regional government to deal with many problems that can only be solved on a metropolitan basis and sub-units of various sizes to permit decentralization and local decision-making. But, while such a model might have its own internal logic, it would not necessarily jibe with experience or real life. With all of the conforming influences in American life, there is still enough diversity in the political and economic situations in various states and regions to suggest that there is no single governmental structure that is appropriate and that will work. Hopefully there are many.

The danger, of course, is not that the Federal Government will seek, successfully or not, to impose a uniform plan for the reconstruction of local governments, but that it will continue its present policy of turning monies over to the states without any basic ground rules. The current concrete political manifestation of this danger lies in legislative proposals for revenue sharing. Initiated

by economist Walter Heller, the concept of revenue sharing contemplates use of the powerful and efficient revenue-raising capacity of the Federal Government as a means of channeling
needed funds to the states.[25] Unlike the categorical grant-in-aid
programs now in effect, a revenue-sharing plan would make a
designated portion of funds available to the states on an unre-
stricted basis, allowing them to select their own priorities and
programs.

The Heller plan appeals to people who are concerned about the
planless bureaucracy created by present grant-in-aid programs
and who are seeking ways of reinvigorating state government.
Under the Nixon Administration, which has embraced revenue
sharing, the rhetorical banner has been raised even higher with
much Presidential talk about "returning power to the people."

In its presently proposed form, revenue sharing would do no
such thing. Rather it would return power to the states with no
guarantee that the people would be treated fairly or equally. It
would not even impose the elemental condition that states reform their own revenue systems to stop discriminating against
the poor. In fact, it would compound existing inequities through
a formula providing that each local government would receive a
portion of state revenue-sharing grants corresponding to its present share of total local government revenues. For example, in
Wisconsin, in recent years, the affluent suburbs in the Milwaukee
metropolitan area received a per capita share of $100.94 of the
state's personal income tax while the central city's per capita
share was $18.62.[26] Under the Nixon program, not only would this
kind of distribution of state revenues be permitted to continue,
but Federal revenue would be allotted in the same outrageous
proportions.

Despite these terrible inequities, there is at least a fair prospect
that the Nixon revenue-sharing program will become the law. The
states, naturally enough, want it. And mayors, who are desperate
for federal assistance, may be impelled to accept anything that
guarantees them some revenue even at the price of being seriously shortchanged. If this comes to pass, it is not difficult to pre-
dict what will follow. After a few years elapse and a substantial
amount of money has been spent, the urban crisis will not have
abated. Conservatives will cite this as further proof that govern-

ment is inherently incapable of helping the poor and that the poor are congenitally incapable of benefiting from government assistance. Radicals, having absented themselves from the original legislative struggle, will say it is confirmation that government always serves the interests of the establishment. And, amid the new set of mutual recriminations, the poor and the black will retain their status as victims.

There can be no guarantee, of course, that the alternative approach urged here will solve all the problems. Like the "one man —one vote" decisions, the ground rules proposed here are something of a paradox—an exercise of national authority intended not to detract from but to strengthen state and local authority. But states can only avail themselves of this opportunity to exercise more authority by becoming more responsive to public needs. To do so they will have to change the archaic procedures (part-time legislators, one-term limitations on the governor, the absence of staff assistance in the executive and legislature, etc.) that have made them ineffectual institutions and create incentives for the most able people to come to the states, to metropolitan planning councils, urban development corporations, regional governments, or whatever other new instrumentalities may be established. While the Federal Government can furnish assistance and prodding in this area as well, ultimate success or failure will depend largely on community and political efforts at the local level to bring about change.

The outlook, however, is far from hopeless. In city governments, in universities, in local political and civic organizations and elsewhere there is to be found a growing cadre of young people who are dedicated and innovative, and who have the energy to put their ideas into practice. They are being frustrated now not simply by an inability to change the institutions they work for but by the fact that even when they can, the institutions as presently constituted cannot make much of a difference. If we are able to make a collective national decision that new institutions of government shall be created, we may unleash a flow of talent and energy sufficient to give these new institutions flesh and meaning. It is even possible that together we may fashion a government so structured that "local control" and "equality of opportunity" become harmonious terms.

Can Our National Machinery Be Made to Work?

One last issue requires some examination. Simply stated, it is this: assuming that broad public support can be mobilized for the basic policy changes needed, is the national government capable not only of making the decisions but of assuring that they will be carried out?

The question is not an idle one. In Part II, we saw that civil rights laws and social welfare enactments have fallen far short of achieving their purposes because of critical failures in implementation. A part of the answer has already been given; a major reason for failure has been the treatment of the interests of the poor and black as privileges rather than rights and the delegation of basic decision-making authority to state and local authorities. If the new mandate for change is broad enough to remedy these basic flaws, there is every prospect that the laws can be administered to achieve their purpose.

But this answer is not entirely sufficient. For we have also observed that laws in which interests were clearly defined as rights and authority was entirely within the Federal Government have been undermined by failures in executive management and by the intrusion of special interests.

Thus, we must also examine what changes in the structure and operation of the national government are necessary to remedy these failures and what hopes there are that the changes will be achieved.

In the Congress, the most urgently needed reform is a *major revision of the seniority system* so that the principal committees will no longer be baronies run without restriction by the oldest and often the most conservative men elected to office. Such a change is probably more needed to assure that laws once passed are fairly administered than it is to assure their enactment in the first place. Although the handicaps are still great, it is becoming increasingly less difficult to move through the Congress legislative proposals that enjoy popular support, even when they are opposed and bottled up by Congressional elders. But there is probably no way, short of changing the seniority system and limiting the authority of committee chairmen, to restrain the power that these men have to distort the purposes of a law and bend its administration to the service of special interests.

What are the prospects for such reform? Some change is coming, whatever Congress does, because a two-party system is developing in the South and its advent will deny to southern Democrats the dominance over committees that their secure Congressional seats have given them up to now. And the chances for action within Congress are better than they have been in the past because there is an increasing number of young congressmen chafing under a system that reduces their influence to minuscule proportions and no longer willing to wait patiently in line until their turn comes.

In the executive branch, no set of structural reforms is as important as the exercise of Presidential and cabinet leadership. In Chapter 5, evidence was cited that despite the difficulty that a cabinet officer has in moving his own bureaucracy and despite the pressures that can be brought to bear by powerful congressmen and special interest groups, a determined leader who has the support of his president can sometimes mobilize the resources at his disposal to bring about real social change. The trouble is that under present circumstances even the most courageous cabinet officer can win only a few such victories before his influence, credit, and energies are exhausted. This is likely to remain the case until, through reform of Congress and other means, the influence of special interest groups is moderated.

Nevertheless, there are steps that can be taken within the executive branch to bolster a president and his cabinet in efforts to accomplish their major social goals. While much attention has been directed to the need to strengthen the capacity of the executive office of the President to provide overall policy guidance, it would also be useful to strengthen the staffs of agency heads so that they can exercise closer supervision over the implementation of the laws they are charged with administering. Such a step would give a cabinet officer more leverage in seeking to overcome the inertia of his own bureaucracy and its receptivity to the pleadings of special interest groups. It would also be helpful in many cases to have a consolidation under a single cabinet officer of grant programs designed to deal with the same problem. For example, a transfer of food programs from the control of the

Agriculture Department to Health, Education and Welfare would make it more likely that the programs would be administered in the interests of poor people and as part of an overall effort to achieve welfare reform.

In many cases, however, it is impossible to consolidate all of the programs that should be directed toward a unified objective. The theory of the Model Cities program—that efforts to achieve decent shelter can only be successful if linked with a variety of social services—means that the Secretary of Housing and Urban Development must rely upon the assistance of HEW, the Office of Economic Opportunity, and other agencies. In cases of this kind, the remedy lies not in consolidation but in the President delegating authority to the Secretary of Housing and Urban Development (or whatever cabinet officer has the principal interest) in terms clear enough to enable him to impel the cooperation of the other agencies.

So, too, it would be useful to establish a system of social accounting along the lines suggested in Chapter 5. Such a system would assist in the establishment of goals and priorities, and, equally as important, would impel both Congress and the executive to evaluate periodically the success or failure of programs in achieving their stated goals. If government can force itself to examine what works and what doesn't, it is possible that practical planning and experimentation may replace the games that Congress and the executive branch now play with each other.

All of these reforms in executive management (and others that are needed) are no substitute for the exercise of political leadership and efforts to curb the influence of special interest groups. Some, in fact, are apt to follow rather than to precede more fundamental changes. Nevertheless, there is some comfort to be derived from a knowledge that if other things can be made to happen there are some tools at hand to make our laws and policies work.

One final key element in making the Federal machinery work should be noted—the need to strengthen the role of public interest groups in securing fair administration of the laws. Traditionally, the attention of civil rights groups and other public interest organizations has been devoted almost exclusively to securing the passage of new laws. Once the laws have been enacted very little time and effort have been expended in monitoring enforcement and in countering the work of groups seeking to thwart the law or bend it to their own purposes. While this is understandable—since resources are few, the struggle to obtain passage of laws has been long and hard, and many of the laws have been enacted only recently—this gap in the efforts of public interest groups has been damaging.

Recently the situation has begun to change. Young lawyers and other professionals have come to Washington for the specific purpose of representing before Federal agencies the interests of people previously unrepresented and have managed to scrape together enough money to start several new operations. And the success of Ralph Nader in representing consumer interests has shown that the vaunted power of the special interests in influencing the administration of the laws does not always survive public exposure and a few well-directed efforts at reform.

Here, as elsewhere, the crying need is for more resources. But the prospects are not entirely bleak. One of the many curious aspects of our schizophrenic society is that the same corporate sources that generate wealth that is often employed for narrow gain also produce wealth that is sometimes used for more benevolent purposes. In the coffers of foundations and church groups there resides a great deal of "benevolent wealth," still largely untapped, for supporting public interest lobbying. While the traditional caution of foundations has been reinforced by a 1969 law barring them from financing efforts to influence legislation, the law does not prohibit subsidies for monitoring executive action, and a few foundations have exhibited some understanding of the need and an inclination to help.

Assistance may also come from the Federal Government itself. A precedent has already been set in the legal services program of the war on poverty which has financed challenges to arbitrary government action at the community level, sometimes involving Federal as well as local officials. This precedent might well be extended to provide representation for the poor not only at the local level but before Federal agencies in Washington as well. True, it would be paradoxical for government, after allowing its policies to be undermined by the intrusion of special interests, to seek to compensate by financing efforts to nullify the impact of those interests. But in a society like our own where power and influence are diffused and often exercised by informal means, it is precisely through such paradoxes that progress is often made.

In short, our national government reflects all of the conflicting impulses and interests that now exist in institutions, communities, and within individuals themselves. The crucial issue is whether strong political leadership will emerge that can mobilize all of the positive instincts discussed in Chapter 7 into a commitment for basic social change. If this happens—if the will can be mustered to support national policy decisions of the kind outlined—there is no flaw in the machinery of national government so serious or irremediable as to prevent the decisions from being carried out.

10

HANGING TOGETHER

IF AN EPITAPH is ultimately to be written for American society, it may well read as follows:

> In a nation in which men came closer than any before them to acknowledging racial injustice and determining to eradicate it, they were ultimately defeated by a paralysis of will, an inability to change ancient institutions and political structures that inhibited mobility and freedom in their cities.

Or, with equal justification, the inscription might read:

> In a society in which men sought to make their cities free and livable places, they were ultimately defeated by their inability to throw off the shackles of racism that had plagued them throughout their history.

A strong case can be made for either epitaph. America *is* a less racist nation than it was two decades ago. The record in recent years of government action to deal with racial injustice *is* impressive. The social ills that still afflict us have been exposed with perception and candor by many of the nation's best minds. In light of this recent record of progress, it is interesting to speculate on where we might be today if, when the mass migration of black people to cities began, the cities had not been places uniquely unsuited to meeting the needs of newcomers—if there had not been an ongoing movement of jobs and people to the suburbs propelled by forces other than race, if there had been provision for equalizing resources and services in metropolitan areas, if there had not been restraints upon the location of poor people outside the central city. It is conceivable that while many of the same battles against race and class discrimination would have had to be fought, the situation would not be nearly as drastic as it seems today. If, for example, jobs had been accessible to Negroes in the cities in the 1950s and 1960s when civil rights breakthroughs were made, some of the optimism that was generated by those victories might have been sustained.

But this, of course, was not the case. Negroes came to cities in which the process of deterioration had already begun, cities that had solved the problem of providing opportunity and mobility for many European immigrants but that had left others relatively disadvantaged. The system that had evolved maximized the possibilities for racial conflict. By throwing impoverished blacks and low-income whites together in declining cities, it almost ensured that the worst in people would be brought out —that people who in other circumstances might have reached an accommodation would behave like racists. If, then, the struggle is ultimately lost, it may not be because white Americans are incurably racist but because we did not have the wisdom and energy to restructure the urban system in a manner that would allow our decent instincts to prevail.

The situation, however, may also be viewed from a different perspective. For the first time in our history, many Americans seem ready to face up to the problem of creating livable cities. We now have the technology, the capacity, and the abundance to build cities which both realize the advantages of bigness and give contemporary meaning to the old values of "grass-roots democracy." Having seen the consequences of anarchic growth, we are no longer afraid of the idea of public planning. Recognizing the dangers of overpopulation, we are beginning to realize that religious dogma must yield to the need for survival. Having reaped the advantages of industrial progress, we have developed into a people on the whole sufficiently educated and affluent to compel action against the evil consequences of industrialization —the exploitation of consumers and workers and the destruction of the environment.

If we could wish away our whole tragic history of slavery and injustice or if, alternatively, we were further along the way toward establishing a measure of racial understanding, there would be few doubts about the success of efforts to make our cities places that are livable and free. Instead, with all of our abundance and technology, we may fail because we allow our capacity for rational planning to be undermined by our inability to conquer racial fear.

In short, if we fail, the reason may not be that racism was endemic in the nation or that we were incapable of reforming urban structures and institutions, but that these two great problems came to a crisis point at the same time and overwhelmed us.

There is, of course, ample reason for pessimism. The capacity of many white Americans to delude themselves seems limitless. For years we have excluded Negroes from participation in American society. Now, in bitterness and frustration, some black people have said, "Okay, since you reject us, we reject you and we will build our own society." And in response, many whites have eagerly seized upon a new rationalization, saying piously, "See, that's the way *they* like it themselves."

While many young people have developed a striking capacity for exposing this and other brands of hypocrisy, some of the most perceptive are afflicted with a kind of tunnel vision of their own. They can see clearly enough critical flaws in the character of individuals and institutions and they have become adept at laying bare these defects, but they seem unable to focus on the strengths that remain in society and how these strengths can be used to revitalize the institutions that they scorn.

And it is possible that even if our major institutions were to receive infusions of new talent and energy, they would be incapable of renewal and change. A republic that has not yet celebrated its two-hundredth anniversary may be seen as still young in the long view of history, but it is old enough for its arteries to harden and to become incapable of meeting new challenges. It has, after all, required only thirty years for many labor unions to convert themselves from spearheads in the movement for social and economic justice to defenders of the status quo.

The pressures of time are also enormous. The residuum of traditional American optimism that survives in many of us leads people to talk glowingly of the possibilities for the year 2000. It still sounds like a remote time in which all things *are* possible. But a child born today in Bedford-Stuyvesant or in rural Alabama will just be reaching his most productive age in the year 2000. What happens *now* and in the next few years will determine whether he will really be a productive person—and part of a better and more just society. If, indeed, dealing with racial deprivation, poverty, and urban decay is not yet beyond our capacity, it will require only a few more years of neglect for the problems to become totally insoluble.

But amid all the reasons for despair there may still be room for hope. In the evidence, albeit fragmentary, that neither the task of conquering racial injustice nor that of creating livable cities is insurmountable alone, there is ground for at least a bit of confidence that the two can be overcome together.

And we still have a good deal going for us. The nation has not lost the capacity to analyze its own ailments. In the reports of a Kerner Commission, a Kaiser Commission, a Douglas Commission, a Heineman Commission, an Eisenhower Commission, almost all of the critical flaws in our society have been spread on the public record. If the failure of these reports to impel action warrants cynicism, the fact that one after another group of business, university, union, and government leaders has reached almost identical conclusions shows that many among the nation's affluent have not yet succumbed to either complacency or fear. If the diagnoses and prescriptions are available, so too are the resources. In this society, the interests of affluent and poor, white and black are not inherently irreconcilable. The means are at hand, if only we would use them to create genuine opportunity within the context of a better life for all. And in the thorough shaking up that society is receiving from many of its young, there lies the opportunity to liberate ourselves from past rigidities and constraints and to become a more open, just, and compassionate people.

There is, then, at least the hope that we can get ourselves together not just as individuals or members of groups, but as a nation. It may be possible that an epitaph for a free society need not be written at all.

Notes

1: Goals and Reality

1. In 1959, most poor people in the nation still lived outside metropolitan areas. But by 1967, most poor people—including 55 per cent of the Negro poor—lived in metropolitan areas. U.S. Bureau of the Census, Department of Commerce, Series P-23, No. 27, *Trends in Social and Economic Conditions in Metropolitan Areas*, p. 53. Unless otherwise indicated, the statistics used in this chapter are drawn from this report and another Census Bureau report, Series P-20, No. 189, *Selected Characteristics of Persons and Families: March 1969*. As results from the 1970 Census are analyzed and reported, many of the figures cited here are being updated. But the preliminary reports on the census do not indicate changes significant enough to alter the conclusions drawn from the data used here.
2. Report of the National Advisory Commission on Civil Disorders, p. 125 (hereinafter cited as Kerner Report).
3. U.S. Commission on Civil Rights, *A Time to Listen . . . A Time to Act*, p. 104 (hereinafter cited as *A Time to Listen*).
4. Kerner Report, *op. cit. supra* note 2, pp. 126–127.
5. *Ibid.*, p. 124.
6. The criteria were developed by the Social Security Administration. In 1968, the poverty threshold for a nonfarm family of four was $3,553.
7. Kerner Report, *op. cit. supra* note 2, p. 128.
8. The results are summarized in U.S. Commission on Civil Rights, *Racial Isolation in the Public Schools*, p. 14 (hereinafter cited as *Racial Isolation*).
9. Brimmer, "The Negro in the National Economy," in *The American Negro Reference Book*, pp. 251, 260–261. The comparisons are of expected lifetime earnings.

10. Frieden, "Housing and National Urban Goals," in *The Metropolitan Enigma,* pp. 148, 158.
11. Kerner Report, *op. cit. supra* note 2, pp. 258–259.
12. See Taueber and Taueber, *Negroes in Cities.*
13. Kerner Report, *op. cit. supra* note 2, pp. 136–137.
14. *A Time to Listen, op. cit. supra* note 3, pp. 20–21. The report also summarizes conditions in other cities. Similar disparities exist in other health services. A recent survey reported that the ratio of doctors to residents in ghetto areas is from one-fifth to one-half of what it is for the city as a whole. See *The New York Times,* Nov. 23, 1969, p. 60.
15. *A Time to Listen, op. cit. supra* note 3, pp. 18–19; Kerner Report, *op. cit. supra* note 2, p. 138.
16. See discussion, Chapter 4 *infra.*
17. *A Time to Listen, op. cit. supra* note 3, pp. 19–20.
18. President's Commission on Law Enforcement and the Administration of Justice, *The Challenge of Crime in a Free Society,* p. 38 (hereinafter cited as Crime Report).
19. *Ibid.,* p. 39. See also Kerner Report, *op. cit. supra* note 2, pp. 133–135.
20. Crime Report, *op cit. supra* note 18, p. 40.
21. The testimony is summarized in *A Time to Listen, op. cit. supra* note 3, pp. 21–26.
22. *Ibid.,* p. 24.
23. *Ibid.,* p. 23.
24. *Ibid.,* pp. 36–39; Kerner Report, *op. cit. supra* note 2, pp. 139–141. See also U.S. Federal Trade Commission, *Economic Report on Installment Credit and Retail Sales Practices of District of Columbia Retailers.*
25. Kerner Report, *op. cit. supra* note 2, p. 123.
26. Galbraith, *The Affluent Society,* pp. 286–287.
27. U.S. Bureau of the Census, Department of Commerce, Series P-60, No. 59, *Income in 1967 of Families in the United States,* p. 24.
28. Fein, "An Economic and Social Profile of the Negro American," in *Daedalus,* Vol. 94, pp. 815–846.
29. Clark, *Dark Ghetto,* pp. 81–110.
30. *Ibid.,* p. 106.
31. See Liebow, *Tally's Corner.*
32. Brown, *Manchild in the Promised Land.*
33. *The Autobiography of Malcolm X.*
34. Ellison, *Invisible Man.*
35. Clark, *Dark Ghetto.*
36. *A Time to Listen, op. cit. supra* note 3, p. 6.
37. *Ibid.,* p. 7.
38. *Ibid.,* p. 9.
39. *Ibid.,* pp. 7–8.

40. "Transcript, Hearing Before the U.S. Commission on Civil Rights in Cleveland, Ohio," p. 352.
41. *Ibid.*, p. 354.
42. *Ibid.*, pp. 352–353.
43. *A Time to Listen, op. cit. supra* note 3, p. 5.
44. *Ibid.*, p. 10.
45. Tocqueville, *Democracy in America,* Vol. 1, pp. 408–409.

2: The Immigrant Myth

1. See, e.g., Kristol, "The Negro Today is Like the Immigrant Yesterday," *The New York Times Magazine,* Sept. 11, 1966, p. 50.
2. Report of the National Advisory Commission on Civil Disorders, p. 117 (hereinafter cited as Kerner Report).
3. Sio, "Interpretation of Slavery: The Slave Status in the Americas," in *American Negro Slavery,* pp. 314–315. See also Elkins, "Slavery and Negro Personality," *ibid.*, p. 245.
4. Sio, *supra* note 3, pp. 321–322.
5. Litwack, *North of Slavery,* pp. 113 ff.
6. Klein, "The Slave Economies of Cuba and Virginia," in *American Negro Slavery, op. cit. supra* note 3, pp. 112–128. In the view of some historians, such as Elkins and Tannenbaum, slavery in the United States was in many other ways a far more repressive institution than Latin American slavery, but this is a conclusion on which not all agree. A summary of some of the varying views appears in Sio, *op. cit. supra* note 3.
7. A summary of some of the testimony of Negro parents at public hearings held by the Commission in several cities appears in U.S. Commission on Civil Rights, *A Time to Listen . . . A Time to Act,* pp. 41–49 (hereinafter cited as *A Time to Listen*).
8. See generally Glazer and Moynihan, *Beyond the Melting Pot.*
9. Litwack, *op. cit. supra* note 5, pp. 162–166.
10. See U.S. Commission on Civil Rights, *Freedom to the Free,* pp. 51 ff. The concessions were made to the South by Republicans in order to secure the election of their candidate, Rutherford B. Hayes, in the disputed Presidential election of 1876.
11. See, e.g., Glazer and Moynihan, *op. cit. supra* note 8.
12. Tocqueville, *Democracy in America,* Vol. 1, pp. 371–373.
13. U.S. Department of Labor, *Manpower Report of the President.* The growth in the labor force will be more than 20 per cent. The estimates are predicated on an assumption that the civilian unemployment rate will be 3 per cent.
14. *Ibid.* The overall growth rate expected is about 32 per cent.
15. See discussion, Chapter 6, pp. 184–185 *infra.*
16. See Chapter 6, pp. 173–174 *infra.*
17. Kain, "The Distribution and Movement of Jobs and Industry," in *The Metropolitan Enigma,* pp. 22–23. For most cities, this has

meant an absolute decline of the number of jobs in central cities. In manufacturing alone the drop has been estimated at 300,000 jobs between 1958 and 1963. See "Loss Continues in Big-City Jobs," *The New York Times,* June 16, 1969, p. 69.

18. See *A Time to Listen, op. cit. supra* note 7, pp. 123–124, and sources cited therein. In New York City, it is estimated that it would cost a worker who lived in Harlem about $40 a month to commute by public transportation to a job in an aircraft plant in Long Island, in a parts plant in Westchester, or in a chemical plant or shipyard in Staten Island.

19. *Ibid.*

20. See, e.g., Kain, "Housing Segregation, Negro Employment, and Metropolitan Decentralization," 82 *Quarterly Journal of Economics,* pp. 175, 179.

21. See discussion, Chapter 3 *infra.*

22. *Washington Post,* Sept. 22, 1969, p. 1.

23. See Chapter 3 *infra.*

24. U.S. Commission on Civil Rights, *For ALL the People . . . By ALL the People,* p. 4. The report is a survey of equal opportunity in state and local employment in seven metropolitan areas—Detroit, Philadelphia, San Francisco–Oakland, Memphis, Houston, Atlanta, and Baton Rouge. In all cities except Baton Rouge, Negroes were better represented in government jobs than in private industry and were employed in at least roughly the same proportion as they represented in the population.

25. *Ibid.,* pp. 10–14.

26. *Ibid.,* pp. 37–54.

27. *Ibid.,* pp. 21–22.

28. *Ibid.,* pp. 14–16.

29. *Ibid.,* pp. 86–90.

30. In the first seven months of 1969, it is estimated that 654 businesses failed in New York City alone. From 1958 to 1963, a decline of 25,000 was reported in the number of owners of unincorporated retail stores in New York City (lowering the number of such businesses from 84,000 to 59,000). *The New York Times,* Sept. 29, 1969, p. 49.

31. See the *Wall Street Journal,* Oct. 8, 1968, p. 34.

32. The effectiveness of training programs assisted by the government is assessed in Chapters 3 and 4 *infra.*

33. Letter from Thomas Jefferson to Mr. Correa, Nov. 25, 1817, in *The Writings of Thomas Jefferson,* Vol. 7, pp. 94–95.

34. Twelfth Annual Report of Horace Mann as Secretary of the Massachusetts Board of Education (1848), in *Documents of American History,* Doc. No. 173, p. 318.

35. U.S. Commission on Civil Rights, *Racial Isolation in the Public Schools,* pp. 77–81 (hereinafter cited as *Racial Isolation*) and sources cited therein.

36. U.S. Office of Education, Department of HEW, *Equality of Educational Opportunity,* pp. 21-23, 302–310 (hereinafter cited as Coleman Report).
37. *Ibid.,* p. 304.
38. "Transcript, Hearing Before the U.S. Commission on Civil Rights in Boston, Mass.," p. 65 (testimony of Dr. Charles Pinderhughes) (hereinafter cited as Boston Hearing).
39. "Transcript, Hearing Before the U.S. Commission on Civil Rights in Rochester, N.Y.," p. 63 (testimony of Norman Gross).
40. *Ibid.,* p. 234 (testimony of David Jaquith).
41. Brogan, *The American Character,* p. 170. See also Chapter 7, p. 199 *infra.*
42. Goodlad, "Desegregating the Integrated School," in *Education Parks,* p. 14.
43. *Brown* v. *Board of Education,* 347 U.S. 483, 494 (1954).
44. *Racial Isolation, op. cit. supra* note 35, p. 193. The Commission concluded that the racial composition of a school has a relationship to student performance that is distinct from that associated with socioeconomic composition. *Ibid.,* pp. 89–106, 204.
45. *Ibid.,* pp. 103–106.
46. "Transcript, Hearing Before the U.S. Commission on Civil Rights in Cleveland, Ohio," p. 308 (testimony of Charles Bohi).
47. See *Racial Isolation, op. cit. supra* note 35, p. 207. Since 1967, when the report was issued, there has been an increase in desegregation in the South while segregation has increased in the North.
48. *Ibid.,* pp. 93–94. See also *Hobson* v. *Hansen,* 269 F. Supp. 401, 434–436 (D.D.C. 1967), dealing with inequalities in the Washington, D.C., school system.
49. Boston Hearing, *op. cit. supra* note 38, pp. 26, 27, 29 (testimony of John Callahan).
50. *Racial Isolation, op. cit. supra* note 35, p. 93. The report summarizes the results of teacher examinations in St. Louis, Philadelphia, and Atlanta, and of a vocabulary test administered to teachers as part of the Coleman Report.
51. See, e.g., Kohl, *36 Children;* Kozol, *Death at an Early Age.*
52. See Clark, *Dark Ghetto,* pp. 132–133. A summary of studies indicating a relationship between teacher expectation and students' attitudes and performance is found in *Racial Isolation, op. cit. supra* note 35, p. 99.
53. See testimony summarized in *A Time to Listen, op. cit. supra* note 7, p. 44.
54. *Ibid.,* p. 48.
55. U.S. Advisory Commission on Intergovernmental Relations, *Fiscal Balance in the American Federal System,* Vol. 2, pp. 64–70. In addition to the disparities between per pupil expenditures in urban and suburban school districts, it has been found in some cases

that even *within* a city school district less money is spent on predominantly Negro schools than on white schools. See, e.g., *Hobson* v. *Hansen, op cit. supra* note 48, pp. 437–438, where Judge Wright found differences of $100 to $132 in expenditures in the Washington, D.C., public schools.

56. The Illinois figures are contained in Plaintiff's Brief in Opposition to Defendant's Motion to Dismiss, *McInnis* v. *Ogilvie,* 293 F. Supp. 327 (N.D. Ill., 1968), aff'd, 394 U.S. 322 (1969). The California statistics are in the Complaint, *Serrano* v. *Priest,* No. 93854, Super. Ct. Cal, L.A. County (dismissed, Jan. 8, 1969).

57. See *Racial Isolation, op. cit. supra* note 35, pp. 26–30, and the discussion, Chapter 4, pp. 127–130 *infra.*

58. See the *McInnis* and *Serrano* cases, *op. cit. supra* note 56. The New York information is from Allen, "The State, Educational Priorities and Local Financing," in *Integrated Education,* p. 55.

59. See Benson, *The Cheerful Prospect.*

60. See *Racial Isolation, op. cit. supra* note 35, p. 30. A more important key to attracting better teachers may be a general upgrading of their salaries and status and a change in current professional practice which now makes advancement dependent largely upon seniority to one which rewards merit and achievement.

61. *Buchanan* v. *Warley,* 245 U.S. 60. In a few places, racial zoning ordinances continued in force long after the Supreme Court held they were unconstitutional. It was not until 1950 that the racial zoning law of Birmingham, Alabama, was challenged and held unconstitutional. *City of Birmingham* v. *Monk,* 185 F. 2d 859 (5th Cir. 1950), cert. denied, 341 U.S. 940 (1951).

62. *Shelley* v. *Kraemer,* 334 U.S. 1.

63. See generally Taueber and Taueber, *Negroes in Cities;* Lieberson, *Ethnic Patterns in American Cities.*

64. See discussion, Chapter 4, pp. 114–116, 137–138, *infra.*

65. The key decision was that of the Supreme Court in *Village of Euclid* v. *Ambler Realty Co.,* 272 U.S. 365 (1926).

66. Report of the National Commission on Urban Problems, part III, pp. 1–29 (hereinafter cited as Douglas Report).

67. *Ibid.,* pp. 1–43, 44. See also discussion, Chapter 6, pp. 175–176, *infra.*

68. *Ibid.,* pp. 1–41. See also President's Committee on Urban Housing, *A Decent Home,* pp. 140–142 (hereinafter cited as Kaiser Report). Other forms of land-use controls that may have a similar impact are laws that exclude multiple dwellings and mobile homes, minimum house-size requirements, and subdivision regulations that sometimes are applied to require newcomers to pay for services that will benefit the whole community by forcing builders to dedicate excessive amounts of land for improvements. Douglas Report, *op. cit. supra* note 66, pp. 1–43, 49.

69. *Introduction* to Douglas Report, *op. cit. supra* note 66, p. 64.
70. *Ibid.*, p. 75. See also Von Eckhardt, "Building Crisis," *Washington Post*, Oct. 27, 1968, p. 1, and subsequent articles through Nov. 3.
71. See discussion, Chapter 6, pp. 179–180, *infra*.
72. Kaiser Report, *op. cit. supra* note 68, p. 135.
73. Kerner Report, *op. cit. supra* note 2, p. 145.
74. *Ibid.* See also Glazer and Moynihan, *op. cit. supra* note 8.
75. U.S. Commission on Civil Rights, *Cycle to Nowhere*.

3: The Civil Rights Effort

1. The Unemployment Relief Act of 1933, for example, stipulated that there should be no discrimination because of race, creed, or color. Other laws and regulations are collected in U.S. Commission on Civil Rights, *Employment*, pp. 7–8.
2. See Weaver, *Negro Labor*, pp. 1–15; Ruchames, *Race, Jobs and Politics*, pp. 11–14.
3. Schlesinger, *The Age of Roosevelt: The Politics of Upheaval*, Vol. 3, pp. 431–432.
4. *Ibid.*
5. See U.S. Commission on Civil Rights, *Housing*, pp. 14–17.
6. 347 U.S. 483.
7. Greenberg, "The Supreme Court, Civil Rights and Civil Dissonance," 77 *Yale Law Journal* 1520, 1522.
8. The exceptions to this general rule include a couple of school cases (e.g., in New Rochelle) and a few public housing cases where it was proved that government authorities had a clear intent to discriminate.
9. Remarks of the President at Howard University, Washington, D.C., "To Fulfill These Rights," June 4, 1965.
10. The amount is now about $18 billion.
11. *Shelley* v. *Kraemer*, 334 U.S. 1. The FHA then decided that it would not insure properties on which there were new restrictive covenants. But this was still a long way from either sponsoring or requiring a policy of open occupancy.
12. These were the figures as of 1966. The 76 units were outside Cincinnati, the only place where the city housing authority has been permitted to build outside the city.
13. A study by the American Friends Service Committee cited the experience of a Negro home-seeker in Prince Georges County, Md., who made sixty-nine telephone calls, attended thirteen meetings, wrote ten letters, and hired a lawyer before he could obtain a house in an FHA-insured development.
14. In 1966, the Attorney General reported that eleven builders had been placed on an ineligible list, of whom four had been re-

instated, and that "about 118 complaints" had been received and "about twenty-nine complainants" got their housing.

15. *Jones* v. *Mayer,* 392 U.S. 409.
16. Some of the early successes in implementing the order are recounted in Sovern, *Legal Restraints on Racial Discrimination in Employment,* pp. 106–112.
17. The talents of the public relations man were important to the operation of "Plans for Progress." After an agreement had been negotiated, the president or another high company official ordinarily flew to Washington for a public signing ceremony conducted by then Vice-President Johnson.
18. In a survey conducted by the Southern Regional Council in 1963, it was reported that officials of several of the Plans for Progress companies were only vaguely aware of the agreement, thought it only covered blue collar jobs, or were indifferent to it. The limited nature of the gains was revealed in a report on 103 Plans for Progress companies issued in 1964. It was reported that during a two-year period, the percentage of Negroes employed had increased from 5.1 to 5.7 per cent. The gain in salaried employment was from 1.5 to 2.1 per cent. And the total increase in employment for Negroes was about 41,000 as against 300,000 new jobs for whites.
19. For example, Martin Kilbane, chairman of the Joint Apprenticeship Committee of the Plumbers Local of Cleveland, stated that "There is a tendency for us to take care of our own . . ." "Transcript, Hearing Before the U.S. Commission on Civil Rights in Cleveland, Ohio," p. 470 (hereinafter cited as Cleveland Hearing).
20. Testimony of George Fink, Cleveland Hearing, p. 466.
21. The measures included assistance to minority youth to enter apprenticeships, and publicizing equal opportunity policies to subcontractors.
22. Registered programs also benefit from Federal grants to vocational schools under the Vocational Education Act of 1946.
23. Section 8(f) of the National Labor Relations Act (49 Stat. 452, as amended, 29 U.S.C. 158, 1964) provides that it is not an unfair labor practice for an employer in the building trades and construction industry to make an agreement with a labor organization which requires referral by the union. But a strong argument can be made, and has already been accepted by one court, that such a collective bargaining agreement should be disregarded where union control over the hiring process results in the exclusion of Negroes.
24. Among the recent cases are two in which courts have taken into account past practices of discrimination in defining the present rights of Negro workers. *Quarles* v. *Phillip Morris, Inc.,* 279 F. Supp. 505 (E.D. Va., 1968); *U.S.* v. *Local 189, United Paper-*

makers and Paperworkers, 282 F. Supp. 39 (E.D. La., 1968). In each, Negroes who had been employed in segregated job departments were given the benefit of the plant seniority they had accrued when they moved to integrated departments. The courts found this was equitable and necessary to protect them from layoffs and provide an opportunity for promotions. In other cases, however, courts have refused to take past discrimination into account in deciding present rights. See, e.g., *Griggs* v. *Duke Power Co.,* 292 F. Supp. 243 (M.D. N.C., 1968).

25. Section 703 (h).

26. There appears to have been some recent improvement in this situation. In 1968, about half of the 125,000 on-the-job trainees had fewer than four years of high school and came from families with incomes below the poverty line. Economic Report of the President, 1969, p. 163.

27. A Labor Department analysis showed that only 55 per cent of nonwhites completing institutional training in 1966 were employed in training-related jobs three months after the courses. Thirty per cent were either unemployed or not in the labor force. The average earnings for nonwhites completing MDTA programs was $1.60 an hour compared with $1.32 before they entered training.

28. See Interview with Lee White, quoted in Orfield, "The Enforcement of Title VI."

29. In 1961, a Federal court held that the school board in New Rochelle, N.Y., had drawn school district boundaries with the deliberate intent of segregating Negro students and had maintained a segregated system through the years. *Taylor* v. *Board of Education,* 191 F. Supp. 181 (S.D.N.Y., 1961), aff'd, 294 F. 2d 36 (2d Cir.), cert. denied, 368 U.S. 940 (1961).

30. Some of the institutional factors which may help to explain the failures of the Federal Government are explored more fully in Chapter 5.

4: Economic and Social Programs

1. Information extracted from 1967 and 1968 Budget Messages of the President.

2. *The New York Times,* May 27, 1968, p. 1.

3. Report of the National Advisory Commission on Civil Disorders, p. 260.

4. Smart, Rybeck, and Shuman, *The Large Poor Family—A Housing Gap,* pp. 1–2. It was assumed in the study that a family of five or six needed three bedrooms. The 12,000 new units planned in the seven cities still left a gap of 71,000 units. And nonwhites constituted more than 60 per cent of the families in need.

5. Some studies show a relationship between occupancy of public

housing or other standard housing and improvements in health. Connections between improved housing and other improvements in status or aspirations have proved harder to establish. See Wilner and Walkey, "Effects of Housing on Health and Performance," in *The Urban Condition*, p. 224.

6. Mangum, "Manpower Programs in the Antipoverty Effort," p. 246.
7. Lecht, *Manpower Requirements for National Objectives in the 1970's*, pp. 201–202.
8. See Advisory Council on Public Welfare, *Having the Power, We Have the Duty*, p. 7.
9. *Ibid.*, p. 16.
10. In this analysis, mention has been omitted of poor people who do not participate at all in the AFDC program. It is estimated that of 21.7 million people who in 1966 were poor but not aged, only one-third received assistance from the major public welfare programs. Many of the families not participating were headed by fathers who either were unemployed or whose earnings were below the poverty line. (Although Federal assistance is available to families with unemployed parents, participation in the program is up to each state and the majority of states have not accepted it.) While many of these families receive some form of general assistance provided by states and localities without Federal aid, the level of support generally is below that provided by AFDC. Although it has been argued that public welfare is not the best alternative for assisting families with employable men, until a meaningful alternative is provided, many of these families are in straits even more dire than those who are receiving public welfare. (Unemployment insurance in its present form does not constitute an alternative because it is based on the theory that the unemployed will be reabsorbed in the labor market after a short interval and accordingly does not provide benefits of long duration.) In addition, an undetermined number of people who are eligible for public welfare do not participate, in some cases because they are unaware that they are eligible, in others because, for reasons to be discussed *infra*, they feel that participation would degrade them.
11. See "Transcript, Hearing before the U.S. Commission on Civil Rights in Cleveland, Ohio," pp. 173 ff. (hereinafter cited as Cleveland Hearing).
12. This was the Wooster Square project which cost the Federal Government $19.3 million. It is estimated that the cost of having one such project in every major city would be $13 billion. *Time*, March 4, 1966, p. 31.
13. See Cleveland Hearing, pp. 174–175; Abrams, *The City Is the Frontier*, pp. 132 ff. For a rosier view of relocation, see Community Relations Service, U.S. Conference of Mayors, Experience Report 104, *New Patterns in Urban Housing*.

14. See Abrams, *op. cit. supra* note 13.
15. See discussion, *supra,* Chapter 3, pp. 91–92.
16. In part, the financial problems of the school lunch program are attributable to the fact that as farm surpluses have dwindled, the value of commodities donated to the program has declined. For a detailed review of the deficiencies of the school lunch program, see *Their Daily Bread,* a publication of the Committee on School Lunch Participation. See also Citizens' Board of Inquiry into Hunger and Malnutrition, *Hunger U.S.A.*
17. The district abandoned its practice and decided to accept Title I funds when confronted with a novel lawsuit brought by parents which claimed that refusal to accept such aid violated the equal protection clause of the Fourteenth Amendment. *Silvas* v. *Santa Ana Unified School District* (Calif. Superior Ct. Orange Co., No. M-0945, 1968), II CEB *Legal Services Gazette,* No. 10, July 1968, p. 306.
18. As noted previously, the Housing and Urban Development Act of 1968 eliminates the explicit veto power of suburban jurisdictions over most programs designed to provide housing for people of low and moderate incomes. Thus, in theory, builders who wish to take advantage of the subsidies provided in the legislation may locate developments anywhere they are able to find sites without obtaining the approval of the local governing authorities. But suburban zoning controls still operate and may prohibit particular types of developments such as multi-family housing, or raise land costs so high that builders cannot construct housing within the income limits specified in the statute. In practice, then, suburban governments continue to exercise an effective veto power through their control of the use of the land.
19. See generally, Benson, *The Cheerful Prospect.*
20. See U.S. Commission on Civil Rights, *Racial Isolation in the Public Schools,* pp. 25–30.
21. See National Advisory Council on the Education of Disadvantaged Children, 1968 Report to the President, pp. 7 ff.
22. See The White House Conference, *To Fulfill These Rights,* pp. 58–59.
23. Some of the old statutes are cited in Riesenfeld and Maxwell, *Modern Social Legislation,* p. 709. In the residence cases, the Supreme Court affirmed the rulings of three district courts which had held that such requirements violated the Constitution. *Shapiro* v. *Thompson,* 394 U.S. 618 (1969).
24. A general account of the Coronet Village story by Gilbert Cornfield, an attorney who represented the tenants' union, is found in *Civil Rights Digest,* Summer, 1968, p. 1.
25. See e.g., testimony of Mrs. Hattie Mae Dugan, Cleveland Hearing, p. 31.

26. See U.S. Commission on Civil Rights, *A Time to Listen . . . A Time to Act,* pp. 15–16.
27. For a discussion of the origins of the community action program and a review of its successes and failures, see Kravitz, "The Community Action Program in Perspective," in *Power, Poverty and Urban Policy,* pp. 259 ff. See, also, Hallman, "The Community Action Program, An Interpretative Analysis," in the same volume at p. 285; Metropolitan Applied Research Center, *A Relevant War Against Poverty.*

5: The Politics of Failure

1. See "Transcript, Hearing Before the U.S. Commission on Civil Rights in San Francisco, Calif.," pp. 177 ff. (hereinafter cited as Bay Area Hearing). In fact, Tuggle's concern about FHA losing its share of the new housing market was less well grounded in the Bay Area where it insured 51 per cent of new housing as opposed to other sections of the nation, where FHA's share is only 15–20 per cent.
2. "Local FHA Criticized on Bias Order," *San Francisco Chronicle,* Nov. 30, 1967. It is not being suggested that FHA is totally responsive to the interests of the housing industry. Builders frequently complain about the delays entailed in getting applications through FHA "red tape."
3. A recent effort is the Concentrated Employment Program (CEP) established in 1967 to bring together "such diverse services, as remedial education, special counseling, work experience, institutional and on-the-job training . . ." State employment service personnel can be used for these programs, but this is not necessarily done.
4. See "Transcript, Hearing Before the U.S. Commission on Civil Rights in Cleveland, Ohio," pp. 475 ff.
5. Levitan and Mangum, *Making Sense of Federal Manpower Policy,* p. 18.
6. See, e.g., U.S. Commission on Civil Rights, *Equal Opportunity in Farm Programs.*
7. U.S. Commission on Civil Rights, *Cycle to Nowhere,* p. 25.
8. Bay Area Hearing, p. 501.
9. "Transcript, Hearing Before the U.S. Commission on Civil Rights in Montgomery, Ala.," p. 456.
10. See testimony of Mr. Manuel Rodriguez and Mr. Charles Mitchell, Bay Area Hearing, p. 540.
11. Rosenman, *The Public Papers and Addresses of Franklin D. Roosevelt,* Vol. 1, p. 646.
12. See Hearings, Subcommittee on Government Research, Committee on Government Operations, U.S. Senate, on S. 843, 1967; see,

also, "Social Goals and Indicators for American Society," 371 *Annals,* May 1967.
13. See Pearson and Anderson, "Rural Poor Cut, Rural Rich Aided," *Washington Post,* Oct. 14, 1968, p. 11.
14. See *The New York Times,* March 2, 1969, Section 4, p. 12.
15. Shuman, "Behind the Scenes . . . and Under the Rug," *Washington Monthly,* July 1969, pp. 14, 19–20.
16. Slitor, *The Federal Income Tax in Relation to Housing.* Moreover, as Stanley Surrey, former Assistant Secretary of the Treasury, has pointed out, the accelerated depreciation and capital gains features of these laws provide a tax shelter for landlords that costs the government about $750 million in revenues each year, an amount which could be used to make a significant dent in the problem of providing housing for low-income people. *The New York Times,* Oct. 29, 1968, p. 17. The Tax Reform Act of 1969 may provide some partial redress of these inequities, but it does not fully correct them.
17. Figures for the highway program are derived from Hearings before a Subcommittee of the Committee on Appropriations, House of Representatives, 90th Cong., 2nd Sess. (1968), p. 347.

6: A Bad Trip into the Future

1. Hodge and Hauser, *The Challenge of America's Metropolitan Population Outlook—1960 to 1985.*
2. *Ibid.,* pp. 5–10. A metropolitan area is defined generally as an area comprised of a central city of 50,000 or more people and contiguous counties related in various ways to the central city. The census people have dubbed such places as Standard Metropolitan Statistical Areas (SMSAs) and there are now some 212 of them in the United States.
3. *Ibid.,* pp. 13–18. The assumption here is that central city boundaries will not be changed by annexation. The assumption does not seem unreasonable since in recent years there has been very little shifting of boundaries in metropolitan areas.
4. *Ibid.,* p. 26.
5. U.S. Bureau of the Census, *Recent Trends in Social and Economic Conditions of Negroes in the United States,* p. 5. Here the figures used are for Negroes rather than nonwhites.
6. Hodge and Hauser, *op. cit. supra* note 1, pp. 25–27. These overall figures obscure some striking regional differences. In the older cities of the Northeast and North Central regions, Negroes would continue to be very highly concentrated in the central cities, the percentages being 82 and 89, respectively, and representing little change from 1960. In the South and West, where patterns of racial concentration are not yet so hardened, roughly two-thirds of

the nonwhites in metropolitan areas are likely to reside in the central city.

7. *Ibid.*
8. The Hodge–Hauser report does not spell out these trends. Much of the discussion which follows is drawn from Vernon, *Metropolis 1985,* which projects trends in the New York metropolitan area to 1985.
9. Vernon, *op. cit. supra* note 8, pp. 232 ff.
10. Regional Plan Association, *Spread City,* p. 11. One-half of all zoned land requires lots of one acre or larger.
11. *Ibid.,* p. 21.
12. Vernon, *op. cit. supra* note 8, p. 182.
13. *Ibid.,* p. 91.
14. *Wall Street Journal,* Feb. 20, 1969, p. 1. The figures, compiled by the International Council of Shopping Centers, are for Canada as well as the United States. But the percentage of retail business accounted for by shopping centers would not be altered significantly if limited to the United States.
15. *Ibid.*
16. Netzer, *Impact of the Property Tax,* p. 1. In Maryland, for example, only 27 per cent of the state's population lived in Baltimore, but the city accounted for 71 per cent of all people receiving AFDC assistance. In Massachusetts, the figures for Boston were 14 per cent and 38 per cent. U.S. Advisory Commission on Intergovernmental Relations, *Fiscal Balance in the American Federal System,* Vol. 2, p. 5.
17. In thirteen of fifteen major cities, for example, more than one-third of all public school buildings were at least forty-five years old. *Fiscal Balance, op. cit. supra* note 16, p. 67.
18. Netzer, *op. cit. supra* note 16, pp. 1–2. Among other factors placing a strain on city budgets is the long overdue increase in the salaries of teachers and other government employees who are organizing to press for economic gains.
19. *Ibid.,* p. 18.
20. *Ibid.,* pp. 22–24.
21. *Ibid.,* p. 26.
22. See Vernon, *op. cit. supra* note 8, pp. 124–125.
23. From 1961 to 1966, only two major cities, New York and Los Angeles, had an increase in their property tax base greater than that of their surrounding areas. Several other large cities experienced an absolute decline in assessed valuation. *Fiscal Balance, op. cit. supra* note 16, p. 82.
24. For a discussion of the effect that differentials in tax rates may have upon the location of economic activity, see Netzer, *op. cit. supra* note 16, pp. 30–33.
25. *Fiscal Balance, op. cit. supra* note 16, pp. 6, 105.

26. *Ibid.*, pp. 67–74. For the thirty-seven largest cities, average expenditures for the central city for education were 32.6 per cent of total general expenditures, while for the suburbs they were 53.2 per cent. In Cleveland, 43 per cent of the property tax levies went for schools, while the average for the suburbs was 60 per cent, and some suburban jurisdictions were able to devote 80 per cent of their property tax revenues to schools.

27. Netzer, *op cit. supra* note 16, pp. 49–51.

28. *Ibid.*, pp. 39–43.

29. Hodge and Hauser, *op. cit. supra* note 1, pp. 33 ff.

30. National Commission on Technology, Automation, and Economic Progress, *Technology and the American Economy*, Vol. 1, pp. 22, 30 (hereinafter cited as Technology Report).

31. Lecht, *Manpower Requirements for National Objectives in the 1970's*, pp. 63–79.

32. Technology Report, *op. cit. supra* note 30, p. 31.

33. It is estimated that there were 3 million nonwhites in white collar jobs in 1960 and 4.3 million in 1967, a gain of about 7 per cent a year. U.S. Bureau of the Census, *Recent Trends in Social and Economic Conditions of Negroes in the United States*, p. 15.

34. *Ibid.*, p. 11.

35. Lecht, *op. cit. supra* note 31, pp. 92–93.

36. *Ibid.*, p. 92.

37. For example, in 1968 in Illinois there were four Negro state senators and ten representatives; in Michigan three senators and nine representatives; in New York three senators and eight representatives; in California one senator and five representatives. See U.S. Commission on Civil Rights, "Roster of Negro Elected Officials," in *Civil Rights Digest*, Spring 1968, pp. 35–39.

38. Dixon, *Democratic Representation*, p. 585.

39. The argument does not seem valid in situations where there is only one ascendant political party. In parts of the South when Negroes registered in large numbers after the enactment of the Voting Rights Act of 1965, southern officials sought to dilute the impact of their votes by abolishing wards or precincts as units for electing local officials and moving to a system of at-large elections. See U.S. Commission on Civil Rights, *Political Participation*, pp. 21 ff.

7: Glimmers of Hope

1. Myrdal, *An American Dilemma*, Vol. 1, pp. 8–12. The creed, he said, had strong roots in the European enlightenment of the eighteenth century, in the drive for religious liberty and basic teachings of the Christian church, and in the English common law.

2. *Ibid.*, Vol. 2, p. 1009.

3. *Ibid.*, Vol. 1, pp. 21–22.

4. Brogan, *The American Character*, pp. 170, 174–175.

5. It is a view that will be rejected also by many blacks and whites who see out-and-out racism, rather than the more complex processes described here, as the major force in keeping Negroes down.

6. Report of the National Advisory Commission on Civil Disorders, p. 1.

7. *Ibid.*, p. 5.

8. Rustin, "The Anatomy of Frustration."

9. In a detailed review of violence in labor disputes over the past century, Ross and Taft conclude that labor violence has almost always been harmful to the union, and that the gains achieved during the New Deal probably would not have occurred had there been widespread violence on the part of the unions. Taft and Ross, "American Labor Violence: Its Causes, Character and Outcome," in *Violence in America*, Vol. 1, pp. 221, 288–294.

10. Gans, *The Levittowners*, pp. 271–272. A few, principally well-educated women, also said they missed downtown cultural opportunities. And perhaps because Levittown had not yet fully developed a shopping center, many people said they missed downtown shops.

11. Brogan, *op. cit. supra* note 4, pp. 109–114.

12. Walinsky, "A Rough Autopsy on Democrats," *Washington Post*, Oct. 20, 1968, p. B2.

13. Some of the best work has been done by journalists. See Hamill, "The Revolt of the White Lower Middle Class," *New York*, p. 24; Schrag, "The Forgotten American," *Harper's*, p. 27.

14. Wood, *Suburbia*.

15. *Ibid.*, Chap. 3.

16. Gans, *op. cit. supra* note 10, Chap. 2.

17. Wood, *op. cit. supra* note 14, p. 106.

18. *Ibid.*, pp. 158–166.

19. *Ibid.*, p. 264.

20. See, e.g., Barbara Ward, "Remarks: National Growth and Its Distribution," p. 26.

21. The sources for the material which follows are cited in U.S. Commission on Civil Rights, *Racial Isolation in the Public Schools*, pp. 167–177. Papers on education parks, commissioned from educators including John Fischer, Francis Keppel, and John Goodlad are collected in U.S. Commission on Civil Rights, *Education Parks*.

22. *Education Parks, op. cit. supra* note 21, p. 54.

23. See, e.g., Mumford, *The City in History*, pp. 482 ff; Gans, *op. cit. supra* note 10, Chap. 2 and p. 286.

24. He added, "I do not give all these opinions as true, but as American opinions." Tocqueville, *Democracy in America*, Vol. 1, pp. 409–410.

25. Myrdal, *op. cit. supra* note 1, Vol. 2, pp. 1023–1024.

8: Strategies for Change: Together *and* Autonomous

1. The polls are summarized in Pettigrew, "Racially Separate or Together," in *Integrated Education,* pp. 36, 51–52 (Jan.-Feb. 1969). See also Campbell and Schuman, "Racial Attitudes in Fifteen American Cities," in *Supplemental Studies of the National Advisory Commission on Civil Disorders;* "Report from Black America," *Newsweek,* June 30, 1969.
2. In the Campbell and Schuman survey it was concluded that even on questions where the appeal to separation was strongest, more than 75 per cent of the respondents indicated a clear preference for integration. Among young black men sixteen to nineteen years of age, the pro-separatist responses ranged from 11 per cent to 28 per cent. Campbell and Schuman, *op. cit. supra* note 1, pp. 5, 18–19.
3. See Pettigrew, *op. cit. supra* note 1, p. 52.
4. Funnyé, "The Untogether People: Separate but Gilded," *Village Voice,* Sept. 26, 1968.
5. See, e.g., "Transcript, Hearing Before the U.S. Commission on Civil Rights in Jackson, Miss.," Vol. 1, p. 169 (testimony of Charles Evers).
6. Ellison, "An American Dilemma: A Review," in *Shadow and Act,* p. 302.
7. The terms "ghetto dispersal" and "ghetto enrichment" are those used by Anthony Downs in a pioneering analysis of the strategies that may be employed to deal with racial inequality in the cities. Downs, "Alternative Futures for the American Ghetto," in *Daedalus,* Vol. 97, pp. 1331 ff.
8. See Alsop, "No More Nonsense About Ghetto Education," *New Republic,* July 22, 1967, pp. 18 ff., and "Ghetto Education," Nov. 18, 1967, pp. 18 ff.; Cloward and Piven, "Desegregated Housing: Who Pays for the Reformers' Ideal?," *New Republic,* Dec. 17, 1966, pp. 17 ff.
9. See the discussion of these issues in Chapter 3 *supra.*
10. Howe, "National Ideals and Educational Policy," in *National Conference on Equal Educational Opportunity in America's Cities,* pp. 769, 775.
11. See, e.g., Tyler, "Investing in Better Schools," in *Agenda for the Nation,* pp. 207, 235–36.
12. See U.S. Commission on Civil Rights, *Racial Isolation in the Public Schools,* pp. 177–179 (hereinafter cited as *Racial Isolation*).
13. See discussion, Chapter 6 *supra.*
14. On the higher costs of land in the central city, see President's Committee on Urban Housing, *A Decent Home,* pp. 140–142. A further, very practical problem in following ghetto development strategies is that there simply is not enough vacant land in most

central cities to provide decent housing for more than a small percentage of those who need it. *Ibid.*, pp. 138–140.

15. Levitan and Taggart, *Developing Business and Entrepreneurs in the Ghettos.*
16. *The New York Times*, April 28, 1968, Section 4, p. 4.
17. Jack Faucett Associates, *A Preliminary Analysis of the Economic Effects of the Urban Employment Opportunity Development Act.*
18. Levitan and Taggart, *op. cit. supra* note 15.
19. U.S. Federal Trade Commission, *Economic Report on Installment Credit and Retail Sales Practices of District of Columbia Retailers,* pp. 20–21.
20. Levitan and Taggart, *op. cit. supra* note 15. A summary in the April 1970 Bedford-Stuyvesant Restoration Corporation Newsletter shows an expansion of operations since the Levitan and Taggart report. It states that more than $4 million has been invested, 43 businesses financed and 1,161 jobs created. The observation on the limited job-producing potential of such efforts still seems valid.
21. See Hunter, "The New Black Businessmen," *Saturday Review*, Aug. 23, 1969, p. 27.
22. Brimmer, "Opportunity and Choice in an Expanding Economy," Commencement Address, Clark College, Atlanta, Ga., June 3, 1968, p. 17.
23. See, e.g., Dahl, *Who Governs?*
24. See discussion, Chapter 6 *supra*.
25. These points were demonstrated clearly in several investigations conducted by the U.S. Commission on Civil Rights. The Commission studies and other research are summarized in Pettigrew, *op. cit. supra* note 1, pp. 39–42.
26. *Racial Isolation, op. cit. supra* note 12, pp. 151–154. More recent reports showing a continuation of encouraging progress are summarized in New York State Education Department, *Racial and Social Class Isolation in the Schools,* pp. 245 ff. (December 1969).
27. The original plans for the school are reported in *The New York Times*, Sept. 4, 1968, p. 28.
28. Downs, *op. cit. supra* note 7, pp. 1370–1372.

9: Elements of a Program

1. See, e.g., U.S. Commission on Civil Rights, *Cycle to Nowhere.*
2. For a detailed discussion of income maintenance approaches, see President's Commission on Income Maintenance Programs, *Poverty Amid Plenty* (hereinafter cited as Heineman Report); Tobin, "Raising the Incomes of the Poor," in *Agenda for the Nation*, pp. 77 ff.
3. Tobin, *op. cit. supra* note 2, p. 99.
4. See Heineman Report, *op. cit. supra* note 2, pp. 61–62.
5. *Ibid.*, pp. 92–102.

6. National Commission on Technology, Automation, and Economic Progress, *Technology and the American Economy*, Vol. 1, pp. 35–37.
7. Tobin, *op. cit. supra* note 2, p. 89.
8. See U.S. Commission on Civil Rights, *Schools Can Be Desegregated.*
9. See Washington Research Project *et al.*, *Title I of ESEA: Is It Helping Poor Children?*
10. The suggestion is that of Edward Logue, head of New York's Urban Development Corporation, and is cited in *The New City.*
11. President's Committee on Urban Housing, *A Decent Home*, p. 213 (hereinafter cited as Kaiser Report).
12. *Ibid.*, pp. 22–24.
13. *The New City, op. cit. supra* note 10.
14. Fleming, "Social Strategy and Urban Growth" in *The New City, op. cit. supra* note 10, pp. 41 ff.
15. Downs, "Moving Toward Realistic Housing Goals," in *Agenda for the Nation*, pp. 141, 160–162.
16. *Ibid.*, p. 154.
17. Schultze, "Budget Alternatives after Vietnam," in *Agenda for the Nation*, pp. 13, 16.
18. *Ibid.*, pp. 28–29.
19. See, e.g., Kaysen, "Military Strategy, Military Forces and Arms Control," in *Agenda for the Nation, op. cit. supra* note 15, pp. 549 ff.
20. Schultze, *op. cit. supra* note 17, p. 19.
21. *Ibid.*, p. 13.
22. The ratio of taxes to gross national product is about 27.5 per cent in the United States. In Austria, Norway, Germany, Sweden, and France, it ranges from 34.5 per cent to almost 38 per cent. Only a few nations, notably Japan and Switzerland, have tax ratios significantly lower than that of the United States. See Goode, "The Tax Burden in the United States and Other Countries," 379 *Annals* 83–93.
23. See Schultze, *op. cit. supra* note 17, p. 48. He notes that the United States adds the equivalent of a West Germany to its tax base every five years.
24. The argument against taxing interest on municipal bonds is that it would make funds for financing local public needs even scarcer than they now are. In answer, proposals have been developed to enable local governments through Federal subsidies to continue to issue bonds at competitive rates even though interest would no longer be tax-exempt. It is estimated that the revenue recaptured by closing the tax loophole would more than make up for the subsidy. See Haar and Lewis, "Where Shall the Money Come From?" in *Public Interest*, Vol. 18, pp. 101 ff.

25. See Heller, *New Dimensions of Political Economy,* pp. 117 ff.
26. U.S. Advisory Commission on Intergovernmental Relations, *Urban America and the Federal System,* p. 14.

Selected Bibliography

Historical

Brogan, D. W., *The American Character* (Time Inc., 1956)

Elkins, Stanley, "Slavery and Negro Personality," in *American Negro Slavery*, p. 245 (Weinstein and Gattell eds., Oxford, 1968)

Jefferson, Thomas, *The Writings of Thomas Jefferson* (Taylor B. Maury, Washington ed., 1854)

Klein, Herbert S., "The Slave Economies of Cuba and Virginia," in *American Negro Slavery*, p. 112 (Weinstein and Gattel eds., Oxford, 1968)

Litwack, Leon F., *North of Slavery* (University of Chicago, 1961)

Mann, Horace, "Twelfth Annual Report as Secretary of the Massachusetts Board of Education (1848)," in *Documents of American History*, Doc. No. 173 (Commager ed., 4th ed., Appleton-Century-Crofts, 1958)

Mumford, Lewis, *The City in History* (Harcourt Brace, 1961)

Rosenman, Samuel, *The Public Papers and Addresses of Franklin D. Roosevelt* (Random House, 1938)

Ross, Philip, and Taft, Philip, "American Labor Violence: Its Causes, Character and Outcome," in *Violence in America*, p. 221 (Report to the National Commission on the Causes and Prevention of Violence, Government Printing Office, 1969)

Schlesinger, Jr., Arthur, *The Age of Roosevelt: The Politics of Upheaval* (Houghton Mifflin, 1960)

Sio, Arnold, "Interpretation of Slavery: The Slave Status in the Americas," in *American Negro Slavery*, p. 314 (Weinstein and Gattell eds., Oxford, 1968)

Tocqueville, Alexis de, *Democracy in America* (Vintage, 1945)

U.S. Commission on Civil Rights, *Freedom to the Free* (Government Printing Office, 1963)

General—Cities and Race

Brown, Claude, *Manchild in the Promised Land* (Macmillan, 1965)

Campbell, Angus, and Schuman, Howard, "Racial Attitudes in Fifteen American Cities," in *Supplemental Studies for the National Advisory Commission on Civil Disorders*, p. 1 (Government Printing Office, 1968)

Clark, Kenneth, *Dark Ghetto* (Harper Torchbooks, 1967)

Dahl, Robert, *Who Governs?* (Yale University, 1961)

Downs, Anthony, "Alternative Futures for the American Ghetto," in *Daedalus,* Vol. 97, p. 1331 (Fall 1968)

Ellison, Ralph, "An American Dilemma: A Review," in *Shadow and Act*, p. 290 (Signet, 1966)

Ellison, Ralph, *Invisible Man* (Random House, 1947)

Funnyé, Clarence, "The Untogether People: Separate but Gilded," *Village Voice*, Sept. 26, 1968.

Gans, Herbert, *The Levittowners* (Pantheon, 1967)

Glazer, Nathan, and Moynihan, Daniel, *Beyond the Melting Pot* (Massachusetts Institute of Technology, 1964)

Hallman, Howard, "The Community Action Program, An Interpretative Analysis," in *Power, Poverty and Urban Policy*, p. 285 (Bloomberg and Schmandt eds., Sage Publications, 1968)

Hamill, Pete, "The Revolt of the White Lower Middle Class," *New York*, April 14, 1969, p. 24

Kravitz, Sanford, "The Community Action Program in Perspective," in *Power, Poverty and Urban Policy*, p. 259 (Bloomberg and Schmandt eds., Sage Publications, 1968)

Kristol, Irving, "The Negro Today is Like the Immigrant Yesterday," *The New York Times Magazine*, Sept. 11, 1966

Malcolm X, *Autobiography* (Grove Press, 1964)

Metropolitan Applied Research Center, *A Relevant War Against Poverty* (1968)

Myrdal, Gunnar, *An American Dilemma* (McGraw-Hill, 1964)

National Advisory Commission on Civil Disorders, *Report* (Government Printing Office, 1968)

Netzer, Dick, "New York City's Mixed Economy: Ten Years Later," in *The Public Interest*, p. 188 (Summer 1969)

Pettigrew, Thomas, "Racially Separate or Together?," in *Integrated Education*, p. 36 (Jan.-Feb. 1969)

"Report from Black America," *Newsweek*, June 30, 1969

Rustin, Bayard, "The Anatomy of Frustration" (Address to the Anti-

Defamation League of B'nai B'rith, May 6, 1968)

Schrag, Peter, "The Forgotten American," *Harper's,* Aug. 1969, p. 27

U.S. Commission on Civil Rights, *A Time to Listen . . . A Time to Act* (Government Printing Office, 1967)

U.S. Commission on Civil Rights, *Cycle to Nowhere* (Government Printing Office, 1968)

Vernon, Raymond, *Metropolis 1985* (Harvard University Press, 1960)

Walinsky, Adam, "A Rough Autopsy on Democrats," *Washington Post,* Oct. 20, 1968, p. B2

Ward, Barbara, "Remarks: National Growth and Its Distribution," p. 26 (A symposium sponsored by the U.S. Department of Agriculture, Dec. 1967)

Wood, Robert, *Suburbia* (Houghton Mifflin, 1959)

General—Government, Civil Rights

Comment, "Title VI–Civil Rights Act of 1964," 36 *George Washington Law Review* 824 (1968)

Dixon, Robert, *Democratic Representation* (Oxford, 1968)

Goode, Richard, "The Tax Burden in the United States and Other Countries," 379 *Annals* 83 (Sept. 1968)

Greenberg, Jack, "The Supreme Court, Civil Rights and Civil Dissonance," 77 *Yale Law Journal* 1520 (1968)

Grodzins, Morton, *The American System* (Rand McNally, 1966)

Haar, Charles, and Lewis, Peter, "Where Shall the Money Come From?," in *The Public Interest,* Vol. 18, p. 101 (Winter 1970)

"Hearings on S. 843 Before the Subcommittee on Government Research of the Senate Committee on Government Operations," 90th Cong., 1st Sess. (1967)

Heller, Walter, *New Dimensions of Political Economy* (Harvard University Press, 1966)

Johnson, Lyndon, *"To Fulfill These Rights,"* Remarks of the President at Howard University, Washington, D.C., June 4, 1965

Kallenbach, Joseph E., *The American Chief Executive* (Harper & Row, 1966)

Kaysen, Carl, "Military Strategy, Military Forces, and Arms Control," in *Agenda for the Nation,* p. 549 (Gordon ed., Doubleday, 1969)

Netzer, Dick, *Impact of the Property Tax,* Research Report No. 1 (National Commission on Urban Problems ed., 1968)

Orfield, Gary, "The Enforcement of Title VI" (Unpublished doctoral dissertation, University of Chicago, 1968)

President's Commission on Law Enforcement and the Administration
of Justice, *The Challenge of Crime in a Free Society* (Government
Printing Office, 1967)

Schultze, Charles, "Budget Alternatives After Vietnam," in *Agenda for
the Nation*, p. 13 (Gordon ed., Doubleday, 1969)

"Social Goals and Indicators for American Society," 371 *Annals* 1 (May
1967)

U.S. Advisory Commission on Intergovernmental Relations, *Fiscal Balance in the American Federal System*, Vol. 2 (Government Printing
Office, 1967)

U.S. Advisory Commission on Intergovernmental Relations, *Urban
America and the Federal System* (Government Printing Office,
1969)

U.S. Commission on Civil Rights (Government Printing Office):
Political Participation (1968)

"Roster of Negro Elected Officials," in *Civil Rights Digest*, p. 35
(Spring 1968)

"Transcript, Hearing Before the U.S. Commission on Civil Rights:
—in Cleveland, Ohio" (April 1–7, 1966)
—in Jackson, Miss." (Feb. 16–20, 1965)
—in Montgomery, Ala." (April 27–May 2, 1968)
—in San Francisco–Oakland, Calif." (May 1–3, 1967)

White House Conference, *To Fulfill these Rights* (June 1–2, 1966)

Education

Allen, James, "The State, Educational Priorities and Local Financing,"
in *Integrated Education*, p. 55 (Sept.–Oct. 1968)

Alsop, Joseph, "No More Nonsense About Ghetto Education!," *New
Republic*, July 22, 1967, p. 18

Alsop, Joseph, "Ghetto Education," *New Republic*, Nov. 18, 1967, p.
18

Benson, Charles, *The Cheerful Prospect* (Houghton Mifflin, 1965)

Brown v. *Board of Education*, 347 U.S. 483 (1954)

Goodlad, John, "Desegregating the Integrated School," in *Education
Parks*, p. 14 (U.S. Commission on Civil Rights ed., 1967)

Hobson v. *Hansen*, 269 F. Supp. 401 (D.D.C. 1967)

Howe, Harold, "National Ideals and Educational Policy," in *National
Conference on Equal Educational Opportunity in America's Cities*,
p. 769 (U.S. Commission on Civil Rights ed., 1967)

Kohl, Herbert, *36 Children* (Signet, 1968)

Kozol, Jonathan, *Death at an Early Age* (Houghton Mifflin, 1967)

Mayer, Martin, *The Schools* (Anchor Books, 1963)

National Advisory Council on the Education of Disadvantaged Children, Report to the President (Jan. 31, 1968)

Tyler, Ralph, "Investing in Better Schools," in *Agenda for the Nation*, p. 207 (Gordon ed., Doubleday, 1969)

U.S. Commission on Civil Rights (Government Printing Office):
Education Parks (1967)
Racial Isolation in the Public Schools (1967)
Schools Can Be Desegregated (1967)
"Transcript, Hearing Before the U.S. Commission on Civil Rights:
—in Boston, Mass." (Oct. 4–5, 1966)
—in Rochester, N.Y." (Sept. 16–17, 1966)

U.S. Office of Education, Department of HEW, *Equality of Educational Opportunity* (Government Printing Office, 1966)

Washington Research Project *et al., Title I of ESEA: Is It Helping Poor Children?* (1969)

Employment and Economic Security

Advisory Council on Public Welfare, *Having the Power, We Have the Duty*, Report to the Secretary of Health, Education, and Welfare (1966)

Brimmer, Andrew, "Opportunity and Choice in an Expanding Economy," Commencement Address, Clark College, Atlanta, Ga., June 3, 1968

Brimmer, Andrew, "The Negro in the National Economy," in *The American Negro Reference Book*, p. 251 (Davis ed., Prentice-Hall, 1966)

Citizens' Board of Inquiry into Hunger and Malnutrition, *Hunger U.S.A.* (New Community Press, 1968)

Committee on School Lunch Participation, *Their Daily Bread* (1968)

Economic Report of the President (1969)

Jack Faucett Associates, *A Preliminary Analysis of the Economic Effects of the Urban Employment Opportunity Development Act* (mimeo, August 1967)

Fein, Rashi, "An Economic and Social Profile of the Negro American," in *Daedalus*, Vol. 94, p. 815 (Fall 1965)

Galbraith, John K., *The Affluent Society* (Houghton Mifflin, 2nd ed., 1969)

Hunter, Charlayne, "The New Black Businessmen," *Saturday Review*, Aug. 23, 1969, p. 27

Kain, John, "The Distribution and Movement of Jobs and Industry," in *The Metropolitan Enigma*, p. 1 (Wilson ed., U.S. Chamber of Commerce, 1967)

King v. *Smith*, 392 U.S. 309 (1968)

Lecht, Leonard, *Manpower Requirements for National Objectives in the 1970's* (National Planning Association, 1968)

Levitan, Sar, and Mangum, Garth, *Making Sense of Federal Manpower Policy* (The Institute of Labor and Industrial Relations, University of Michigan and Wayne State University, 1967)

Levitan, Sar, and Taggart, Robert, *Developing Business and Entrepreneurs in the Ghettos* (mimeo, April 17, 1969)

Liebow, Elliot, *Tally's Corner* (Little, Brown, 1966)

Mangum, Garth, "Manpower Programs in the Antipoverty Effort," in *Subcommittee on Employment, Manpower, and Poverty of the Senate Committee on Labor and Public Welfare, 90th Cong., 1st Sess., II Examination of the War on Poverty* 235 (Committee Print 1967)

National Commission on Technology, Automation, and Economic Progress, *Technology and the American Economy*, Vol. 1 (Government Printing Office, 1966)

President's Commission on Income Maintenance Programs, *Poverty Amid Plenty* (Government Printing Office, 1969)

Reich, Charles, "Individual Rights and Social Welfare: The Emerging Legal Issues," 74 *Yale Law Journal* 1245 (1965)

Riesenfeld, Stefan, and Maxwell, R. C., *Modern Social Legislation* (Foundation Press, 1950)

Ruchames, Louis, *Race, Jobs and Politics* (Columbia University Press, 1953)

Shapiro v. *Thompson*, 394 U.S. 618 (1969)

Sovern, Michael, *Legal Restraints on Racial Discrimination in Employment* (Twentieth Century Fund, 1966)

U.S. Commission on Civil Rights, *Employment* (Government Printing Office, 1961)

U.S. Commission on Civil Rights, *Equal Opportunity in Farm Programs* (Government Printing Office, 1965)

U.S. Commission on Civil Rights, *For ALL the People . . . By ALL the People* (Government Printing Office, 1969)

U.S. Department of Labor, *A Sharper Look at Unemployment in U.S. Cities and Slums* (Government Printing Office, March 1967)

U.S. Department of Labor, *Manpower Report of the President* (Government Printing Office, April 1968)

U.S. Federal Trade Commission, *Economic Report on Installment Credit and Retail Sales Practices of District of Columbia Retailers* (Government Printing Office, 1968)

Weaver, R. C., *Negro Labor* (Harcourt, 1946)

Housing and Urban Development

Abrams, Charles, *The City Is the Frontier* (Harper and Row, 1965)

Bailey, James, "Housing, Yes, Cities, No," in *Architectural Forum,* p. 37 (Sept. 1968)

Cloward, Richard, and Piven, Frances, "Desegregated Housing: Who Pays for the Reformers' Ideal?," *New Republic,* Dec. 17, 1966, p. 17.

Cornfield, Gilbert, "Tenants Save Their Community," in *Civil Rights Digest,* p. 1 (U.S. Commission on Civil Rights ed., Summer 1968)

Downs, Anthony, "Moving Toward Realistic Housing Goals," in *Agenda for the Nation,* p. 141 (Gordon ed., Doubleday, 1969)

Euclid v. *Ambler Realty Co.,* 272 U.S. 362 (1926)

Fleming, Harold, "Social Strategy and Urban Growth," in *The New City,* p. 41 (Canty ed., Praeger, 1969)

Freiden, Bernard, "Housing and National Urban Goals," in *The Metropolitan Enigma,* p. 148 (Wilson ed., U.S. Chamber of Commerce, 1967)

Jones v. *Mayer,* 392 U.S. 457 (1968)

Kain, John, "Housing Segregation, Negro Employment, and Metropolitan Decentralization," 82 *Quarterly Journal of Economics* 175 (May 1968)

National Commission on Urban Problems, "Building the American City," H.R. Document No. 91–34, 91st Cong., 1st Sess. (1968)

The New City (Canty ed., Praeger, 1969)

President's Committee on Urban Housing, *A Decent Home* (Government Printing Office, 1969)

Regional Plan Association, Second Regional Plan, *The Region's Growth* (May 1967)

Regional Plan Association, *Spread City,* Bulletin 100 (Sept. 1962)

Shelley v. *Kraemer,* 334 U.S. 1 (1948)

Shuman, Howard, "Behind the Scenes . . . and Under the Rug," *Washington Monthly,* July 1969, p. 14

Slitor, Richard, *The Federal Income Tax in Relation to Housing,* Research Report No. 5 (National Commission on Urban Problems ed., 1968)

Smart, Walter, Rybeck, Walter, and Shuman, Howard, *The Large Poor Family—A Housing Gap*, Research Report No. 4 (National Commission on Urban Problems ed., 1968)

Sudman, Seymour, Bradburn, Norman, and Gockel, Galen, "The Extent and Characteristics of Racially Integrated Housing in the United States," 42 *University of Chicago Business Journal* 50 (Jan. 1969)

Tobin, James, "Raising the Incomes of the Poor," in *Agenda for the Nation*, p. 77 (Gordon ed., Doubleday, 1969)

U.S. Commission on Civil Rights, *Housing* (Government Printing Office, 1961)

Von Eckhardt, Wolf, "Building Crisis," *Washington Post*, Oct. 27–Nov. 3, 1968

Wilner, Daniel, and Walkey, Rosabelle, "Effects of Housing on Health and Performance," in *The Urban Condition* (Duhl ed., Basic Books, 1963)

Demographic Analysis

Hodge, Patricia, and Hauser, Philip, *The Challenge of America's Metropolitan Population Outlook—1960 to 1985*, Research Report No. 3 (National Commission on Urban Problems ed., 1968)

Lieberson, Stanley, *Ethnic Patterns in American Cities* (The Free Press, 1963)

Taueber, Karl, and Taueber, Alma, *Negroes in Cities* (Aldine Publishing Co., 1965)

U.S. Bureau of the Census, Department of Commerce (Government Printing Office):

Series P–20, No. 189, *Selected Characteristics of Persons and Families: March 1969* (Aug. 18, 1969)

Series P–23, No. 26, *Recent Trends in Social and Economic Conditions of Negroes in the United States* (July 1968)

Series P–23, No. 27, *Trends in Social and Economic Conditions in Metropolitan Areas* (Feb. 7, 1969)

Series P–23, No. 29, *The Social and Economic Status of Negroes in the United States, 1969* (1970)

Series P–60, No. 58, *Year-Round Workers with Low Earnings in 1966* (April 4, 1969)

Series P–60, No. 59, *Income in 1967 of Families in the United States* (April 18, 1969)

Index

INDEX

Ability tests, 60, 101, 102
Abortion reform, 189
Administrative incompetence,
        154–55
Agricultural subsidies, 162, 164
Aid to Families of Dependent
        Children (AFDC),
        117–18
    eligibility for, 132
        disqualification, 134n
Alabama
    defense contractors in, 155
    State Extension Service of, 153
Alienation, suburban, 214–17
Alsop, Joseph, 235
American Arbitration Association,
        136
American Dilemma, An
        (Myrdal), 196
American Federation of Labor-
        Congress of Industrial
        Organizations (AFL-
        CIO), 150
Aptitude tests, 60, 101
Assimilation, 55

Atlanta, Ga.
    nonwhite population of, 188
    school enrollment in, 173

Baltimore, Md.
    nonwhite population of, 188
    school enrollment in, 173
Berkeley, Calif., education park
        in, 220n
Birmingham, Ala., protests in, 198
Birth rate, nonwhite, 171
Black entrepreneurship, 241–44
Black separatism, 49, 228–32, 233
Blue collar employment, 185
Boston, Mass., education in, 252
Brimmer, Andrew, 29, 243–44
Brogan, D. W., 68, 199, 209
Brooks, Calvin, 42
Brown, Claude, 41
Brown v. *Board of Education*
        (1954), 43, 69, 86–88,
        106, 109, 110
Building industry, 146–48
    employment in, 61–62

333

Federal government (*cont.*)
economic incentives for builders
by, 222–23
economic and social programs
of, 113–44
administration by state and
local governments of,
125–31
community participation in,
135–39
goals of, 120–24
inadequate resources in,
114–19
receipt of benefits under,
131–35
War on Poverty, 139–43
education and
change in school
environment, 270–71
financial assistance, 126–27,
238, 272, 273, 275
school integration policy,
271–72
evaluation and experimentation
by, 158–62
financing of welfare by, 261–62
incompetence and insensitivity
in, 154–55
increased spending by, 283–87
innovation and imagination in,
156–58
integration policies of, 235
local control and, 287–92
priorities and commitments of,
162–64
private investment in ghetto
and, 239–41
proposed housing program of,
276–83
special interests and, 146–54
building industry, 146–48
employers, 148–49

Federal government (*cont.*)
labor unions, 149–50
subsidies to suburbs by, 216
suburban location of
installations of, 265
taxes of, 182
growth in revenues from,
285–86
increased rates of, 286
training programs of, 103, 113,
116–17, 267
Federal Home Loan Bank Board,
91n, 136, 281
Federal Housing Administration,
90, 92, 93n, 147–48
credit to middle-income people
by, 163
economic policy of, 122–23
pressure of liberals on, 152
racial homogeneity policy of,
123
restrictive covenants
encouraged by, 91
Federal Reserve Board, 91n
Federal Savings and Loan
Insurance Corporation,
135–37
Fein, Rashi, 39
Financing
of cities and suburbs, inequities
in, 180–83
of education
Federal, 126–27, 272, 238,
273, 275
inequities in state, 275
of programs, Federal capacity
for, 283–87
"Fiscal zoning," 181
Fleming, Harold, 282
Flexible classroom space, 219
Food programs, Federal, 123–24,
126, 294–95

About the Author

William L. Taylor, born in New York in 1931, was educated at Brooklyn College and Yale Law School. He was a staff attorney for the NAACP Legal Defense Fund before he joined the U.S. Commission on Civil Rights in 1961. He was appointed Staff Director of the Commission in 1965 and served in that capacity until 1968. Mr. Taylor is currently on the faculty of Catholic University Law School and is Director of the Center for National Policy Review located in Washington, D.C.